HOLLYWOOD'S HOLLYWOOD

HOLLYWOOD'S

HOLLYWOOD

THE MOVIES ABOUT THE MOVIES

by Rudy Behlmer and Tony Thomas

THE CITADEL PRESS   SECAUCUS, N.J.

ACKNOWLEDGMENTS

For their various courtesies and generous cooperation, the authors wish to thank the following individuals and organizations (in alphabetical order).

Academy of Motion Picture Arts and Sciences Library
    Mildred Simpson and Staff
The American Film Institute
    Lawrence F. Karr
Blackhawk Films
    David H. Shepard
DeWitt Bodeen
Jerome Hellman
Sally Hope
Bob Lee

Museum of Modern Art
    Eileen Bowser
    Charles Silver
Colleen Moore
The New York Public Library, Lincoln Center:
Theatre Collection
Adela Rogers St. Johns
John Schlesinger
Sidney Skolsky
Mel Tormé

Second paperbound printing
ISBN 0-8065-0680-6

Published by Citadel Press
A division of Lyle Stuart, Inc.
120 Enterprise Ave., Secaucus, N.J. 07094
In Canada: George J. McLeod Limited
73 Bathurst St., Toronto, Ont.
Manufactured in the United States of America
Designed by A. Christopher Simon
Library of Congress catalog card number: 75-20357
ISBN 0-8065-0491-9

Library of Congress Cataloging in Publication Data

Behlmer, Rudy.
    Hollywood's Hollywood.

    Includes index.
    1. Moving-picture industry in motion pictures.
2. Moving-pictures—United States.   I. Thomas,
Tony, 1927-   joint author. II. Title.
PN1995.9.M65B4   791.43'0973   75-20357

CONTENTS

INTRODUCTION

When you mention fictional feature films that deal with Hollywood and the movies, most people immediately think of *Sunset Boulevard* or *Singin' in the Rain*, *A Star Is Born*; perhaps *The Bad and the Beautiful*. Senior citizens might vaguely recall *Merton of the Movies*, *Show People* or Kaufman and Hart's *Once in a Lifetime*. The contemporary filmgoer may talk about the recent *Day of the Locust* and one or two others. Then comes silence. Some people, if they give it any thought at all, will assume there may have been about twenty or thirty feature films produced on the general subject of film-making over the years. They hardly expect to hear that there have been some two hundred feature movies about the movies—and that entries on the list go all the way back to a little Vitagraph item of 1908! Many of these films were polished "A" productions: *Doubling for Romeo* with Will Rogers in 1921; Harold Lloyd's *Movie Crazy* in 1932; *What Price Hollywood?*; the 1932 forerunner of Selznick's 1937 *A Star Is Born*; Marion Davies and Bing Crosby in *Going Hollywood*; Humphrey Bogart as a producer in *Stand-In*, a screen writer in *In a Lonely Place* and a director in *The Barefoot Contessa*; James Cagney as a gangster-movie star in *Lady Killer*, a wild scenarist in *Boy Meets Girl* and as Lon Chaney in *Man of a Thousand Faces*; Jean Harlow doing a composite

take-off on Clara Bow, Gloria Swanson, Constance Bennett and herself in *Bombshell*; Bette Davis as a has-been in *The Star* and *What Ever Happened to Baby Jane?*; W. C. Fields trying to sell a script in *Never Give a Sucker an Even Break*; Erich von Stroheim playing a nightmare caricature of himself as the murderous director in *The Lost Squadron*; and on and on.

This book is a panorama of the many films which have dealt with the motion picture colony, its inhabitants, myths, scandals, burlesques, power-plays, morality plays, mysteries, melodramas, musicals, romances—even the Westerns about the making of Westerns.

Here are the less than accurate (to say the least) movie star biographies covered in a chapter, which we think has appropriately been titled "Any Similarity to Actual Persons, Living or Dead, Is Purely Coincidental." Even their own mothers would be hard-pressed to recognize Pearl White in *The Perils of Pauline*, Buster Keaton in *The Buster Keaton Story*, the screen versions of *Harlow*, *Valentino*, F. Scott Fitzgerald and Sheliah Graham in *Beloved Infidel* and so on.

The alcoholic, degraded women of stage and screen are reviewed here—Lillian Roth in *I'll Cry Tomorrow*, Diana Barrymore (with her father, John

Barrymore) in *Too Much, Too Soon*, Helen Morgan and the rest. The text delves into the real-life people (such as Marilyn Monroe) upon whom certain characters in films are based, the actual Hollywood situations used as a springboard for plotting in fictional films and other prototypes for composite scripting.

The Thalbergs, Louis B. Mayers, Selznicks, Harry Cohns, Zanucks, DeMilles mix it up in these pages with the extra players, stunt men, agents, talent scouts and drugstore cowboys.

There, too, is the Hollywood cavalcade of people, places and events—upper and lower echelons—as shown in the numerous films of their day: the spectacular premieres at Grauman's Chinese Theatre; the evenings on the town at the Cocoanut Grove, Ciro's and the Trocadero; the has-beens and the never-will-bes in the run-down apartment hotels; the radio broadcasts with Louella Parsons and Dick Powell at the legendary Hollywood Hotel; the front gate at Paramount, the back lot at Metro; "Norman Maine" making a drunken spectacle of himself at the Hollywood Bowl and the Biltmore Bowl; "Merton" leaving the Midwest to become a star in tinsel town; the compromised starlet from Peoria and the lecherous producer from Europe; the ex-commanding general of the Czar's army—now a pitiful extra in the breadline of Hollywood; Hedda Hopper on the scene after "Norma Desmond" has killed her lover at the Sunset Boulevard mansion; DeMille racing back from location in Griffith Park to a studio in flames in order to incorporate the actual fire into his filming; the wild party with Carroll Baker as "Rina Marlowe" swinging from a chadelier; "Vicki Lester" receiving the Academy Award while "Norman Maine," her husband, drunkenly humiliates her; Mack Sennett in the Los Angeles suburb of Edendale dreaming up his Keystone Cops, custard pies and bathing beauties. The cowboys hanging around Gower Gulch; Gene Kelly, Donald O'Connor and Debbie Reynolds turning the silent "Dueling Cavalier" into "The Dancing Cavalier"—an all-singing, all-talking, all-dancing smash; "Norman Maine" wading to his death in the Pacific. . . .

Love stories, spoofs, social dramas, musicals, epics—they have all made use of the Hollywood scene. With such a long span of time involved—1908 to the present—the movies about movies tellingly reflect the changing attitudes of the film people about themselves: seldom objective, usually coated with syrup, acid or some kind of spice.

The authors have opted to eliminate the many later short subjects in the genre. A flood of them were made by Mack Sennett alone. These could easily take up another volume. We have somewhat arbitrarily chosen 1916-17, after the feature-length film had become standard, as the cut-off point of the relatively brief one- or two-reel entries, thereby making sure that the earlier milestone productions in this category, regardless of length, would be discussed. Even a serial (*The Third Eye*) with a movie background is included.

The film purist scanning this volume will wonder what *A Vitagraph Romance* made at the Vitagraph Studios in Brooklyn; *A Girl's Folly*, produced at the World Studios in Fort Lee, New Jersey; *Shooting Stars*, an English film; or, for that matter, *Day for Night*, photographed at the Victorine Studios in France, to name a few, have to do with *Hollywood's Hollywood*. Well, ninety percent of the movies about the movies included here were made and took place in Hollywood, but to show how this subject was treated elsewhere and at other times in the various film centers we have included some of the more interesting and historically important films. After all, before the emergence of Hollywood as the movie capital of the world, most of the activity in America took place in New York and New Jersey.

Incidentally, although we hope that all of the major movies about the movies (and a great many of the minor for that matter) have been included in this book, there are some films that either deal in a very marginal way with the subject, or for one reason or another didn't seem necessary to discuss or perhaps even mention. Then again, it's just possible that the authors didn't know about a few, or their research and alert friends in the field missed a title here and there. So, Film Detectives, stand by to make notes!

RUDY BEHLMER
TONY THOMAS

2

HOLLYWOOD'S HOLLYWOOD

CHAPTER ONE

ANY SIMILARITY TO ACTUAL PERSONS, LIVING OR DEAD.... *

For the general public the most interesting of the films about the film world are those dealing with celebrated personalities, and they are also of interest to film buffs because they usually reveal aspects of picture-making in the careers of these personalities. However, with very few exceptions, these biographical treatments are glib and false, and while there are good reasons why they cannot be completely accurate, it is nonetheless disappointing that so many of them choose to stray so far from the facts. The films about Jean Harlow and Rudolph Valentino ignore major facts in their lives and invent fiction in their place, and the movies supposedly intended as tributes to Pearl White and Buster Keaton fall far short of the worth of their subjects. In almost every Hollywood pseudo-biography there is too much about the generally invented personal life and too little about the actual career.

* . . . is purely coincidental

In defending themselves from the criticisms of film historians, the producers point out that this kind of movie is not intended as documentary but as entertainment for the widest possible audience, and whether the film deals with an admirable figure like Will Rogers or a tragic figure like John Barrymore, the rules of entertainment are the same as those applying to all commercial pictures. Sidney Skolsky, the veteran Hollywood columnist and the producer of *The Jolson Story* and *The Eddie Cantor Story* explains: "You cannot put something on the screen as it really is, and in telling a life story in a film you cannot possibly cover all the points. In a book you can take hundreds of pages to explain the development of your character. In a film you usually have less than two hours, and you therefore decide on a point of view about your character and what it is you want to say about him. This is drama, not literature. The true dramatist knows what to take out and not lose the essence of the character, and

5

Valentino: Richard Carlson as the director, Anthony Dexter and Patricia Medina.

how to use those incidents that best illustrate the kind of person you're dealing with. Making this kind of film has many problems. Bear in mind that nobody leads his or her life with the idea that it will eventually be made into a movie; you don't live to a script, and entertainers make mistakes like everybody else. This is a tough business and it's hard to stay in it. In making a film about an entertainer you have to get these points across without offending those who were associated with your personality. The important thing is to arrive at the essence of your character, to decide what it is you want to say and to do it within a dramatic framework."

Perhaps it is impossible to relate the life story of a famous entertainer in a film intended purely as entertainment. Even in the case of Will Rogers, where there is nothing detrimental to say about the man, it still remains difficult to cover every aspect of a long career and a complicated development of style and ability. In the many instances of tragedy in the lives of these people the producers must proceed with caution, since the surviving associates do not wish to be depicted in a less than favorable manner. Legal action can cost the studios a great deal of money. The Hollywood biographies are therefore easy films to criticize.

The legalistic complications of filming life stories were pointed out by Gladwin Hill in the December 4, 1960, edition of *The New York Times:* "Movie-makers have a problem opposite that of historians. This is because our law says, with respect to factual reporting, that virtually everything that ever happened is, in the interest of freedom of information, subject to chronicling, however discomforting it may be to anyone. But when it comes to dramatizing the same facts, the law injects two obstacles, the right of privacy and property rights. Living persons who are depicted on the screen—except for their participation in news events—must have given their permission. And the courts have held that the careers of prominent people no longer living are property belonging to their estates, as far as narrative exploitation is concerned. This is the major reason for Hollywood's frequent fictionalization of life stories."

The most accurate of Hollywood's biographies is *The Story of Will Rogers,* directed by Michael Curtiz for Warners in 1952. In this instance there was no need to alter the facts drastically; Rogers' life was free of scandal, strife or hardship, and he was a classic example of the American Dream. His widow had written his biography and Warners purchased the rights in 1941, largely because Curtiz had been a friend of Rogers and wanted to make a film about him, according to some sources. The project was delayed when Will Rogers, Jr., the logical choice for the role, entered the service for war duty. The studio did not consider it a top priority item, and as the years drifted by, young Rogers made a living as a newspaper publisher, with active interest in the Democratic Party. James Stewart, Gary Cooper, Spencer Tracy and Bing Crosby were all considered for the part but common sense prevailed and Rogers, Jr., finally stepped before the cameras. He was not interested in being an actor, but he realized that if he didn't do the role, the film would never be made.

The film ranges from Rogers' early days as a cowboy in Oklahoma to his death in an Alaskan air crash in 1935. His was not a life of dramatic struggle; his rancher father was wealthy and at one time a senator of the Cherokee Nation. Rogers had a hankering to be an entertainer and spent a few years as a rope-trick artist with Wild West shows and playing the vaudeville circuit. He reached success with his appearances on Broadway in the *Ziegfeld Follies of 1916,* by which time he was thirty-seven, and he was thereafter secure financially and in the affection of the public. The film relates his conflict with his father—a conflict of two equally firm-minded men with differing views—and his ideal marriage to Betty Blake, warmly played by Jane Wyman, and his friendship with aviator Wiley Post, a fellow Oklahoman, played by Noah Beery, Jr. Had Rogers, Jr., not been playing his father, the next best choice would have been Beery, Jr., whose appearance and manner are close to those of Rogers. The film flashes scenes from Rogers' early days in the *Follies,* with Eddie Cantor appearing as himself, and gives particular emphasis to his involvement in the Democratic Convention of 1932, in which he declined a nomination for the Presidency.

The Story of Will Rogers pays little attention to Rogers' activities in Hollywood. While he was only moderately successful in silent movies, Rogers did make a number of them beginning with *Laughing Bill Hyde* in 1918. And he was extremely popular after the coming of sound. Among his best talking pictures were *A Connecticut Yankee* (1930), *State Fair* (1933), and *David Harum* (1934). His last film was *Steamboat 'Round the Bend* (1935), made just before his ill-fated flight with Wiley Post. It was Rogers who said, "The movies are the only place where you can sit in the audience and applaud yourself," and it is fair to assume he would have liked this movie treatment of his life, particularly the performance of his son. Rogers, Jr., confessed that he

Life Begins at 40 (1935): Jane Darwell, Rochelle Hudson and Will Rogers.

The Story of Will Rogers (1952): Jane Wyman and Will Rogers, Jr.

The Story of Will Rogers: Eddie Cantor and Will Rogers, Jr.

The Story of Will Rogers: Will, Jr., as his father, taking time out to write a newspaper column during the filming of *A Connecticut Yankee* (1930).

The Perils of Pauline (1947): Betty Hutton.

7

really didn't like acting for the cameras: "Dad's speechmaking I found easy. I never felt ill at ease about making any of his monologues. The love scenes I found very difficult . . . and I could never get used to the frozen-faced extras while I was saying something funny."

The two Hollywood biographies which reveal interesting but not entirely accurate aspects of the early years of the industry are *The Perils of Pauline*, the fabricated story of Pearl White, and *Man of a Thousand Faces*, dealing with the career of Lon Chaney. The latter is by far the more reliable account. Paramount's 1947 version of Pearl White was couched as a vehicle for the antic Betty Hutton, with four songs by Frank Loesser, the only memorable one of which is "I Wish I Didn't Love You So." The lively Hutton was a good choice for White, but as written for this fictionalized version of her adventures in the movies, Hutton was required to be more gauche and clownish than White acutally was.

Pearl White is here called "The Queen of the Silent Serials," but the title also could refer to Ruth Roland, who began starring in serials in 1915 and continued making them until 1923. Pearl White retired from the American screen in 1922, and lived in Paris until she died of a liver ailment in 1938.

According to the Hutton *Perils of Pauline*, Pearl was a seamstress in a sewing machine shop, who was required to deliver costumes to a Shakespearean company. Attracted to the idea of being hired as a performer, she auditions for the company and gains employment with a knockabout comedy song. Thereafter she is given bit parts, which she mangles. Her movie career begins when a director realizes she is fearless and has the idea of using her in cliff-hanging serials. So far the film is completely false. White went on the stage when she was sixteen and was hired in 1910 to play in films, which led to her being given the lead four years later in a serial called *The Perils of Pauline*, the first of many serials and (later) features in which she appeared over the next eight years. The Hutton picture deals with these years with particular attention to the re-creation of various White stunts and antics and even "salutes" in the credits Charles W. Goddard, who wrote the original *Perils*. But the film goes off-course in relating a fictional White love affair with a stuffy actor, played in a lackluster manner by John Lund. The screenplay has White leaving for Paris to pursue another career as a revue artist (partially true) and dying as the result of a stage accident (false).

Of interest is the fact that *The Perils of Pauline* was directed by George Marshall, who entered the

The Perils of Pauline: William Demarest (with megaphone) directing one of the perils.

8

The Perils of Pauline: News of the Armistice arrives during the shooting of a scene. Betty Hutton and Constance Collier share the general enthusiasm. Only the hard-pressed director (Demarest) seems to resent the interruption.

The real Pearl White.

The Perils of Pauline: A reproduction of a row of early silent sets, circa 1914.

The Perils of Pauline: Betty Hutton and John Lund, and the balloon that went awry.

movies in 1912 as an actor. He began directing in 1917, and his knowledge was put to good use. Several of Ruth Roland's serials were directed by Marshall. Especially interesting in the Hutton film are the scenes which show the making of early silent pictures, with several of them in simultaneous production alongside each other. Paramount duplicated the assembly line methods, with a row of single sets and cameras fixed to the floor. In each room actors perform a variety of comedic and dramatic business. For these sequences a number of famous oldtimers were hired to re-create the bits for which they become famous. On one set we see Creighton Hale, the hero of Pearl White's most successful serial, *The Exploits of Elaine,* which thrilled audiences for thirty-six weeks in 1915. Next we see Paul Panzer, the unctuous villain of the original *Perils,* intimidating a helpless maiden. Then comes William Farnum, the brawny hero of early film dramas, shooting it out in a barroom brawl with other veterans of those days—Snub Pollard and Francis McDonald. On a fourth set are Mack Sennett graduates Chester Conklin, James Finlayson and Hank Mann lobbing custard pies. Aiding this somewhat fanciful harkback to bygone days was the use of genuinely old equipment, such as hand-cranked cameras, mercury lamps, and megaphones.

As for Pearl's perils as depicted in the film: she hung from cliffs, was tied to a railroad track, was confronted by a large circular saw, climbed up fire ladders, jumped from a horse onto a speeding train, brawled on the cowcatcher of a train, was trapped in a burning building and clung to the basket of a runaway baloon. This last was based on an actual incident in which the serial queen was caught in a balloon which broke away from its mooring during filming and came to earth miles away. In its moments dealing with movie-making *The Perils of Pauline* is entertaining, although exaggerated and partially anachronistic, but most of the rest of the picture is tiresome and hollow.

Man of a Thousand Faces, produced by Universal in 1957, is a respectable tribute to Lon Chaney and fairly accurate in its outline of his career and his personality. Chaney did a good deal of his film work at Universal and it was therefore easy for that studio to reveal some of its past history—without alluding to the fact that Chaney spent the last six years of his life at MGM.

As a film about Hollywood this is one of the most interesting, dealing as it does with a man who was unique in his artistry as a pantomimist, a genius with make-up, and a giant figure in the early history of the industry. James Cagney was not an obvious choice to play Chaney, being a far different type physically and an actor with his own very distinct image, but it is Cagney's performance that gives this picture most of its value. Chaney was an enigmatic man, quite complex in personality and so averse to publicity that he once said, "Between pictures there is no Lon Chaney." Since he almost always appeared on the screen in varying disguises the public could only take him at his word. Cagney, through his own skill and sympathy, revealed Chaney as a complicated but honest and compulsively hard-working man.

Chaney died on August 26, 1930, of cancer of the throat, not long after he had made his first sound film and conclusively proven that he was one silent star who had no reason to worry about the future. He was forty-seven. *Man of a Thousand Faces* begins a few days after his death as his young boss and friend, Irving Thalberg, arrives at a memorial service to deliver a eulogy. Thalberg at this time in his life was thirty-one and well established as a production executive. The two men had become friends during the making of *The Hunchback of Notre Dame* in 1923, and a year later when Thalberg took office at MGM one of the first things he did was to sign Chaney to a contract. The role of Thalberg in

10

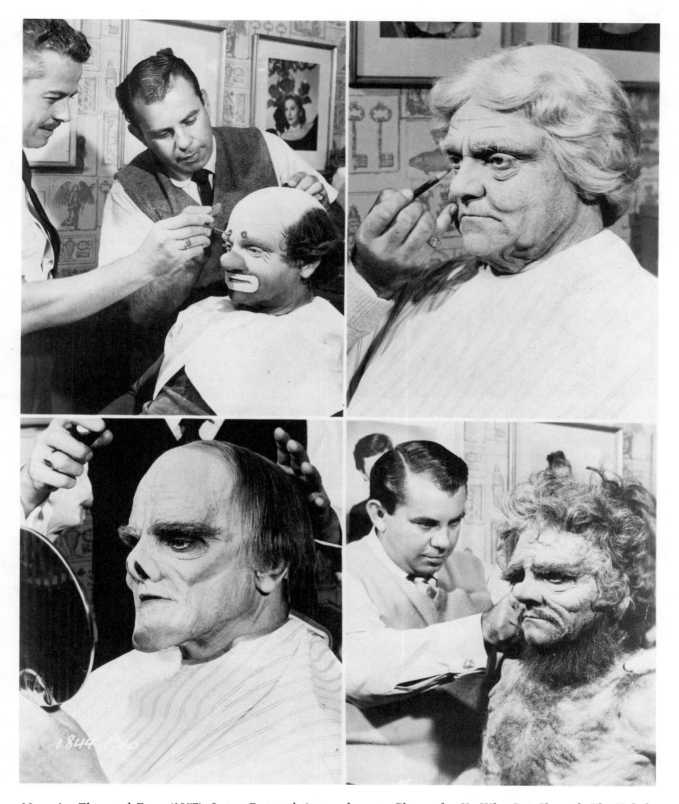

Man of a Thousand Faces (1957): James Cagney being made up as Chaney for *He Who Gets Slapped, The Unholy Three, The Phantom of the Opera* and *The Hunchback of Notre Dame.*

Lon Chaney and Betty Compson in *The Big City* (1928).

this film is played by Robert Evans, who was suggested for the part by Thalberg's widow, Norma Shearer. Evans was born the year Chaney died and years later he assumed a Thalberg-like position in the industry by becoming head of production at Paramount in 1966.

Thalberg begins his tribute to Chaney: "The actor is a very special human being. . . . We cannot replace these personalities—there can only be one of each." These words lead to a flashback to Chaney's boyhood in Colorado where he is taunted by other boys because his parents are deaf-mutes. His gentle mother calms him and sympathizes in sign language. Next we see him as a clown in vaudeville, with a young singer-wife, Cleva Creighton (Dorothy Malone), who is fired when she fails to arrive on time for her act. She tells Chaney she is pregnant and asks him to take her to his parents, whom she has never met. He hedges but agrees, his hedging due to his failure to tell his wife of his parents' affliction. When Cleva meets them she is shocked and behaves unkindly, expressing fear about the health of her child. Their son, Creighton, is born free of affliction, but problems arise between the Chaneys when Cleva insists on pursuing her career. Chaney objects to his son being left with strangers and takes the boy to the theatre in the evenings. An attractive entertainer,

Hazel Hastings (Jane Greer), takes it upon herself to care for the boy.

When he suspects that his wife is having an affair, Chaney turns his back on her and assumes control of the child. To spite him, Cleva appears during one of his performances and swallows a vial of acid in view of the audience. This results in her permanently impairing her voice and causing a scandal, which Chaney fears will end his stage career. A friend suggests he aim for work in the movies. Chaney raises his eyebrows—"What's that got to do with acting?" The friend points out that it has a lot to do with pantomime, of which Chaney is a master.

When next seen, he is outside Universal Studios on Lankershim Boulevard, lining up for possible work. A studio cop replies to an elderly actress (Marjorie Rambeau) when she points to Chaney: "He claims he's an actor," to which she remarks, "An actor? That's a novelty around here." She persuades Chaney that a good living can be made as an extra, since hordes of them are employed every day for the several films in constant production.

Chaney quickly realizes the possibilities of make-up in the movies. "If a guy can be enough things, he can make a good living. I grew up on stories without words." However, as an actor he finds he has little social standing, and loses custody of his son to a state home when he cannot prove permanent employment. Hazel visits Chaney, obviously long in love with him, and suggests a way for him to get the boy back—to get married. The marriage is a good one, and Creighton grows up in good surroundings, content until the day he learns his real mother is alive and in need. Then he leaves Chaney. Earlier, when the boy has expressed his own interest in becoming an actor, Chaney dissuades him. He quotes Richard Mansfield: "Actors are not made. Actors—and idiots—are born."

Chaney's career at Universal continues without fear of unemployment, due to his ability to make up for whatever part is needed. With putty, plaster, collodion-created scars, false teeth, wigs, facial clamps, cotton stuffing and dilaters Chaney creates amazing and sometimes fearful effects. In time he reaches stardom, and the film recreates moments from *The Miracle Man*, *The Hunchback of Notre Dane* and *The Phantom of the Opera*. His second marriage brings him the support and contentment he needs but his happiness is marred when he turns his back on his son, who resents his severe treatment of his mother. Not until Chaney is dying does he admit that the boy had done the right thing in caring for her.

12

Man of a Thousand Faces: Dorothy Malone, James Cagney and Jane Greer.

Man of a Thousand Faces: The set of *He Who Gets Slapped* with Cagney as the clown and Robert Evans (as Irving Thalberg) at left.

Signs of ill health appear as Chaney works on his first sound film, *The Unholy Three*, a remake of his silent version of 1925. Chaney develops a sore throat, and the sound engineers complain of not being able to get a good pick-up on the delivery of his lines. He is hospitalized for examination and a friend later tells his wife that Chaney has terminal cancer. The decision is made not to tell Chaney, and the actor proceeds to his mountain cabin for a fishing vacation. There he is reunited with his son and it is there he finally collapses. On his deathbed, his voice gone, he resorts to sign language to ask his son to bring him his makeup kit. Chaney takes a white crayon and adds the letters "Jr." to his name, and hands the kit to Creighton.

Man of a Thousand Faces is particularly interesting for its insight into Chaney's involvement in the art of make-up, and the splendid re-creations in this film are credited to Bud Westmore and Jack Kevan. The facts of Chaney's private life are softened, but the contradictory character of the man is expertly portrayed by Cagney, showing his jealous, obstinate and hard aspects as well as his honesty and his generosity. But the film fails to indicate the enormous quantity of work Chaney achieved in Hollywood. Following his bits in dozens of pictures during his first year, he appeared in approximately a hundred and fifty films between 1913 and 1930. However, his relationship with Universal was not as smooth and easy as this film suggests. Chaney was not fully appreciated until he had been at the studio

Man of a Thousand Faces: Robert Evans and James Cagney.

Man of a Thousand Faces: Cagney as Chaney as The Phantom.

for about six years. They let him go when he asked for more money, then rehired him after he had made a few pictures for other studios, one of which was the superb *The Miracle Man* for Paramount, in which he played a crook who disguises himself as a helpless cripple. Cagney did a little of this creature in *Man of a Thousand Faces,* and learned firsthand of the painful contortions to which Chaney subjected himself in order to realize his parts. Cagney, it should be noted, was fifty-seven at the time of making this picture.

It was Creighton Chaney who sold Universal the story of his father's life, having written the screenplay himself. In reality he did not assume the name Lon Chaney, Jr., until 1935, and then only because producers insisted he use the name in order to get work as an actor. Chaney, Jr., who earned much of his screen fame working for Universal in generally routine horror movies, bemoaned the fact that once he had sold his script to the studio they assigned a team of writers to rewrite it and that he had no say in the final outcome. This, he felt, was "typical Hollywood."

The Buster Keaton Story, produced and written by Robert Smith and Sidney Sheldon, and directed by Sheldon for Paramount in 1957 is not a very good tribute to the great screen comic, and it misses the real poignancy of the man. It also misses something not known at the time of production, that Keaton would find steady employment in the last few years of his life, bringing him wide and justly deserved recognition. By the time of his death in 1966, film buffs were hailing him as one of the three greatest comics produced by the film world, and there are many who now think Keaton was better than Charlie Chaplin and Harold Lloyd. The 1957 film is at its best when re-creating famous moments from Keaton comedies and at its dullest during those stretches purporting to tell about his private life. Its assets are Donald O'Connor, in a sympathetic and studied performance, and Keaton himself as the film's technical advisor, a job that consisted mainly of coaching O'Connor in his routines.

The Buster Keaton Story, minus its famous name, could be any of many show-biz movies about entertainers rising from the ranks of vaudeville to become stars and enjoy great wealth, then falling from grace and wallowing in bad luck before being restored to esteem. In its bare bones the plot is true. Keaton was born into a theatrical family of comic acrobats and himself performed almost from infancy. It was Fatty Arbuckle who persuaded Keaton to join his movie company in 1917 and from whom

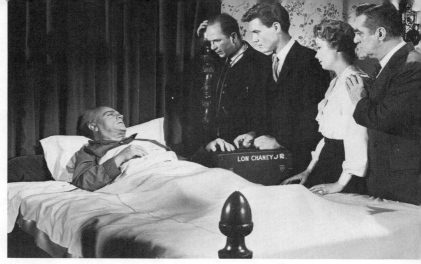

Man of a Thousand Faces: James Cagney, Jack Albertson, Roger Smith, Jane Greer and Jim Backus.

Keaton learned about silent-movie comedy in several two-reelers. The film makes no mention of the tragic Arbuckle but concentrates on the great period of Keaton's success with his films of the 1920s, many of which are now considered classics. Keaton went into decline with the coming of sound, and he was fired by MGM in 1932, thereafter drifting along with spotty employment, marital problems and bouts of alcoholism.

The film touches upon all this but not with complete accuracy, particularly in regard to his marriages. It omits his first marriage to Natalie Talmadge, which produced two sons, and invents a lady named Gloria, a studio casting director played by Ann Blyth, who loves him and helps him at "Famous Studios" without his being fully aware of her devotion. Not until he has fallen into unemployment and taken to the bottle do they get married. Keaton's actual second wife sued Paramount for five million dollars damages, claiming that the film depicted her falsely as a conniving woman who married the comedian while he was in a drunken state and that the film made her appear disreputable. Keaton married dancer Eleanor Norris in 1940, and he credited her for the happiness of the remainder of his life.

Keaton was approached in 1956 by Paramount for the film rights to his story, and Robert Smith brought him a check for $50,000 while he was in the hospital recovering from stomach surgery. He and Donald O'Connor became close friends during the planning and production of the picture, and O'Connor later admitted that despite intense study and coaching there were a few Keaton tricks he could not master. Among the sequences used in this film are Keaton's

15

Klondike fishing antics from *The Frozen North*, the launching of a motorboat from *The Boat*, in which Keaton stands on the prow of his craft as it is being launched and goes down with it as it sinks, and the scene from *The Balloonatic* involving a canoe. The picture also employs bits of comic car chases, pie-throwing brawls, pratfalls and juggling acts. However, some of the re-created bits filmed were deleted prior to release. Keaton's unique talents as a pantomimist, his physical dexterity and his superb timing are properly conveyed. His deadpan humor and his characterization as a sad little man who unemotionally faces and overcomes all life's mean tricks are admirably captured by Donald O'Connor in *The Buster Keaton Story*.

Keaton had nothing but praise for the actor, who he said was first-rate in the part—although he kept his feelings about the film in general to himself. He probably shared the disappointment of critics and admirers who believed his story was more interesting than the Paramount film suggests. But a true accounting would have put many Hollywood people in a poor light, as can be gathered by reading Keaton's autobiography, *My Wonderful World of Slapstick* (Doubleday, 1960) and Rudi Blesh's *Keaton* (Macmillan, 1966).

In discussing the Keaton film, Donald O'Connor does not hesitate to denounce it for its dishonesty: "It wasn't Buster's life. They called him a technical advisor, but they never listened to him. I remember talking to him right after we'd shot a scene of him as a boy in the circus going on for his father who had just died. I asked Buster, 'What kind of a circus was it?' He looked at me and said, 'I never was in a circus.' So I asked him, 'Well, how old were you when your father died?' 'Forty-five,' he said."

Among Keaton's own pictures is *The Cameraman* (1928), and while it does not deal with Hollywood, it does give a comic look at life in another segment of the picture business—the making of newsreels. In this Keaton is an ambitious tintype photographer who fails to get a job as a cameraman with the MGM newsreel company in New York. They laugh at him and his primitive equipment, but a pretty receptionist (Marceline Day) takes pity on him and suggests he try covering a few events as a free-lancer. His attempts are ludicrous, as he double-exposes shots of a battleship sailing down the Hudson with New York street scenes. At the launching of a ship he is so eager to get close footage that he mounts his camera on the cradle that slides the ship into the water, and as it is launched he goes into the water with it. Later an organ grinder's monkey attaches

itself to Keaton. When Keaton leaves his camera to jump into the water to save his girl from drowning, the monkey—trained to grind the organ—cranks the handle of Keaton's camera and gets a record of the deed, which when projected at the newsreel company makes Keaton a hero and gets him his job. *The Cameraman* ranks with *The General* and *Sherlock, Jr.* as among his funniest and most inventive feature films. The picture was remade by MGM in 1950 with Red Skelton and called *Watch the Birdie*, but with many changes—none of which made it half as amusing as the original. The same can be said of *The Buster Keaton Story*.

The complicated lives and sad endings of John Barrymore and his daughter Diana were legally impossible to translate into a thoroughly accurate film. For all that, it should have been feasible to produce something more pertinent than the bland and hollow *Too Much, Too Soon*, made by Warners in 1958. In her candid autobiography, written with Gerold Frank, Diana Barrymore confessed to alcoholism and gross behavior, and offered some explanation for her failure to come to terms with her life. The film offers little that is believable. Its hopeful ending, with Diana finding love in the arms of an old boy friend, proved to be tragically false when she died in 1960, having wrecked her health at the age of thirty-eight. She was the product of the marriage of Barrymore and a poet who called herself Michael Strange (Blanche Oelrichs), but she saw little of her father. By the mid-twenties John Barrymore had given up his stage career for Hollywood. He married Dolores Costello, who divorced him after six hectic years, unable to cope with his drinking and his erratic ways. In the last two years of his life, 1940-42, he was married to a young starlet, Elaine Barrie. But neither of his last two wives is alluded to in the film version of *Too Much, Too Soon*. Here Barrymore, as played by Errol Flynn, lives in a large and almost furnitureless mansion with a male nurse.

Diana Barrymore began her Hollywood career in 1941 under contract to Universal, making a number of films for them, including *Eagle Squadron*, *Between Us Girls* and *Nightmare*. Although she had ability as an actress, her personality did not register with the public, and as a result her film career shortly came to an end. Both the book and the film suggest that her restlessness and her insecurity came from her parents; her mother being too busy socially and with her writing career to give her the attention she needed, her father being a famous, roistering actor, seemingly barely aware of her existence.

The Buster Keaton Story (1957): Donald O'Connor and Ann Blyth.

The Buster Keaton Story: Donald O'Connor recreating the launching from Keaton's *The Boat* (1921).

The Buster Keaton Story: Buster and Donald O'Connor on a break during the filming.

The Buster Keaton Story: Donald O'Connor and Cecil B. DeMille.

17

The Buster Keaton Story: Technical advisor Keaton setting up a routine from *The Balloonatic* with Donald O'Connor.

Buster Keaton and Marceline Day in *The Cameraman* (1928).

In the film she is greeted by Barrymore on her arrival in Hollywood, and he persuades her to live with him. Against her mother's advice, she does. Barrymore in this account still seems to be in love with Diana's mother and eager for a reconciliation, but his ex-wife coldly rejects him. This sends him back to hard drinking, which in turn causes his daughter to move out of the house. He thereafter dies in loneliness and despair, with Diana feeling guilty. There is no mention of the fact that Barrymore was busy in the last few years of his life in films and in radio, and was tended by a group of close friends. In this film there is some talk of his making a film comeback and possibly co-starring with Diana, but it never happens.

Diana's unhappy, and eventually sordid, lovelife is tackled in *Too Much, Too Soon* in soap-opera fashion. Her first husband, actor Bramwell Fletcher is fictionalized as Vincent Bryant (Efrem Zimbalist, Jr.) and he loses her to a slick, sadistic tennis player (Ray Danton), to whom she is married for a painful while. She next marries another actor, Robert Wilcox (Edward Kemmer). Wilcox, correctly

named in the picture, is a reformed alcoholic, but their weaknesses prove too much in combination and together they sink into drunken oblivion. Leaving him and drifting aimlessly, she one day bumps into Lincoln Forrester (Martin Milner), who had courted her in her young society days, and his continued love inspires her to believe in herself. Would that this were truly the turn of events in the story of Diana Barrymore. In fact, she never regained health or professional esteem, and possibly the pitiful truths about Diana and her gifted father were too unpleasant to present in a commercial movie.

The best things about *Too Much, Too Soon* are the performances of Dorothy Malone and Errol Flynn. Malone is somewhat too refined in her playing and a more attractive woman than Diana, but the characterization is as sincere as the scripting and direction allow. And except for one drunken fit in which he has to be restrained by his nurse, Flynn is also more subdued than Barrymore at this harrowing time in his life. Flynn himself had trod the Barrymore path, and here, bloated and bleary, he was really playing himself, prematurely aged and close to death. He was a problem during the making of the picture, drinking from early morning onward, and his scenes had to be done in short takes and over and over. For all that, it is Flynn's portrayal of an actor he greatly admired and befriended that gives *Too Much, Too Soon* its most memorable quality.

The George Raft Story (1961) made little impression on the public. The film points up Raft's (Ray Danton) independence, his hot temper and his efforts to break away from being typecast as a gangster. The most dramatic aspects of Raft's career are his associations with racketeers and gamblers, and the film allows for this, showing him as a sharp young dancer on the fringes of the New York underworld. Hovering between the choice of a life in crime or as an entertainer, he is advised by his criminal friends to go "straight" and take his chances in Hollywood. The tough, glib Raft finds work fairly easily in pictures and gets a big break when he is selected to play a hood in *Scarface* (1932). He advises the director that the part as written is phony and proceeds to show how such a man really conducts himself, which interpretation includes the nonchalant flipping of a coin. The film shows his rise and decline in movies, and ends with his faithful agent (Herschel Bernardi) coaxing him into playing the mob leader in *Some Like It Hot* (1959).

The screenplay points to his friendship with Texas Guinan (Barbara Nichols), Al Capone (Neville

John Barrymore.

Robert Cummings and Diana Barrymore in *Between Us Girls* (1942).

Too Much, Too Soon (1958): Errol Flynn and Dorothy Malone.

Brand), and Bugsy Siegel (Brad Dexter) and fictitiously deals with his love life as played by Barrie Chase, Jayne Mansfield and Julie London, all of them treated in cavalier fashion by Raft. *The George Raft Story* is a rather tepid picture and fails to make much of a case for its subject. How close it is to the truth is known only to Raft, who laconically and characteristically declines comment.

It was Darryl F. Zanuck's idea to make a film about Jean Harlow and to have Marilyn Monroe play her. It was an obvious piece of casting, since the two blonde sex symbols shared similarities in their careers and personal lives. Zanuck instructed Adela Rogers St. Johns to write the screenplay, but before she could finish it Monroe's then husband, Arthur Miller, advised Zanuck that Monroe would not play the part. She had accepted the idea eagerly, but Miller considered it trash and unworthy of his wife, and she adhered to his opinion. When Joseph E. Levine produced his version of Harold Robbins' *The Carpetbaggers*, purportedly inspired by the career of Howard Hughes, he selected Carroll Baker to play the role of the Harlow-like actress. The film was trounced by the critics, but it did well, and Baker's performance as a slinky, amoral actress captured the public's imagination. Levine at this time had also acquired the rights to Irving Shulman's biography of Harlow, and it seemed logical to cast Carroll in the part. Levine issued enormous publicity on the project prior to its filming and took Baker across the Atlantic on the *Queen Mary*, complete with press corps, to attend the London premiere of *The Carpetbaggers* in the guise of Harlow.

Levine's plans to film *Harlow* were knocked somewhat awry by the announcement of producer Bill Sargent that he was going into production with a film about Jean Harlow, and that he intend to call it *Harlow*. The irate Levine was unable to stop Sargent, who hastily put together a company and employed the "Electronovision" process of shooting with live television cameras and transferring to film. Directed by Alex Segal, Sargent's *Harlow*, with Carol Lynley in the title role, was shot in eight days at a cost of $600,000 and rushed into the theatres. It did poorly. The public was disappointed with the dull, grainy quality of the black and white picture and the less than interesting script. Some of the announced leading players dropped out of the problem-fraught enterprise just prior to shooting and others were quickly brought in, later to complain that there was no time to develop convincing characterizations.

Neither version of *Harlow* presents a true story of

20

The George Raft Story (1961): Ray Danton, Barrie Chase and Jayne Mansfield.

George Raft.

the actress and neither Lynley nor Baker convey just what it was that made Harlow an exceptional figure in Hollywood history. Both actresses were made up to resemble Harlow, but neither had the sensual fullness of body and the manner necessary for the part. Karl Tunberg wrote the Sargent script and John Michael Hayes the Levine. Both outline her early years as an extra, her luck in being chosen to play in Howard Hughes' production of *Hell's Angels* in 1930, and the seven frantic years that remained to her. Both present her trying home life with a selfish mother and an ambitious stepfather, but neither shows that she was married three times—first at the age of sixteen. Both pictures dwell upon her traumatic marriage to MGM film executive Paul Bern (Hurd Hatfield in the Sargent and Peter Lawford in the Levine), who committed suicide, presumably for reasons of sexual inadequacy. Neither film mentions that she was afterwards married to MGM cameraman Harold Rosson, whom she divorced.

Tunberg's original screenplay for the Sargent version sticks fairly close to the outlined but edited facts, and dwells more than the Levine on Harlow's tragic relationship with Paul Bern. It also points to her friendship with Marie Dressler (Hermione Baddeley) and the counseling she received from the esteemed Maria Ouspenskaya (Celia Lovsky). It presents her unhappy life with an ambitious mother (Ginger Rogers) and an opportunistic stepfather (Barry Sullivan), and places further tragedy on her unrequited love for a famous movie star, William Mansfield (Efrem Zimbalist, sounding and acting like Ronald Colman, in a part fusing Harlow's love for William Powell and her friendship with Clark Gable).

The Levine version is somewhat more interesting, if only because of the production values allowed by a fairly big budget. Hayes based his screenplay on the Shulman book, and since the book was largely written with the cooperation of Harlow's agent, Arthur Landau, he assumes a large, warm-hearted, solicitous role (Red Buttons) in this film. Those who knew Harlow felt Shulman had maligned her, and that his book was questionable in both fact and taste. Many of the titles of Harlow's films, as referred to in this picture, are false. Louis B. Mayer is thinly disguised as Everett Redman (Martin Balsam). In the Sargent version he is called Louis B. Mayer and played by Jack Kruschen. In both versions he is caricatured unsympatheticly and not very accurately. Howard Hughes is called Richard Manley (Leslie Neilsen) and Harlow's unrequited love is

Jean Harlow.

Carol Lynley as Jean Harlow.

Harlow (Lynley version, 1965): Efrem Zimbalist, Jr., Hurd Hatfield and Carol Lynley.

Harlow (Lynley version): Barry Sullivan, Ginger Rogers and Carol Lynley.

23

Harlow (Baker version, 1965): Carroll Baker, Raf Valone, Angela Lansbury and Red Buttons.

Harlow (Baker version): Carroll Baker duplicating one of Harlow's earliest roles—in a 1928 Hal Roach comedy.

The real Harlow, with her mother and step-father.

Carroll Baker as Jean Harlow.

24

Harlow (Baker version): A fictitious title.

called Jack Harrison (Michael Connors). The parents are well played by Angela Lansbury and Raf Vallone.

Jean Harlow died at the age of twenty-six of uremic poisoning, which caused a cerebral oedema. In Levine's film she dies of pneumonia, as a maudlin ballad about lost love drones from the sound track.

Valentino, produced by Edward Small and directed by Lewis Allen for Columbia in 1951, is so ridiculously untrue that it is difficult to believe it was actually made in Hollywood by people with knowledge of the film industry. It is a fictional account of Rudolph Valentino's brief period of super-stardom, and it presents him as a glib, brazenly confident ladykiller. Full of clichés and platitudes about love and success, the film might well have been written by his most doting fan. Producer Small claims to have spent years preparing the picture—there were supposedly eighteen versions of the script before he settled for the one written by George Bruce. The most obvious problem was to steer clear of libel action from the women with whom Valentino was involved. Another was to maintain his legendary image of virility, in spite of some gossip to the contrary.

To play Valentino, Columbia interviewed almost two thousand actors and screen-tested a vast number of them. (At one time 20th Century-Fox planned to produce a film about Valentino with Tyrone Power.) Finally chosen was a stage actor, unknown to film, who changed his name from Walter Fleischmann to Anthony Dexter. He trained for the part for three years, but was defeated by a naïve plot and hackneyed dialogue. Dexter was made up to look remarkably like Valentino, but as directed he could only charm his way through the ridiculous characterization. At the time of filming, Dexter was thirty-two, one year older than Valentino at the time of his death in 1926.

According to the film, Valentino was a mature young man by the time he arrived in America. He is seen as a dancer in a professional troupe sailing from Naples to New York on what appears to be a rusty tramp steamer. He romances an attractive woman (Eleanor Parker), who is actually a Hollywood star traveling incognito. This Valentino, who speaks American English fluently, tells her one evening in the moonlight, "You know how to use a woman's most powerful weapon—her mystery." She reminds him that until six days ago they had never met and he replies, "The world was created in six days." And when she cautiously suggests they restrain themselves until they get to know each other better, he

Valentino (1951): Richard Carlson, Eleanor Parker and Anthony Dexter.

26

Valentino: Eleanor Parker and Anthony Dexter.

Valentino: Eleanor Parker and Anthony Dexter recreating the famous scene from *The Sheik* (1921).

advises, "Tomorrow is a poor excuse for people who are afraid to live today." Valentino drips slick philosophy as smoothly as he dances, but the attention he pays the lady arouses the jealousy of his employer, who also happens to be a woman (Rita Moreno), and he blithely severs his contract.

In New York the penniless Valentino takes a job as a dishwasher but loses it when he hits a fellow worker for referring to him as a "greaseball." It then occurs to him he can make an easier living as a gigolo in a swank dance hall. With his shiny black hair slicked down it is easy to understand why his rival tutors refer to him as "Vaselino." The lady he dazzled on the boat now reappears, and Valentino

discovers she is Joan Carlyle and that her escort is famed director Bill King (Richard Carlson).

King informs him that "Miss Carlyle has had a tough day at the studio," but this doesn't stop him from sweeping her around the floor in a tango. She tells him that their previous meeting has no meaning for her, and he asks, "Then why is your heart pounding as it did that night on the boat?" King senses that Valentino "has something," and invites him to appear at the studio at Fort Lee, New Jersey. Valentino does a bit as an apache dancer in a café sequence, causing the director to exclaim, "Rudy, that was just great!"

This opinion is shared by a friendly actress, Lila

Agnes Ayres and Rudolph Valentino and the actual scene from *The Sheik*.

Reyes (Patricia Medina), but Valentino's eyes are on Joan, who chooses not to return his attentions. Believing he has a chance in the movie world, he borrows fifty dollars from a friend and leaves for Hollywood.

In Hollywood Valentino has no luck as he makes the rounds of the studios, but he is spotted and picked up by Lila, who tells him she is on her way to get a script. She parks her car outside the studio and while she is gone Valentino looks up at a billboard. It advertises a forthcoming production of *The Four Horsemen of the Apocalypse* and asks the question, "Who will play Julio—John Barrymore, John Gilbert, Douglas Fairbanks or. . . ?"

Valentino studies the part, but cannot get an interview with producer Mark Towers (Otto Kruger), so he turns up at the producer's birthday party with a group of musicians and boldly announces to Towers that he will now perform his impression of a dance prologue to the picture. His heel-clicking, whip-snapping tango wins immediate approval and Towers gives him the role of Julio. A re-creation of *The Four Horsemen*'s closing scene in the trenches is then shown. Newpaper headlines scream, "A Star Is Born!" as fan mail pours in by the ton. Valentino goes from picture to picture and we see flashing scenes of him as a bullfighter in *Blood and Sand*, a cossack in *The Eagle*, and a dueling

Natacha Rambova, Valentino's second wife.

aristocrat in *Monsieur Beaucaire*. Valentino takes all the successes in casual stride, the only apparent objective of his life being to win the love of Joan Carlyle, who does her brave best to resist him.

Valentino sets himself up in splendor and buys a magnificent home, which he calls Falcon Lair. Producer Towers now proudly announces that he has bought *The Sheik*. "I bought it for you—and with Joan Carlyle as your costar, it'll be a box-office earthquake!"

Valentino is pleased to get *The Sheik*, but both he and Joan realize the danger in their appearing together as lovers on the screen. Bill King is assigned to direct them, and he is puzzled by the reserve of the matinee idol in his love scenes with Joan, who is King's wife. He persuades them to invest their moments with "real feeling," and they do. Set musicians play "The Kashmiri Love Song" to create a mood as The Sheik seduces his lovely captive in his tent. Afterwards Rudy confesses to his secret love, "We should never have made this picture together." When the two bridle at the idea of doing a sequel, perplexed producer Towers rages, "An acute attack of success—once they get on top they lose their sense of balance."

While driving his car, Valentino swerves off the road when a sudden jab of pain hits his stomach. He takes to his bed to recuperate, but Joan telephones and pleads to see him. When he appears, she flies to his arms and they kiss passionately, no longer able to sublimate their feelings. Says Rudy, "Let me look at you." Says Joan, "I can't fight it anymore. I have nothing left to fight with." Unknown to Joan, she has been trailed to his home by a vicious newspaper columnist and his photographer. A flashbulb explodes in their faces as they leave the house, and Valentino grabs the camera and smashes it. He thrashes the two journalists, but in the course of the fight he receives a number of severe punches in the stomach, any one of which would badly wind any man, let alone one suffering apparent appendicitis. This incredible scene is topped off with the sneers of the columnist, "The great lover—he betrays the man who made him," referring to director King. As for Joan Carlyle: "And what I'll do to her!"

Nobly, Valentino leaves Hollywood for New York, thereby avoiding further harm to Joan. But first he calls the columnist to his home and squelches his forthcoming story by telling him that he is about to elope with Lila. He pretends to Joan that he doesn't love her, but she knows otherwise.

Valentino is hospitalized in New York with his increasing stomach pains. Lying in bed, he asks a friend to "Pull up the shade and let the sun shine in." As the sunlight falls across his face, Valentino dies. His death is reported in huge newspaper headlines, and crowds surge around the funeral parlor in which he lies. In Hollywood the sympathetic Bill King puts an arm around his grieving wife and tells her, "Yes, I knew." The film ends with a scene at Valentino's tomb twenty-five years later, as a woman dressed and veiled in black places a wreath. An off-screen narrator intones that the visit of this lone, mysterious figure is an annual event and that no one knows who she is. Then the narrator refers to Valentino's talent for making hearts beat a little faster and "made warm with the magic of his personality."

Valentino is an incredibly inaccurate film. It suggests that Valentino came to America after the First World War, whereas he had arrived before the war and made his first appearance in a film in 1914, when he was nineteen. It also manages to ignore the fact that he played parts in at least nineteen films prior to his success as Julio in *The Four Horsemen of the Apocalypse* in 1921. He had been brought to the attention of director Rex Ingram by a writer, June Mathis, and signed by Metro. Following a dispute over money, Valentino went with Paramount. *The*

Sheik, made in 1921, started the Valentino craze and won him multitudes of female fans, but according to this movie biography it was the last of his films. In reality, his final picture was *The Son of the Sheik* in 1926. Dancing, at which he was talented, was his relaxation until he was advised to take it up professionally, and he decided to try his luck in films after a touring theatrical company, in which he was appearing, broke up in Los Angeles.

Valentino presents the actor as a man who loved just one woman, and it completely overlooks his two marriages. His first wife was actress Jean Acker, whom he divorced, and his second was an enterprising, domineering lady, Winifred Shaunessy, who changed her name to Natacha Rambova and took over Valentino's life and career for a time. Had the public been aware that this romantic paragon, whose career was almost ruined by his wife-manager, was a henpecked husband, his decline would have been accelerated. Perhaps to offset this predicament, and possibly because of dire need, Valentino courted the famous vamp, Pola Negri, and their affair was well publicized. Negri fainted on a movie set when she learned of his death, and then caught a train to New York for a final look at the man whose demise had sent thousands of women into hysterics. He died from a perforated ulcer—something the film does not mention.

Despite their attempts to protect themselves by fictionalizing his life, Columbia was hit by a series of lawsuits after the release of *Valentino*. Eleanor Parker's role of Joan Carlyle is a composite of several women. Alice Terry, the widow of Rex Ingram and the star of *The Four Horsemen of the Apocalypse*, instructed her lawyer to prepare a case, and in Milan, Alberto Valentino and Mrs. Maria Strada, Valentino's brother and sister, sued Columbia for $700,000 damages, claiming the film caused them shame and humiliation. They also pointed out that they were not consulted about the film, and that from their standpoint it was completely unauthorized. The Valentino cases were settled out of court for much less than the original sums demanded, as is usually the case.

In 1957 Columbia made another biography, this time of actress Jeanne Eagels, and this brought a suit for $950,000 damages from her family for representing her as a dissolute and immoral person of low character. *Jeanne Eagels*, produced and directed by George Sidney, stars Kim Novak as the tragic actress who was considered to be among the most talented of her time. Daniel Fuchs' screenplay contains a puzzling disclaimer in its credit titles, advising

Jeanne Eagels (1957): Agnes Moorehead and Kim Novak.

31

Jeanne Eagels: Kim Novak and a far from accurate re-creation of the filming of *Man, Woman and Sin* (1927).

Jeanne Eagels: Kim Novak and Jeff Chandler.

The real Jeanne Eagels and Reginald Owen in *The Letter* (1929).

viewers that "all events in this photoplay are based on fact and fiction."

According to this account, Eagels was a waitress in the Midwest who worked as a cooch dancer in a carnival show as the first step in her ambition to be an actress. The carnival owner, Sal Satori (Jeff Chandler), falls in love with her but realizes he cannot stand in her way. In New York she is helped by a drama coach (Agnes Moorehead) and manages to get the role of Sadie Thompson in *Rain*, which becomes her great hit. According to this film, Eagels somehow cheated another actress (Virginia Bruce) out of getting the part and this sad, depressed woman commits suicide, setting up a guilt complex in Eagels which leads to her drinking and becoming irresponsible. Her marriage to a society sportsman (Charles Drake) does not bring her contentment, and her hedonistic ways lead to her being suspended by Actors Equity. Her old love, Satori, spots a loophole in the suspension—that it does not apply to vaudeville—and gets her work. But drink, self-disgust and hard living bring about her early death.

Kim Novak was a good physical choice to play Jeanne Eagels, but neither her acting nor the structure of this film communicates the qualities that made the temperamental Eagels a fascinating actress and a radiant woman. Eagels died in 1929 at the age of thirty-nine, as the result of an overdose of chloral hydrate taken in a doctor's office. She was indeed suspended by Equity for missing performances, but she was never a cooch dancer, there was no Satori in her life, and there is no record of an actress having killed herself on her account. She appeared in a few movies in the late twenties, and her first, *Man, Woman and Sin* with John Gilbert, made in 1927, is shown being filmed in *Jeanne Eagels*. But the hammy acting and the jerky, speeded-up footage presented was not the way silent films were being made or projected in 1927. Also, one gets the impression that *Man, Woman and Sin* was about the Civil War and directed by Frank Borzage, who appears briefly behind the cameras. Actually, the film was a newspaper and courtroom drama directed by Monta Bell. Her last two films, made the year she died, were *The Letter* (later re-made with Bette Davis) and *Jealousy* (also re-made with Davis in a considerably altered version called *Deception*].

The success of *With a Song in My Heart* in 1952, the story of Jane Froman, inspired other movie biographies about female singers who had had some involvement with Hollywood. Jane Froman, well played by Susan Hayward, became popular as a radio star and made two pictures—*Stars Over Broadway* (1935) and *Radio City Revels* (1938) —neither of which gained her much favor with the filmgoing public. This fact was overlooked in *With a Song in My Heart*. Instead, the film concentrates on her shows for servicemen during the war years and her remarkable recovery from severe injuries sustained in an air crash in 1943.

In 1953 Warners made a bio-picture of Grace Moore, who died in an air crash in 1947 at the age of forty-five. The vacuous title of the film, *So This Is Love*, is an indication of its bland treatment of a lady who' was in person pleasantly forceful and humorous. A liking for this film rests almost entirely on a liking for the singing of Kathryn Grayson. It allowed her a wide range of material, from musical comedy to opera, but again there was little mention of Grace Moore's work in movies. To the older general public Grace Moore is now best remembered for the movie operettas in which she appeared in the mid-thirties, particularly for *One Night of Love* and its title song.

The story of Ruth Etting was vividly told in MGM's *Love Me or Leave Me*, produced by Joe Pasternak and directed by Charles Vidor in 1955. Miss Etting's story was one of the few show business yarns to contain genuine dramatic substance. She was a Nebraska girl making a meager living as a nightclub singer in Chicago in the early 1920s when she came under the spell of a minor racketeer named Martin Snyder. Snyder was a crude, ill-tempered, domineering man who limped from a leg wound and was known as "The Gimp." He fell in love with Etting and took over her life, despite her objections,

With a Song in My Heart (1952): David Wayne and Susan Hayward.

Jane Froman with James Melton on the set of *Stars Over Broadway* (1935).

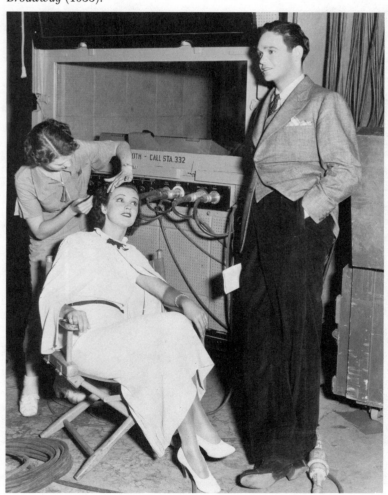

and pushed her career into the upper regions, where she earned big money making records, doing broadcasts, appearing on Broadway in the *Ziegfeld Follies*, and eventually making a few films in Hollywood. She and Snyder were married for seventeen years, during which time she took to drinking to relieve the anguish of her relationship with the jealous, ranting Snyder. When she confronted him with a demand for a divorce in 1938, he shot the man he considered responsible for stealing her affections—pianist Myrl Alderman, who had known her even before Snyder. Alderman recovered from his wounds, Snyder served a year in jail, and Etting decided to retire from her career and settle down with Alderman, who died in 1966.

MGM, contrary to the usual difficulties, managed to get the full permission of Etting, Snyder and Alderman to tell their story with candor, and Doris Day, James Cagney and Cameron Mitchell played the respective parts. Daniel Fuchs won an Oscar for his original screenplay, which hews fairly close to the facts and allows a generous presentation of a dozen or more of the songs associated with Ruth Etting. Doris Day's sympathetic characterization contains some of her best work as an actress, and Cagney's Snyder is yet another example of his great ability.

Grace Moore in *I'll Take Romance* (1937).

So This Is Love (1953): Kathryn Grayson as Grace Moore.

Love Me or Leave Me (1955): Doris Day and James Cagney.

The part is that of a detestable man, but Cagney makes him thoroughly understandable. The real Snyder's only apparent concern with his portrayal on the screen was that Cagney should get his limp right. *Love Me or Leave Me* does not feature references to Ruth Etting's film work, which was not particularly distinguished. She is best remembered for her supporting role in Eddie Cantor's *Roman Scandals* in 1933, in which she sang "No More Love." Her last two feature film appearances were in *Hips, Hips, Hooray* and *Gift of Gab*, both made in 1934.

When asked about *Love Me or Leave Me* by W. Franklyn Moshier in a 1974 interview for *Film Fan Monthly*, Miss Etting replied: "Oh, what a mess that was. . . . I was never at any time a dance hall girl. It was just a means of working in 'Ten Cents a Dance.' They took a lot of liberties with my life, but I guess they usually do with that kind of thing." And this was one of the relatively accurate biographical films!

The most successful of Hollywood's accounts of famous singer-actresses surviving the calamities of their lives is *I'll Cry Tomorrow*, with Susan Hayward giving an excellent performance as Lillian Roth. The 1955 MGM film, directed by Daniel Mann, comes reasonably close to the truth, although

Love Me or Leave Me: Harry Bellaver and James Cagney watching Doris Day and Cameron Mitchell.

Love Me or Leave Me: Doris Day and Cameron Mitchell.

Ruth Etting as she appeared in *Roman Scandals* (1933).

it reduces the number of husbands from five to three. Hayward pulls no punches in depicting the alcoholic despair and degradation of Lillian Roth, who claims to have started drinking when she was twenty and kept at it for sixteen years, during which time she slid from considerable popularity on the stage and screen. Her redemption came about through Alcoholics Anonymous, and her comeback as a public figure began when she agreed to be a subject of the television program "This Is Your Life." She then prepared an autobiography with Gerold Frank, which became a best seller and resulted in offers to work as a television and nightclub singer.

I'll Cry Tomorrow pinpoints Roth's initial problem as being her conflict with her forceful mother (Jo Ann Fleet), who pushed her into show business. Her other problems come from men. She falls in love with a young man (Ray Danton), whose death is a great shock to her. She marries a weakling playboy (Don Taylor) and drinks with him because they have little else in common. Her next marriage is to a sadistic fortune-hunter (Richard Conte), who turns her into a drunk when he wants to get rid of her. Then follows utter despair and groveling for drink in cheap bars, from which she is saved by a sympathetic member of AA (Eddie Albert).

Lillian Roth's career began as a child in movies. In 1918, at the age of seven, she was hailed as Broadway's youngest star. Returning to Hollywood in her late teens (1929), she became a star at Paramount—which studio is actually shown in this MGM picture. Among her films were *The Love Parade* with Maurice Chevalier, *Animal Crackers* with the Marx Brothers, and *The Vagabond King* with Dennis King. *I'll Cry Tomorrow* shows a little of her film-making activities in the early footage, but the picture deals mainly with her personal problems. Susan Hayward did her own singing of the songs identified with Roth, such as "Ain't She Sweet?" and "If I Could Be with You," but Roth herself later made an album for Epic of the songs from the film.

Warners turned to the subject of alcoholic singers in 1957, when they made *The Helen Morgan Story*, to which they had bought the rights in 1942, a year after the singer's death at the age of forty-one. The film is good only as an evocation of the Twenties, with Rudy Vallee and Walter Winchell appearing as themselves, and for the singing by Gogi Grant of the many fine songs associated with Helen Morgan. Miss Grant dubbed for Ann Blyth, whose own singing voice was considered by Warners to sound a little too classical. It might also be said that Miss Blyth herself was a little too classical in appearance to play the frail, wailing torch singer.

Directed by the estimable Michael Curtiz, the screenplay is thin and false. Helen Morgan was an alcoholic, but according to this account she drank because of an unrequited love affair with a prominent married lawyer (Richard Carlson) and because of the cavalier behavior of a roguish racketeer (Paul Newman). Both men were inventions. The film deals with her success as a nightclub singer and her acclaim on Broadway as one of the stars of the original *Showboat* in 1926, but neglects to mention that she also re-created her role in the second film version ten years later. In fact, it completely overlooks her movie career, which ranged from 1929 to 1936 and included Warners' *Go Into Your Dance*, with Al Jolson and Ruby Keeler.

By far the most successful of the show business biographical films is *The Jolson Story*, made by Columbia in 1946. As is sometimes the case with successful pictures, it had severe birth pains. The idea for the film belonged to columnist Sidney Skolsky, who had long been an admirer of Al Jolson. Skolsky believed that despite the decline in Jolson's career, a picture about his many years of enormous fame would find approval with both the old public and the new. Skolsky began presenting the idea to

I'll Cry Tomorrow (1955): Susan Hayward and Don Taylor.

Lillian Roth with Reginald Denny and Roland Young in *Madam Satan* (1930).

I'll Cry Tomorrow: Susan Hayward rendering "Sing You Sinners."

37

The Helen Morgan Story (1957): Ann Blyth.

Helen Morgan at the time of her appearance in *Sweet Music* (1935).

studio heads in 1943, but at every turn it was rejected, and very often with contempt. The brash, egocentric Jolson had made few friends in Hollywood, and there were many who felt his decline was deserved, that not even *his* talent justified his arrogance and insensitivity toward others. However, this would not have been a factor had they believed in the commercial appeal of a movie based on his career. Almost every film executive considered Jolson a has-been with an outdated style. Seldom has any industry been so united in being so wrong.

The only studio not completely opposed to Skolsky's proposal was Columbia, whose tough chieftain, Harry Cohn, was himself a Jolson fan. It took Cohn several months to make up his mind to do *The Jolson Story*, and even when it was in production the rest of Hollywood still scoffed. The studio where Skolsky thought he would get the most sympathetic ear, Warner Bros., turned out to be the least interested. The executives there considered the project absurd, despite the fact that Jolson was a stockholder and an important figure in the history of the studio. It was Jolson who starred in the first talkie, *The Jazz Singer*, in 1927 and set the small, financially shaky company on the road to prosperity.

But Jolson had not starred in a Warner movie since *Go Into Your Dance* in 1936, and after that his film career waned. Three years went by before Jolson next appeared in Hollywood, taking supporting billing to Alice Faye and Tyrone Power at 20th Century-Fox in *Rose of Washington Square*, followed by a guest bit in *Hollywood Cavalcade* and a portrayal of famed minstrel man E. P. Christie in *Swanee River*. Jolson received good notices for his work, but not enough to revitalize his screen career. Again he left Hollywood in partial disgust, to find whatever work he could get on the stage and in radio.

Skolsky's efforts to interest Warners in a film about Jolson took place just after the studio had completed *Rhapsody in Blue*, their large-scaled pseudo-biography of George Gershwin. They had hired Jolson to play himself in the sequence dealing with Gershwin's first hit song, "Swanee," which Jolson made famous on Broadway in 1919. Although he performed the song with great vitality in the picture, it produced no public clamor for more Jolson. Warners could also rightly point to the fact that Jolson's new recording of the song, made to bolster and perhaps cash in on his appearance in *Rhapsody in Blue*, had done very poorly, barely selling enough copies to cover its cost. Nonetheless, Harry Cohn commissioned Sidney Skolsky to produce the film and Stephen Longstreet to write it.

Al Jolson was, as expected, ecstatic at the idea of a film based on his life. He placed himself totally at the disposal of the studio and became cooperative to the point of being a problem. The sixty-year-old entertainer desperately wanted to play himself on the screen, but he was finally convinced that no amount of make-up could possibly present him as a young man. Jolson was present at every stage of pre-production and filming, and he was part of the group sitting in on the auditions of the many actors who were tested to play the lead. No one, in his opinion, had the vitality and the radiance to play Jolson.

One of the first tested was Larry Parks, who had been under contract to Columbia for several years and had made only a minor name for himself. He was dismissed and the part was considered for more famous actors. The only star Jolson thought capable of playing the role was James Cagney, but Cagney politely declined. Finally, Harry Cohn reviewed the situation and decided, over Jolson's objections, that the best available man for the part was Larry Parks.

There was never any question that Jolson's voice would be used in the film. He was paid $25,000 to

Ruby Keeler and Al Jolson in *Go Into Your Dance* (1935).

Sidney Skolsky, Larry Parks, Al Jolson and Columbia Pictures executive Jonie Taps on the set of *The Jolson Story* (1946).

The Jolson Story: Larry Parks and Evelyn Keyes.

record the many songs the film required, and he volunteered to coach Parks in the physical performance of the material. On his own, Parks spent weeks studying Jolson films and recordings, and not until many years later did he admit that working with Jolson was much less fun than he claimed at the time. Jolson was a man of enormous energy, and he almost exhausted the younger man in his demands to approximate his movements in performing the songs. In the case of "Swanee," Jolson—ever compulsive and domineering—demanded to perform the song himself on camera because Parks couldn't give it the exact Jolson supercharge. So in blackface and in long-shot it is Jolson himself who appears in this one sequence of *The Jolson Story*.

As a biography, *The Jolson Story* is a very soft account of his career. While it presents him as a confident, ambitious, forceful entertainer, it presents those qualities only in their more appealing aspects. It barely hinted at his driving conceit and his all-consuming need to perform, but it did communicate Jolson's spellbinding ability to hold an audience in the palm of his hand, with a personality as bright as a searchlight, and a voice and style unlike those of any other singer. He was, even in the admission of those who did not personally like him, a magical performer. The screenplay, however,

omitted many facts and facets of his life, including his brother, his two sisters and the first of his three wives. Jolson's love in *The Jolson Story* is a lady called Julie Benson, played by Evelyn Keyes. The role represented Ruby Keeler, who was married to Jolson from 1928 to 1940, but she refused to allow any mention of her name in connection with the film or any discussion of her opinions of Jolson. However, she accepted a sum of $25,000 not to be involved in the project or to have any say in its outcome.

The Jolson Story is, in a sense, an ideal movie biography, since it presents its subject in the light both he and his admirers preferred. It is a bright, bouncing piece of entertainment and as such it remains one of the biggest successes in the history of Columbia Pictures. It triggered a landslide comeback in the life of Al Jolson. From the depths of an almost collapsed career he went back to the peak of popularity he had known as a Broadway giant. In the remaining four years of his life Jolson continually made recordings and broadcasts, and, not unnaturally, a sequel to *The Jolson Story*. *Jolson Sings Again* (1949) is less than its predecessor simply because so little of Jolson's story was left to tell. It proved popular because once more Larry Parks expertly mimed a slew of engaging songs.

Jolson Sings Again tells the story of the amazing

40

resurgence of his career, and goes into interesting detail about the actual making of *The Jolson Story*. Again Jolson wanted to play himself—and almost did—but Cohn was not completely sold on the idea and again sent for Parks. The film was shot for about half the cost of the first picture, and it utilized a good deal of footage from the original. And it made an enormous profit. The fictitious Julie Benson appears at the beginning of the film, but after she passes out of Jolson's life, a new lady enters, one Ellen Clark (Barbara Hale), a role accurately based on X-ray technician Erle Galbraith, the last Mrs. Jolson. For Jolson enthusiasts the film is a grand slam, and for film buffs it is particularly interesting in showing the manner in which Parks performed to the Jolson voice in dubbing the first picture. It reveals much of the sound stage techniques and gadgetry, and in the scenes of the filming of *The Jolson Story* in *Jolson Sings Again* Larry Parks is seen both as Jolson and himself.

The film also deals with Jolson's admirable work in entertaining the armed forces overseas. He had performed unstintingly for the troops, and despite his age and against the advice of his doctors, Jolson repeatedly toured the battle zones of Korea in the summer of 1950. In September he exhausted himself with a particularly arduous tour in Korea and died of heart failure within a few weeks of arriving home in California. His age was given as sixty-four, but he may have been older since there were no records of his birth in a small Russian town, and he had arbitrarily picked a birthday. Of the many comments about Al Jolson, perhaps the most pertinent is this one by George Jessel, who lost *The Jazz Singer* to Jolson because the money wasn't big enough: "He was a no-good son of a bitch, but he was the greatest entertainer I've ever seen."

Sidney Skolsky tried for a similar success in 1953 with Warners' *The Eddie Cantor Story* and employed Alfred E. Green, who had directed *The Jolson Story*, to guide Keefe Brasselle in a physical impersonation of Cantor as the veteran comic mouthed his famous songs. The results were lamentable. Cantor, who was a kindly man and well liked in Hollywood, summed up his feelings about the picture years later: "If that was my life, I didn't live."

It was Cantor himself who pressed Sidney Skolsky to make a film about his life and offered backing to prepare the screenplay. Skolsky outlined the story and brought in Jerome Weidman and Ted Sherdeman to arrive at a final script. The result was a rather conventional account of a show-biz rise to

The Jolson Story: Larry Parks, William Demarest, Bill Goodwin and Evelyn Keyes.

Jolson Sings Again: Larry Parks and Barbara Hale.

Jolson Sings Again (1949): Barbara Hale, Larry Parks and William Demarest.

Jolson Sings Again: Giving his all for the boys.

fame, its only conflict coming from Cantor's compulsive work habits, which cause him to neglect his wife and five daughters. The film traces his impoverished childhood and his early days as a child performer, through vaudeville and his acclaim on Broadway. It touches on his great success in radio in the thirties, but pays scant attention to his Hollywood career.

A major drawback in *The Eddie Cantor Story* is Keefe Brasselle, who gives the impression that Cantor was a sprightly, eyeball-rolling comic every hour of the day. Part of Cantor's humor played on the fact that he was a man of short stature, but since Brasselle is a six-footer, this point is lost. Cantor and his wife Ida are seen at the opening and closing of the picture as they attend a private screening of his movie biography, but they serve only to accentuate the blandness and the falsity of the picture.

Among the most bland of the biographical pictures is *Beloved Infidel,* an account of the love affair of writer F. Scott Fitzgerald and Hollywood columnist Sheilah Graham. This might have been interesting, but 20th Century-Fox decided it should be a tragic love story aimed at women. As such it offends those who look for insights into Fitzgerald's last sad years. The tone of the film was set with the miscasting of Gregory Peck as Fitzgerald and Deborah Kerr as Sheilah Graham, both very capable actors but quite different in type from the originals. Peck is too robust and Kerr too refined. The point of

Graham's story was that she was a Cockney girl who yearned for life on a higher level of society and in Fitzgerald found a Henry Higgins. She referred to her story as "the education of a woman" and credited Fitzgerald with teaching her much about life and literature. In return she claims to have helped restore his faith in himself at a low period in his life. Little of this is apparent in *Beloved Infidel,* in which Fitzgerald appears as an amiable alcoholic who occasionally becomes violent, and Graham as a budding gossip columnist who becomes his common-law wife.

Fitzgerald and Graham met in 1937 at a party at The Garden of Allah, the fabled residential hotel which was located on Sunset Boulevard at the corner of Crescent Heights, now the site of office buildings. Among the celebrated guests of the hotel was Robert Benchley, who befriended Fitzgerald and Graham and who appears in a slightly disguised form in *Beloved Infidel* as Robert Carter, played by Eddie Albert—yet another example of the film's sad diminishing of potential assets. Fitzgerald was at this time in his life working as a writer for the studios, attempting to earn enough money to maintain his daughter in college and his wife, Zelda, in a sanitarium.

Graham had already bettered herself socially and was intending to marry a titled Englishman, but she was drawn to the bitter Fitzgerald, whose career had almost collapsed due to improvident living, changing times and "emotional bankruptcy." Their life together spanned just three years. Fitzgerald died in 1940 at the age of forty-four. Graham undoubtedly helped Fitzgerald pull himself together in order to write what there is of his last novel, *The Last Tycoon.* Fitzgerald's own failure to come to terms with Hollywood is best summed up in one of his last comments about the place: "A strange conglomeration of a few excellent, overtired men making the pictures and as dismal a crowd of fakes and hacks at the bottom as you can imagine."

The worst thing about *Beloved Infidel* is that it reverses the intent of Graham's book, written with Gerold Frank, which made it clear she was indebted to the intelligent and cultured Fitzgerald and that he had regained his belief in himself. In the film it appears she is the strong but gentle savior of a weakling. Of interest is the studio's partial recreation of The Garden of Allah, with its swimming pool built in the shape of the Black Sea to remind Alla Nazimova, the silent screen vamp who originally owned the property, of her native land. Many parties were held around that pool and many

42

Beloved Infidel (1959): Deborah Kerr and Gregory Peck.

Eddie and Ida Cantor at the premiere of *The Eddie Cantor Story*. The expression on Cantor's face might well express his reaction: "That was *my* story?"

The Eddie Cantor Story (1953): Marilyn Erskine, Jackie Barnett and Keefe Brasselle.

Beloved Infidel: Herbert Rudley, Karin Booth and
Deborah Kerr.

famous people were said to have fallen in fully
clothed. The film could not resist including such a
scene, but here the gaiety seemed very contrived.

The film includes a few scenes in movie studios as
Graham goes about her business as a columnist, and
it touches upon one actual incident. She was once
introduced to Constance Bennett, about whom she
had made a slighting comment in print, and the
actress remarked that Graham was the biggest bitch
in Hollywood, to which Graham replied, "No, the
second biggest." Here the actress was played by
Karin Booth and given the name Janet Pierce.

A feature film for television, *The Screen Test: F.
Scott Fitzgerald in Hollywood*, not yet shown at the
time of the completion of this book, hopefully will
deal with the characters, events and periods with a
reasonable degree of fidelity. The script concerns
itself with two out of three of Fitzgerald's Hollywood
sojourns in 1927 and 1937. Jason Miller portrays the
author, Tuesday Weld his wife, Zelda, and Julia
Foster is Sheilah Graham. In any case, the
photography of the estimable James Crabe will be a
strong asset.

In her book *The Rest of the Story* Sheilah Graham
spelled out her bitter disappointment with the film
version of *Beloved Infidel*, describing it as a complete disaster. She felt the actor best suited to play
Fitzgerald was Richard Basehart, but the studio
rejected the idea on the grounds his name was not
commercial enough. Desperately unhappy with the
script written by Alfred Hayes, Graham asked
producer Jerry Wald if she could write her own
version. Wald agreed, but according to Graham,
none of her material was accepted and she retreated
from further involvement in the production.

She writes: "When you have sold your story to a
motion picture company, you have sold your soul to
the devil. They can change your name, the title, the
story, they can make you fictitious, they can make
you real, they can cut anything they like, add
anything they like, they can sell you to television,
they can sell you down the river. All they cannot do,
according to the contract, is hold you up to public
ridicule and scorn. And 20th Century-Fox managed
this too."

Sheila Graham at the time of filming *Beloved Infidel*.

F. Scott Fitzgerald circa 1934.

CHAPTER TWO

BOMBSHELLS AND GODDESSES

Sharon Kimm and Mickey Reid, childhood sweethearts in a tenement neighborhood, are separated when Sharon is placed in an orphanage. Years later in Hollywood, Sharon works as an extra, but a flair for wearing beautiful clothes results in her being given a chance for Fame by a Great Director. So Sharon—once insignificant and forlorn—is quickly skyrocketed to glory and a place among the stars. Ironically, the movie that made her an overnight sensation was written by her childhood sweetheart, Mickey.

She buys a costly home in Beverly Hills, surrounds herself with a retinue of servants, jewels and limitless luxuries. Her quick rise leaves her self-centered and a spendthrift, so she seeks monetary aid from the Great Director who gave her a break. He offers to help, but with certain—shall we say—conditions. As the title card phrases it: "Then came to Sharon the shock of realization that his interest in her natural art was but a mask to cloak his lust." Sharon goes the way of desire, vanity and debt. Finally, the fallen star goes back to her childhood sweetheart, now aware that she has been a thoughtless and ex-

travagant peacock. Thus, she finds Truth and the ultimate haven in the Right Man's arms. Fade out.

It was a long way from the exploits of Sharon Kimm in *The Skyrocket* (1926) to the fate of the ladies portrayed in *Valley of the Dolls* (1967). The screen's glamour girls, sex symbols, love goddesses, blonde bombshells, barefoot contessas, fading or aging movie queens have been dealt with extensively in the fictions of the films—from Peggy Hopkins Joyce, the dazzling blonde beauty of the 1920s, who portrayed Sharon Kimm in *The Skyrocket*, to Gloria Swanson, the legendary grand lady of many decades, who often has been confused with her portrayal of Norma Desmond, the old-time movie queen living in a world of illusions on *Sunset Boulevard*.

Back in the 1930s Gloria Swanson reportedly confided to an interviewer, "I don't want to be glamorous. I'm tired to death of being glamorous. What does it mean, anyway?"

What, indeed, does it mean? Most assuredly different things to those who are glamorous and those who aren't equipped but would like to be.

Sunset Boulevard: Gloria Swanson and William Holden celebrating New Year's Eve.

Peggy Hopkins Joyce in *The Skyrocket* (1926).

Hollywood Speaks (1932): Pat O'Brien, Genevieve Tobin and Lucien Prival.

Physical beauty by itself can only hold the public a few years. Then there must be something more. For those without something more, trying times are ahead. As somebody once said, to be once adored and then long forgotten is an intolerable state. The director (Cecil B. DeMille) states in *Sunset Boulevard*, "A dozen press agents working overtime can do terrible things to the human spirit."

The conclusion of Hollywood's self-analysis is always that Hollywood destroys. Success gives self-destructive impulses free reign. But the misguided, manufactured sex symbols who half believe and half despise their own publicity inevitably destroy themselves. Hollywood is the catalyst—and a powerful one—that makes it possible for ill-equipped beauties to achieve swiftly, without being provided the education, maturity and perspective to enable them to cope with the "too much, too soon" syndrome built largely on illusions.

The Skyrocket, based on a *Cosmopolitan* magazine story and book by Adela Rogers St. Johns, was the first of two films made by that notorious glamour queen of the 1920s, Peggy Hopkins Joyce. A showgirl in the *Ziegfeld Follies* and Earl Carroll's *Vanities*, she appeared in plays, wrote novels and an autobiography (*Men, Marriage and Me*). The blonde Peggy wed and fled three millionaires in

Hollywood Speaks: The director (Lucien Prival) discussing the role with his star (Genevieve Tobin).

Hollywood Speaks: Genevieve Tobin.

rapid succession and, in all, married six times, including one nobleman. Mrs. St. Johns refers to her as "the mistress of one very rich man after another. She once said to me, 'There are two kinds of women: those who love diamonds and those who don't.' "

Peggy Hopkins Joyce photographed well, but her acting and personality on the screen left something to be desired. Director Marshall Neilan cast her in his independent production of *The Skyrocket*, although their romance of two years earlier was over. The role of Sharon Kimm was said to be based somewhat on Gloria Swanson, and many saw Marshall Neilan himself as the prototype of the star-maker and director played by Earle Williams.

Adela Rogers St. Johns' *Cosmopolitan* story "The Worst Woman in Hollywood" was the basis for Anna Q. Nilsson's 1924 vehicle, *Inez from Hollywood*, which dealt with a screen vamp who is primarily concerned with shielding her younger sister (Mary Astor) from the life and men she knows. That same year Irene Rich played a screen star in *Behold This Woman*, a not particularly noteworthy Vitagraph production. The year before, in *Broadway Broke* Mary Carr was a retired theatrical star with financial problems, but when she sells her plays to a film executive she is rediscovered as a motion picture actress in the bargain.

The Miracle of the Bells (1948): Fred MacMurray and Alida Valli.

The Miracle of the Bells: Fred MacMurray and Lee J. Cobb.

Hollywood Speaks (1932) furthered the general belief that some directors are on the make for pretty actresses. At the film's beginning a young lady played by Genevieve Tobin is about to take poison in the lobby of Grauman's Chinese Theatre because she has been frustrated in her ambition to be a film star. But a newspaper columnist (Pat O'Brien) prevents the suicide and then determines he will help the aspiring actress. By clever press agentry and introductions to the right people, he makes her a star. She flatters a famed director (overplayed by the road-company von Stroheim, Lucien Prival), and gets involved in a scandal when the director's wife (Leni Stengel) commits suicide and blames the actress in a note. Racketeers move in and attempt blackmail. The scandal is broadcast and the star's career collapses. But the columnist marries her anyway.

This rather dull, synthetic picture purports to expose Hollywood rackets, and ventures occasionally in a mild way to give glimpses of the workings of the film capital and its intrigues. But the main point seems to be the naïve glorification of the studios and all who inhabit them.

Eighteen years later, another dull, incredibly naïve and sentimental film, *The Miracle of the Bells* (1948), told of a beautiful Polish-American girl (Alida Valli) from a Pennsylvania coal town who dies just after finishing a big role in a Hollywood epic. The producer (Lee J. Cobb) decides to shelve the film. A publicity man (Fred MacMurray), who was in love with the girl, takes her body back to her home town and attempts to carry out her last wishes

for the funeral. He gains publicity by having the bells of the town ring for four days. Then, as the actress's body lies in state in the dingy church, the statues of St. Michael and the Virgin slowly turn on their bases until they face the coffin. This is regarded as a miracle, and the public's emotional reaction causes the producer to change his mind and release the picture. The priest (Frank Sinatra) of St. Michael's has a realistic explanation for the miracle, but he does not reveal it to the public: Unprecedented crowds, drawn by the publicity, caused the old church to settle, thereby turning the statues.

While on the subject of funerals, *The Barefoot Contessa* (1954) begins in a cemetery in Rapallo, Italy. It is the funeral of Maria Vargas (Ava Gardner). In flashback sequences, a film director (Humphrey Bogart), press agent (Edmond O'Brien), and later an Italian nobleman (Rossano Brazzi) tell how this Spanish Cinderella was discovered dancing in a café in Madrid, how she rapidly became an international star, how she fended off the tyrannical Wall Street wizard turned movie producer (Warren Stevens), how she went off with the amoral heir to a vast South American fortune (Marius Goring) and how she met and tragically loved a proud but impotent Italian nobleman (Brazzi). In the course of all this we also discover that the young lady only feels at home with her feet in the dirt, and she throbs with a loneliness and fear that drive her to keep earthy trysts with every guitarist, Gypsy dancer, or chauffeur who happens along.

Writer-director Joseph L. Mankiewicz loves good talk and does write arresting dialogue, but his characters seem to be forever sounding off—either explaining themselves as if they were in group psychotherapy, or waxing philosophical at the drop of a hat. In this film there is a succession of party scenes in which people get drunk in a sophisticated manner, and in which at twelve o'clock there is a great unmasking of inner secrets. "I'm going home with him," says a blonde starlet (Mari Aldon), described as "Made in Hollywood," who has supinely accepted a proposition from the wealthy young producer. "And you know why? Because I'm a tramp." She also says, "Don't worry about your soul; you must have lost it at some preview a long time ago."

Fans who delight in *films à clef* have a field day with *The Barefoot Contessa.* The lady herself seems to be composed of a bit of Rita Hayworth, a dash of Jean Harlow, a portion of Hemingway's Lady Brett Ashley from *The Sun Also Rises* and a fair amount of the real Ava Gardner. Howard Hughes, naturally, is the model for the millionaire producer, and his press agent, Johnny Meyer, is the springboard for the role played by Edmond O'Brien. Also present are caricatures based on the Duke of Windsor, King Farouk, Elsa Maxwell and probably others too inside to recognize.

Marilyn Monroe appeared to be the prototype for Paddy Chayefsky's study of *The Goddess* (1958), although director John Cromwell seemed to feel that Ava Gardner's life inspired the film. It is an interesting work containing one major miscalculation: the casting of stage actress Kim Stanley in the role of a sensuous sex symbol. As with the casting of Jack Palance in the role of a major star with considerable romantic appeal in *The Big Knife,* regardless of how well the roles are played, the characterizations are impossible to believe because of the physical limitations of the players.

The goddess of the title, Chayefsky protested, is no particular movie queen. The goddess is really William James' bitch-goddess, Success. And the heroine, Chayefsky declared, "represents an entire generation that came through the Depression with nothing left but a hope for comfort and security. Their tragedy lies in that they never learned to love, either their fellow humans or whatever god they have."

Emily Ann Faulkner's (Kim Stanley) father had killed himself when she was four, and a few weeks later she hears her mother (Betty Lou Holland) begging some relatives to take the child. Nobody pays much attention to the girl until she turns six-

The Barefoot Contessa: Rossano Brazzi, Ava Gardner and Humphrey Bogart.

The Barefoot Contessa (1954): Ava Gardner, Humphrey Bogart and Elizabeth Sellars.

The Barefoot Contessa: Edmond O'Brien, Warren Stevens and Humphrey Bogart.

The Goddess (1958): Kim Stanley, Joyce Van Patten and Joanne Linville.

The Goddess: Kim Stanley and Lloyd Bridges.

The Goddess: Lloyd Bridges and Kim Stanley.

teen, and then it seems as though every male in Beacon City, Maryland wants her—and several follow through. While working in the five-and-ten she keeps herself alive by dreaming of Hollywood and how it would be if she became a famous movie star. One day she lures the heavy-drinking son of a Hollywood star (Steven Hill), who happens to be in town, to a hotel and eventually persuades him to marry her. Months later he is off to the wars, and Emily Ann has a baby. "I don't want her!" she screams. "I got a good figure. I want to have some fun."

She leaves the baby with her mother, goes to Hollywood, changes her name to Rita Shawn, gets a divorce, and marries an ex-light-heavyweight champion (Lloyd Bridges), who has no hold on anything except the past. All he does is sit around and watch television while she files her nails.

After that marriage ends, she suddenly clicks in a small part. The producer decides she has something: "the quality of availability." The executive producer asks her for a date. She asks, "Shall I dress?" And he replies, "What does it matter?"

Before long she has everything—four thousand dollars a week, a villa with an indoor pool and a nervous breakdown. She tries religion for a while, but decides she likes liquor better. After that she stumbles along from drink to drink, sleeping pills to waking pills, picture to picture. "Life really is a fraud, isn't it?" she sighs one day through the barbiturate haze.

An even closer parallel with Marilyn Monroe was presented in the 1974 feature film produced for television, *The Sex Symbol*, based on Alvah Bessie's novel. The major roles in this blatant, cliché-ridden and tasteless farrago are thinly veiled caricatures of Monroe, Joe DiMaggio, Arthur Miller, Harry Cohn, a Kennedy-like senator and a combination Hedda Hopper-Louella Parsons Hollywood columnist. Mumbling about Chekhov and Ibsen, the artist-intellectual husband of The Sex Symbol (Connie Stevens) tells her that she "possesses deep spiritual beauty, a brilliant mind and tremendous strength." Snarling about box-office receipts, the no-nonsense producer has a somewhat earthier outlook: "She's a piece of meat that I buy and sell like the rest of them. . . . a pretty face, good rear and nice chest." So much for *The Sex Symbol*.

Whereas *The Goddess* suffered from unlikely casting, Louis Malle's French-Italian co-production of *A Very Private Affair* (1962) benefited considerably from the presence of Brigitte Bardot playing a sex symbol very much like Brigitte Bardot.

A *Very Private Affair* (1962): Marcello Mastroianni and Brigitte Bardot.

Jill (Bardot) is hopelessly in love with a young Italian theatre director (Marcello Mastroianni). She lives with her mother in a villa on Lake Geneva; then, unhappy, she goes off to Paris and a career as a dancer. This fails; she becomes a photographer's model. Suddenly Jill is catapulted into motion picture stardom as a "sex kitten." She has a number of men, is idolized by thousands of film fans, and is mobbed wherever she goes. As her successes on celluloid increase, in like ratio do her amours and her public attention. She finds she cannot have individual solitude and personal affection for herself alone but only for the image she has created. There is no surcease even in the comparative safety of her apartment. Her cleaning lady fills the air with epithets and denounces Jill for ruining men's lives, among other things: "Can't you leave those poor boys alone! You can't sleep with every man in the world! You bitch! You earn millions for running around naked, while my brother's in Algeria!"

Under the strain, her nerves break. She flees and finally finds her old love, the director. Rescued by him, she begins anew her temporarily postponed affair and ultimately follows him to the picturesque Italian city of Spoleto, where he is producing a summer pageant.

There is, throughout the film, the flashing of camera bulbs and the bustle of autograph seekers. It is almost inevitable, therefore, that Miss Bardot's grand finale be associated with the clamor of a crowd and the bursting, blinding light of flashbulbs. As she stands atop a roof watching the play below, the snap of a shutter and the flash of light startle her and make her fall to her death. As the sex kitten falls in slow motion, her long hair loosely undulating, there is a moment of silence—no scream, no shouts, no shrill music. The tormented girl has finally found peace. She is seen with a serene expression on her face as she falls through space.

Incredibly, the project originally was planned as a film version of Noël Coward's *Private Lives* and then evolved into *Bardot's Private Life* as a working title.

Ginger Rogers also played a movie star with an overwhelming desire to get away from it all and escape the incessant autograph hounds in an RKO release of 1935, *In Person*. The movie star Mae West portrayed in *Go West, Young Man* (1937) didn't seem to have that problem. Warren William, as her public relations advisor, had a job primarily consisting of keeping the sex symbol, who is on a personal appearance tour, from getting married in accordance with a clause in her contract. He falls for Mae at the finish.

Since the Hollywood and film-making aspects were minimized in the adaptation of Jacqueline Susann's best-selling novel, *Valley of the Dolls* (1967), it is not necessary to dwell at length on this *magnum opus* of memorable clichés. The story deals with the rise and stumblings of its three female stars: Neely O'Hara (Patty Duke), rising young singing star who gets hung up on pills (or "dolls") to sleep and pills to wake up; New England country girl Anne Welles (Barbara Parkins), who comes to the big city and eventually is seduced by urban social patterns and later pills, and Jennifer North (Sharon Tate), a big-bosomed, untalented, but basically sensitive girl who never finds happiness and, faced with impending breast removal because of cancer, kills herself with pills. Susan Hayward, who replaced Judy Garland in the cast, does an excellent job in giving some depth to the role of the older legit star, Helen Lawson, ever alert to remove threats to her supremacy.

The resemblance to actual persons was extremely thin, but people seemed to want to believe that Barbara Parkins' character was suggested—however vaguely—by Grace Kelly, Patty Duke's by Judy Garland, Sharon Tate's by Marilyn Monroe and Susan Hayward's by Ethel Merman.

The men in their lives are all dull and cardboard; the production is slick and shallow, and most of the sex is off the screen, talked about, or seen in discreet, fleeting silhouettes.

Highlights from the dialogue:

About Neely: "Now you're just like all the rest of them—success is too big for you."
Philosophy: "The stockholders are interested in only one thing—profits."
To Neely: "What about the bad publicity?"
Reply: "It creates sympathy. People love to forgive."
Helen Lawson about Neely: "She doesn't have that hard core. She can't roll with the punches. In this business they come left, right and center."
Also about poor Neely: "Nothing can destroy her talent, but she'll destroy herself."
Advice from Helen Lawson: "Get married and have kids, or one day you'll wake up and wonder what the hell happened—like me."
Neely's disenchanted husband: "The old star sickness begins to reappear—all power and no gratitude."

Closer to Patty Duke's adolescent Neely than Brigitte Bardot's sex kitten Jill, Natalie Wood's Daisy Clover doesn't make much sense. Daisy is fifteen years old when *Inside Daisy Clover* (1965) starts and all of seventeen when it ends. She has been made into an international movie star by a big Hollywood studio, has seen her mother (Ruth Gordon) committed to an asylum by a scheming sister, has married—in ignorance—a homosexual movie star (Robert Redford), has been the mistress of the studio head (Christopher Plummer), has had a breakdown, and has attempted suicide. At the film's conclusion, she decides to use the gas stove to blow up her house instead of doing away with herself, after a comically inept attempt at suicide.

Daisy is described as "a primitive child, adult beyond her years, a rebel with a cause." She is, at the opening of the film, living a life of freedom and poverty on the Santa Monica pier with her addled mother. She has sent a record of her singing voice to the head of the studio and he instantly engages her for grooming to stardom as "America's Valentine."

It is not clear from viewing the film whether the treatment should be regarded as satire, fantasy, up-the-establishment, charcoal-gray humor, social comment, a gross melodrama of manipulation, or, perhaps, a bit of each. Make of it what you will: There are musical numbers, period touches (late 1930s), "inside Hollywood" flourishes and caricatured characters—intentional or not—in profusion. Christopher Plummer, who certainly has

In Person (1935): William Davidson and Ginger Rogers.

Valley of the Dolls (1967): Barbara Parkins, Sharon Tate and Patty Duke.

Valley of the Dolls: Patty Duke in dire straits.

Inside Daisy Clover (1965): Natalie Wood and Robert Redford.

Inside Daisy Clover: Natalie Wood and Christopher Plummer.

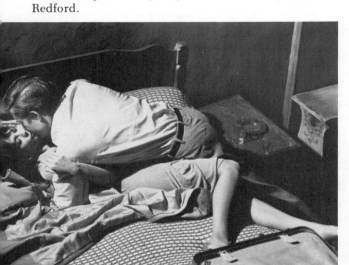

Play It As It Lays (1972): Tuesday Weld and Anthony Perkins.

done excellent work on the stage, contributes a truly strange and heavy-handed performance. He speaks and moves portentously as if he were being photographed and recorded in slow motion. The trimming of the pauses in his speeches alone should take several minutes of running time out of the film.

Not quite fitting into this chapter, nor, for that matter, into any chapter of this book, the "heroine" of *Play It as It Lays* (1972), Maria Wyeth (Tuesday Weld), is perhaps a remote second cousin to Daisy Clover. She is a deeply troubled actress-wife-mother trapped in a totally depressing view of the sick Hollywood scene. The film examines Maria's agonies—a floundering marriage to a director (Adam Roarke), a brain-damaged child, a wrecked career, an abortion, and too many loveless infidelities. Her friends are lechers, procurers, tramps and connivers. Anthony Perkins plays a homosexual producer, a gentle but bitter and amoral cynic, who does everybody favors, and is the one person to whom Maria relates. He finally washes down a lethal dose of pills with vodka and goes to sleep in Maria's arms.

The aimless despair of Maria is handled as a complex mosaic, beautifully photographed by Jordan Cronenweth. As critic Charles Champlin put it: "[The] neurotic, disintegrating heroine, pacing and reminiscing through the stately grounds of a private mental institution as we meet her and leave her, is drawn from a sub-sub-subculture. She is from a rarefied part of Hollywood, which is rare enough to begin with and distinct from Southern California, which is in turn distinct from anywhere else."

On the heels of *Valley of the Dolls* and a year or so after such misfires as *The Oscar* and *Inside Daisy Clover*, came *The Legend of Lylah Clare* (1968)—a sort of nightmare concoction made up of ideas and parts of *Sunset Boulevard*, *Vertigo*, *Persona*, *Rashomon* and *The Barefoot Contessa*. The story revolves around the life of a Hollywood sex queen of the thirties, Lylah Clare (Kim Novak), who died on her wedding night, and the attempts to reincarnate her through the making of a new movie. Kim Novak is the star who plays the star. Actually, she plays two stars, one being the deceased Lylah Clare, the other, Elsa Brinkmann, being a discovery who is to portray Lylah Clare in the screen story of her life. Lewis Zarkan (Peter Finch), as a moody directorial Svengali, works like a man possessed to convert Elsa into an exact replica of his great star and great love, the mysterious and enigmatic Lylah. Elsa has fallen in with his scheme and has also fallen into bed with him. The more she imbues herself with the role of Lylah, the more Elsa speaks with Lylah's pronounced, but rather bizarre, European accent—which seems to suggest Transylvanian with a touch of Swedish.

Bit by bit, unsavory secrets about the departed glamour queen emerge, seen from conflicting points of view. Strangely enough, the new star begins to go the way of the old, and in the end it is apparent that Elsa has become Lylah. Along the way the picture has many supposedly insightful and poignant things to say about Hollywood, its citizens, its newspaper people and columnists, and the system of moviemaking.

Making up a curious mosaic are the Harry Cohn-like studio boss (Ernest Borgnine), who screams every line; a past-obsessed, Lesbian dope addict (Rossella Falk), who stays around director Zarkan's gloomy Jacobean mansion dropping ambiguous hints about the real circumstances concerning Lylah's death; the eager, self-sacrificing "yes man" agent (Milton Selzer), who is told by the complicated, egomaniacal director, "Think of all the people you've had ten percent of. Almost enough to

The Legend of Lylah Clare (1968): Kim Novak, Robert Cornthwaite and Peter Finch.

The Legend of Lylah Clare: Gabriele Tinti, Peter Finch and Kim Novak.

The Legend of Lylah Clare: Make-up man Bob Mills with Kim Novak.

The Legend of Lylah Clare: In a sequence filmed at the Brown Derby on Vine Street, Hollywood—Ernest Borgnine, Kim Novak, Peter Finch, Milton Selzer and (leaning on booth) producer-director Robert Aldrich.

Bombshell (1933): Jean Harlow and Pat O'Brien.

make you a complete person"; the mandatory earthy Latin stud (Gabriele Tinti), who happens to be the gardener (!) on the director's estate; a dress designer (Valentina Cortesa); and for good measure, a monstrously bitchy and crippled columnist (Coral Browne).

Gasping for some kind of comic relief from these dark, somber sagas of sex symbols and decadence, we come upon the one significant comedy in this vein: *Bombshell* (1933), starring Jean Harlow as a bewildered, hectically living film star, who combines a love of exhibitionism with a certain wistful desire for home and babies.

The frantically paced *Bombshell*, based on an unproduced play, kids all kinds of things and people in Hollywood, including the real Jean Harlow. In the film, Lola Burns (Harlow) lives in a Beverly Hills mansion with a platoon of unsavory sycophants whom she supports. There are her boozy race tout father, who is her business manager (Frank Morgan); her gambling and allergic-to-work brother (Ted Healy); a double-crossing secretary who steals (Una Merkel); a casual and disrespectful maid (Louise Beavers); and three enormous sheep dogs.

Lola tells taxi drivers to "charge it," and decides at one point that she would like to play the lead in her studio's version of *Alice in Wonderland*. Somehow she manages to insist that "The mice, the coach and the ball" are part of *Alice*, and not *Cinderella*.

Called to do retakes for *Red Dust* because "The Hays Office censored something," she appears at "Monarch Studios" (MGM) and runs into "Space" Hanlon (Lee Tracy), a studio publicity man who is constantly involving Lola in outrageous exploitation gimmicks. She also finds that an old flame, Jim Brogan (Pat O'Brien), is directing the revised scenes. Lola is engaged to a marquis (Ivan Lebedeff). When she hears him referred to as a "glorified barber," Lola announces, "He's got royal blood in his veins!" And the director barks back, "I don't care if he has a royal flush in his kidneys!" "Space" breaks the engagement by having the marquis arrested as an illegal alien at the Cocoanut Grove while Gus Arnheim and his band play "Lazy Bones" in the background.

Lola then decides to adopt a baby, but "Space," her family, Brogan, the marquis and newspaper reporters manage to nullify that possibility when they all drop in at her home at the same time and make a scene while two lady adoption officials from the orphanage look on in outraged disapproval.

Next Lola walks out of her contract and half-

Bombshell: Louise Beavers, Frank Morgan, Leonard Carey, William Newell, Jean Harlow and Una Merkel.

Bombshell: Jean Harlow and Lee Tracy.

The Fuzzy Pink Nightgown (1957): Robert H. Harris, Adolphe Menjou and Jane Russell.

finished picture and tries to get away from it all in Palm Springs. There she meets a supposed blueblood from Boston (Franchot Tone) and his stuffy and supercilious mother (Mary Forbes) and father (C. Aubrey Smith). After this love affair and pursuit of culture and refinement collapse, she returns to the studio to finish her picture, and then finds out that "Space" planted the bluebloods, who are in reality stock actors. The picture ends with an indication that Lola finally believes that she belongs to the movies and that "Space" really cares for her.

In addition to including certain parallels with Harlow's own life, Lola Burns was composed of a bit of Clara Bow (Lola is referred to as the "If Girl," and the depiction of her secretary is reminiscent of some problems Miss Bow had with her secretary in 1930-31), Gloria Swanson and Constance Bennett (both ladies married the Marquis de la Falaise de la Coudraye and both adopted baby boys).

Bombshell was loud, brash, funny and a good vehicle for Harlow, but it was a little too "in" for the provinces. MGM tried to boost the commercial potential by retitling the picture *Blonde Bombshell*, but it still did not do very well.

United Artists released a not very good comedy in 1957 about a Hollywood glamour star (Jane Russell) who is kidnapped just before her new picture, "The Kidnapped Bride", is to open. Naturally, no one believes the kidnapping is anything but a publicity stunt. The kidnappers (Ralph Meeker and Keenan Wynn) are represented as charming fellows who

aren't really criminals anyway. The police charitably agree to forget the entire matter, and romance triumphs between the star and the character played by Meeker. Incidentally, the irrelevant title of this little item is *The Fuzzy Pink Nightgown*.

The movie star Esther Williams portrayed in *On an Island with You* (1948) is kidnapped, in a manner of speaking, by a Navy lieutenant (Peter Lawford), who is in love with her. He flies her off to the island where he first met her while she was entertaining the boys during World War II. She eventually responds to this rather ingenious but extreme demonstration of ardor.

What happens to the goddesses who manage to survive the glory years and then move on to the emptiness that follows? The classic *Sunset Boulevard* (1950) gives us a full-length portrait of the ex-super star of the silent days (Gloria Swanson) who hasn't made a film in twenty years. A suicidal neurotic in her fifties, with an air of arrogant grandeur once rooted in fame and now propped up by delusion, she lives in an immense, mausoleum-like mansion on Sunset Boulevard with her butler-confidant, Max von Mayerling (Erich von Stroheim), who, it turns out, was one of her three husbands and along with DeMille, one of her major directors. He writes phony fan mail to her, runs the house projector showing her old films night after night, plays Bach on the organ for recreation, and periodically prevents her from completing the suicide act.

Surrounded by framed photographs of herself, the ex-star works tirelessly on her script of "The Story of Salome," the film that will be her next major success after spending "a few years away from the screen." Once a week she plays bridge with her cronies from the old days—portrayed by silent stars Buster Keaton, H. B. Warner and Anna Q. Nilsson—and occasionally she ventures forth into the outside world in an ancient chauffeur-driven, leopard skin-upholstered Isotta-Fraschini. Fortunately, she has considerable income from real estate, oil and stocks.

Enter Joe Gillis (William Holden) a down-on-his-luck hack writer who tries to escape the finance company by driving his car into the garage on Norma Desmond's estate. Norma Desmond and von Mayerling think he is there to make funeral arrangements for her recently deceased pet chimp. But after discovering he is a young, attractive screen writer, she plies him with champagne and urges him to read her tome about Salome. He wades through the incredibly old-fashioned, turgid, long-winded melange of melodramatic clichés, and, sensing some potential loot, suggests that with a little editing, rearranging and rewriting, it could be quite good.

Joe goes to work. At first he has a room over the garage, but later he moves into the main house. Soon he is caught up by a new life style: he works on her masterpiece by day, and by night is entertained with her silent movies ("We didn't need dialogue; we had faces then. They don't have faces any more—maybe one, Garbo") and her impersonations of Charlie Chaplin and herself as a parasol-twirling Sennett bathing beauty. As a kept man, he is given expensive clothes and starts escorting her here and there on occasion. On New Year's Eve their celebration in the mansion consists of a private party—just the two of them, formally attired—a small orchestra and the *de rigueur* champagne.

They dance ("Valentino said 'There's nothing like tile for the tango' ") and eventually quarrel. Joe feels the need to join his old friends at a party at an assistant director's (Jack Webb) apartment that is the complete antithesis of the wake at Norma Desmond's.

The apartment is mobbed and the guests are animated. Songwriters Jay Livingston and Ray Evans are at the piano, and Joe is back in his element. He again meets the assistant director's fiancée, Betty (Nancy Olson), a reader in the story department at Paramount, and they seem to have a warm rapport.

But the festivities come to an abrupt end for Joe when Max von Mayerling tells him on the phone that "Madame got the razor from your room and cut her wrists." Joe returns to the mansion and goes to Norma in her bedroom. With her bandaged wrists, Norma reaches up and engulfs Joe with her arms, pulling him down to her on the large swan-styled bed. Joe gives in and, now more than ever, he is her prisoner.

Later, Norma receives calls from Paramount. She believes it is someone working for DeMille who wants to discuss her Salome script, which had been recently sent to the director. Dressing up in her finest, and accompanied by a solemn and resigned Joe, she is chauffeured by Max in the Isotta-

Sunset Boulevard (1950): On location at the old mansion on Wilshire Boulevard.

Sunset Boulevard: On the set with Buster Keaton, Anna Q. Nilsson, William Holden, Cecil B. DeMille, Gloria Swanson and H. B. Warner.

Fraschini to the entrance of Paramount, where she is recognized by the old gateman. She then goes to the set where DeMille is shooting *Samson and Delilah.* Puzzled by her statements regarding "their working together again" (they made twelve pictures), DeMille discovers that the telephone calls were regarding the rental of her old Italian limousine "for the Crosby picture." Charming and solicitous, DeMille tries to evade the Salome issue ("Pictures have changed quite a bit, Norma"), but she is carried away by being at the studio and on a set again. One of the electricians swings a lamp from above in her direction, bathing her in light. Oldtimers gather around. She is ready to return to the cameras ("But remember, never before 10:00 or after 4:30"). Without telling her the truth or making a commitment, DeMille walks her to the exit and graciously says good-bye.

Later, Joe starts to moonlight—working on his own script with Betty, the Paramount reader, while Norma goes into a crash physical program "to get ready for the cameras." Joe and Betty work nights in her office at Paramount, while her fiancé is on an extended location junket. Over the weeks, they fall in love. She is a third-generation Hollywood girl, who worked her way up from the mail room, to stenographic, to reader.

Then Norma finds out about the script Joe has been working on, about his relationship with Betty, and that the phone calls from Paramount had only to do with renting her car. There is to be no production of "Salome", no DeMille, no return of the cameras.

Joe decides it is time to face reality all the way around. He calls Betty and asks her to come to the mansion, where he bluntly tells her the truth about his situation ("You know, older woman who is well-to-do and younger man who is not doing too well"). She leaves in a state of shock, and he starts to pack. Norma now sees that her whole insulated, deluded world is crumbling. Joe tries to jolt her into reality by being perfectly honest with her, as he was with Betty, after months of shielding, lying, and helping to sustain illusions. He tells Norma, "There's nothing tragic about being fifty—unless you try to be twenty-five."

As he goes out the front door, Norma shoots him in the back and he falls dead into the swimming pool. Then the police, reporters and columnists (including Hedda Hopper) arrive. Norma is in a state of complete mental shock. With the general hubbub and the presence of newsreel cameras and flash-bulbs, the actress, in her unbalanced state, thinks she is getting ready to play Salome.

"Tell Mr. DeMille I'll be right down." Faithful to the end, Max von Mayerling stands by the cameras. "Lights! Are you ready, Norma? This is the staircase of the palace. All right. . . . cameras—action!" Norma descends the staircase as a transfixed Salome. The cameras are rolling, flashbulbs exploding, and the background music swells with a purposefully blatant and distorted Norma Desmond–Salome theme.

The dream she had clung to so desperately has enfolded her.

"This is my life—it always will be. All right, Mr. DeMille, I'm ready for my close-up!"

The music reaches its climax and segues into a pastiche of "Paramount on Parade." Fade out.

Sunset Boulevard was the last film made by the team of Charles Brackett and Billy Wilder, who as scriptwriters had done *Bluebeard's Eighth Wife* (1938), *Midnight* (1939) and *Ninotchka* (1939), among others, before producing (Brackett) and directing (Wilder) their own scripts, e.g., *Five Graves to Cairo* (1943), *The Lost Weekend* (1945), *A Foreign Affair* (1948), etc. After *A Foreign Affair* Brackett and Wilder were joined by a third writer, D. M. Marshman, Jr., who had been a film critic for *Life* magazine. Following discussions, they decided to do a film dealing with Hollywood. One of them came up with the idea of the relationship between a silent movie queen who lives in the past and a young and unsuccessful screenwriter. After a period of gestation, they were discussing a Balzac story one day, and someone suggested the killing of the young man by the older woman. That idea gave them the necessary impetus to move ahead.

Although there had been some talk about Mae Murray or Pola Negri for the Norma Desmond role, Gloria Swanson seemed to be the prime contender all along. Montgomery Clift originally signed for the part of the writer, but two weeks before shooting was to commence he dropped out, giving as his official reason the opinion that his fans would not accept his sleeping with a woman twice his age. Then William Holden did some tests with Swanson. Later she said, "The first tests I did they said, 'You look thirty-five.' [Swanson was then fifty.] Then they did some tests with all top light, and I looked like I had water on my brain. I didn't like that at all. I said, 'You've got to make Holden look younger instead of me older'—and he wasn't any baby! [Holden was then thirty-one.] So they gave him a short, collegiate haircut and painted out the lines under his chin."

Like Norma Desmond, Gloria Swanson had worked for Mack Sennett and DeMille—actually starring in six silent DeMille features. She also lived in a twenty-four-room mansion in Beverly Hills during her heyday in the 1920s. Swanson made *Queen Kelly* with director Erich von Stroheim in 1928, a clip of which is seen briefly during one of Norma's screenings in her home. And she was, in fact, Paramount's leading box-office attraction from 1921 to 1926. But, unlike Norma Desmond, Gloria Swanson made one of her biggest hits after sound arrived (*The Trespasser*, 1929), and appeared in several films after that. She has kept constructively busy during the years, and most certainly is not moored to the past. The eccentricities of Norma Desmond have little or nothing to do with Gloria Swanson, who at the age of seventy-five is still astonishingly healthy, vigorous and professionally active.

The right mansion couldn't be found on Sunset Boulevard, but eventually was located a short distance from the studio, on Wilshire Boulevard at Crenshaw Boulevard. The French-Italian palatial residence was built by a former U.S. consul to Mexico and was owned at the time of filming by J. Paul Getty, one of the richest men in the world. The house was demolished in the late 1950s and the site is now an office building.

According to Billy Wilder: "Originally we shot an opening sequence at the Los Angeles County Morgue of William Holden's body being brought in, and then a dozen corpses discussing with each other how they came to be dead—a boy who drowned off

Sunset Boulevard: William Holden as the hack writer in his Hollywood apartment.

Venice [near Santa Monica], an avocado rancher who had had a heart attack, and then, of course, Holden. When we previewed it, by the time they were putting the name tag on Holden's big toe, the audience was hysterical with laughter. It became a black comedy, which was not precisely what we had in mind."

The revamped opening shows two police cars racing down Sunset Boulevard to the scene of the murder. Joe Gillis' body is discovered floating face down in the pool, and the unusual device of a dead man narrating his own story begins. The film flashes back to the days when he was a struggling writer living in the Alto Nido apartment house on Franklin Avenue and Ivar in Hollywood and goes on from there.

The stylish and truly unique *Sunset Boulevard* is crammed with significant detail, and is one of a handful of films about Hollywood that was and is completely satisfying.

In the disappointing *Three for Bedroom C* (1952), Gloria Swanson played the leading role of a film star rushing back to Hollywood from the East via train because her studio has cast her in a picture she doesn't like.

The problems of an aging movie queen were examined on a superficial and not particularly effective level in Universal's *The Female Animal* (1957). Hedy Lamarr is the fading sex symbol who is feeling her years. When she meets the character played by George Nader on the set of her latest picture, she is intrigued and sets him up as

63

Sunset Boulevard: Gloria Swanson showing William Holden one of her old movies and claiming "We had faces then!"

Sunset Boulevard: On the set—a mock-up of the original Schwab's Drug Store—with director Billy Wilder, columnist Sidney Skolsky and William Holden.

Sunset Boulevard: Gloria Swanson and William Holden.

Sunset Boulevard: The entrance to Paramount.

Sunset Boulevard: Gloria Swanson and Cecil B. DeMille.

Sunset Boulevard: Hedda Hopper.

Sunset Boulevard: Hauling William Holden out of the pool.

68

Sunset Boulevard: Erich von Stroheim and Gloria Swanson.

The Female Animal (1957): George Nader and Hedy Lamarr.

The Female Animal: Jane Powell, Hedy Lamarr and George Nader.

"caretaker" of her lavish beach house. Nader then meets and falls in love with her adopted daughter (Jane Powell) and the problems begin. Jan Sterling plays a has-been movie great who gives a lesson as to what Miss Lamarr can become if she pursues her quest for fleeting youth.

As the debauched and fading movie star Alexandra Del Lago in *Sweet Bird of Youth* (1962), Geraldine Page repeated her stunning performance created for Tennessee Williams' play. The character is a flamboyant and formerly gorgeous creature who reveled in the adulation of millions of fans and who, when she fears she is losing her grasp on her star status, tries to drown herself in gin, dope and sex. Chance Wayne (Paul Newman, who also created the role on Broadway) has been trying to crash Hollywood's inner circles. While serving as a beach boy at a swank Southern California swim club, he has been picked up by the drunken star and becomes her self-appointed driver, booze and dope supplier, companion, caretaker, and lover. His plan is to blackmail her into seeing that he too becomes a star. Although he doesn't wind up castrated, as he does in the play, his face is somewhat disfigured and the picture ends with Alexandra's being given news

that renews her self-confidence and gives her career revived hope—a concession not in the play.

A silent film of 1926, Warners' *Broken Hearts of Hollywood*, is probably the first instance of a picture concentrating on the pitfalls of a "has-been" film actress. It deals with a film star (Louise Dresser) who marries and retires from the screen. But the lure of the cameras causes her to leave her husband and child and return to the studios. Unfortunately, her beauty has faded and, seeking solace in drink, she soon finds herself on the fringes of the film world. Her daughter (Patsy Ruth Miller), winner of a beauty contest back home, heads for Hollywood, where she fails in her first screen opportunity, enrolls in a phony acting school and is arrested in a "wild party" raid. In order to get money to help her injured boy friend (Douglas Fairbanks, Jr.), who has been seriously hurt performing a movie stunt, she offers herself to the Great Lover of the Screen (Stuart Holmes), only to be taken by him to his home, where he introduces her to his wife and daughter. Nevertheless, he does slip her a check and obtains the leading female role in his next film for her. But—irony of ironies—her own mother is cast as her mother in the picture. The ex-star keeps silent about their relationship until the film is completed. The young girl is a hit, but Mama overhears the unscrupulous owner of the acting school (Jerry Miley) arrange to take the girl to his apartment. Apprehensive for her daughter's safety, Mama shoots the man while she is in a drunken stupor and is arrested. At the trial, the girl's testimony saves her mother, and they are then happily reunited.

70

The Star (1952): Bette Davis.

In Monogram's inexpensive *Wife Wanted* (1946), Kay Francis played a fading star who becomes a partner in a real estate firm, which, in reality and without her knowledge, is a front for a lonely-hearts outfit next door.

Bette Davis created an acute, frightening portrait of an actress obsessed with her past and her legend in *The Star* (1952). Miss Davis replaced Joan Crawford (for whom the script had been prepared) in the role of Margaret Elliot, who, a few years before the film's beginning, was one of the top ten. Now she is on the skids, but she won't admit it. "They can't put me out to pasture. Why, I'm an institution. Girls talked like me, imitated my make-up, my hair. . . . I was a *star*. I *am* a star!"

As if to give her the lie, the picture begins with an auction of her belongings. There are arc lights, just like at a premiere, but this is a finale. Margaret Elliot is an Academy Award-winning actress whose last three pictures, produced with her own money, have failed financially, leaving her broke and unemployed. She was married once, but the gentleman "wasn't even Miss Eliott's husband; he was her lover—by appointment—when she wasn't too tired or afraid to muss her hair."

After the auction she goes on a roaring drunk—all alone—in her car, during which she sardonically points out the mansions of Hollywood celebrities, including her own former residence. She winds up in jail and is bailed out by Jim Johannson (Sterling Hayden), who operates a marine supply shop and whom she once made her leading man to spite another leading man. He takes her to his apartment

The Star: Bette Davis and Sterling Hayden.

71

and tries to persuade her to give up a calling, which, as he tells her bluntly, has given her up long since. She refuses to concede that her starring days are over.

When she gets a chance at a fortyish movie role, she tries to play the test as a sexy young girl in the hope of cutting a new, rising star out of the lead. When her test is screened, she watches her unfortunate performance and becomes aware that her glamour days are over. Then another role looms up. The part is such a parallel with her own life that she finally gets a clear perspective on herself and begins to acquire a real sense of values. She picks up her young daughter (Natalie Wood) and rushes to the marina, where she tells Jim, who has loved her for years, that she is ready to fulfill herself as a woman in love.

As opposed to the usual Hollywood dramas of tawdry connivings, back-stabbings, conceits and deceptions *The Star*, in its modest way, presents a Hollywood of legitimate ambitions, fair dealing, realistic evaluations and honest emotions. And Bette Davis avoids her characteristic brittleness to a large degree and contributes a sympathetic performance.

As a kind of Grand Guignol nightmare conglomeration of all the sagas of aging movie queens, *What Ever Happened to Baby Jane?*, starring Bette Davis and Joan Crawford, appeared in 1962 and was a huge box-office success.

A lurid melodrama of hate, revenge and murder, the story, from the novel by Henry Farrell, concerns two aged actresses immured in their Hollywood home. One, Jane Hudson (Davis), was once a singing and dancing child star. Her sister, Blanche (Crawford), was envious and not so pretty as a child, but a great success as a stunning, adult movie star. Baby Jane's failure as an adult actress and her mad belief that her sister deliberately eclipsed her, provides the basis for the corrosive relationship that ties them. Blanche's career was ended when she became hopelessly crippled in an automobile accident. Details are vague, but Blanche's paralyzed legs are blamed on Jane, who had been drinking that night and supposedly was driving. The dislike they have always had for each other has, after many years, blossomed into seething hatred and been given added fuel by the renewed popularity of Blanche's early feature films shown on television (actually, the clips shown are from Crawford's *Sadie McKee*, made by MGM in 1934). The cripple is confined to a wheel chair upstairs; Jane roams the downstairs, answering the buzzer pressed by her sister with complete loathing when she has to, and

The Star: Bette Davis, Sterling Hayden and Oscar.

generally giving way to the psychosis that gradually is turning her into a sadistic killer.

One day Blanche announces that they are running out of money and will have to sell the house. Fearful that she will be put in a sanitarium, Jane at first plans a stage comeback and advertises for an accompanist (Victor Buono) to help her rehearse. Then she decides to get rid of her sister by driving her out of her mind. One of her methods is to serve her roasted rats for dinner, with the result that Blanche begins to starve to death. Jane catches Blanche crawling downstairs to the telephone for help and ties her up. When the maid returns to the house and discovers Blanche bound to her bed and gagged, Jane kills the maid in a moment of panic.

Later Jane takes her sister to Malibu Beach where she intends to bury her in the sand. At dawn, Blanche, close to death, confesses to Jane in a twist ending that she has been responsible for her mental decline, because in a jealous rage she had engineered the automobile accident which resulted in her own injuries, and had deluded Jane into thinking it was her fault. The final scene is strongly reminiscent of the ending of *Sunset Boulevard:* Jane, about to be arrested, imagines that the gathered crowd is an audience from out of the past. She curtsies and performs one of her old numbers from childhood—completely out of touch with the present and reality.

72

Although certainly not at any time a sex symbol, love goddess or the like, Bette Davis has had the kind of driving intensity that is needed to stay at the top over a good many years in a business that is highly uncertain. Fortunately, she is also talented and intelligent. But one pays a price. Miss Davis has said: "I think any career is hard on a woman as regards her personal life, but being an actress is more so. However, if you love it enough and must do it—you do it. I wouldn't advocate being an actress to any woman. I would stop them if I could; but if you care that much, you can't stop anyone. Much of being a career woman in pictures isn't being a woman; you have to become almost a man in many areas of your life, and being a man in your career has to tide over into your personal life. It is, in my opinion, not the happiest life a woman can have, and I'm speaking from deep experience. But I have no regrets, because I've been very fortunate in that at least my goals were realized. To have started out on this kind of career and not to have made the top—this I would never have done. I would have departed long ago. With me, it had to be the most or nothing."

What Ever Happened to Baby Jane? (1962): Joan Crawford and Bette Davis.

What Ever Happened to Baby Jane?: Filming the beach scene. Producer-director Robert Aldrich is lying in front of Crawford and Davis.

CHAPTER THREE

WHAT PRICE HOLLYWOOD?

"If we are to believe this film, the price of Hollywood is the social downfall and degradation of those unable to resist the temptation of drink, and the perpetual agony and thwarted home life of those who, thanks to their eminence, are constantly exposed to public gaze." This was the opinion of critic Alexander Bakshy, writing for *The Nation* in August of 1932, when he had seen *What Price Hollywood?* If the title of the picture were removed from his review, any number of other titles of movies about movies could be inserted and Mr. Bakshy's views would have equal validity.

It is one of the peculiarities of a highly peculiar town-industry that Hollywood seemingly loves to wallow in its own absurdities and agonies. Even comedies and musicals about movie people have drawn their fun from lampooning egocentric actors, pompous and inept producers, eccentric directors, amoral and not very bright starlets, sardonic writers, insensitive financiers and devious agents.

But one thing must be remembered in discussing Hollywood's films about itself—that they were made for the same reason as films about any other place or subject, and that is to entertain the widest possible public. Whether they are genial spoofs or searing melodramas, the movies about the movies cannot be taken as documentaries. For comedic and dramatic reasons, Hollywood has often exaggerated all the obvious facets of its character—although it may seem impossible for them to be more exaggerated than they really are—and willingly opened all its closets in the search for movie material. In doing so, it reveals itself as a tough-minded industry revolving around enormous amounts of money. It is the nature of the picture business to call attention to itself—just as an actor must do the same thing—and it does so by making itself appear interesting, bizarre, glamorous, fascinating, frightening, beguiling, exciting and amusing.

Perhaps the first sound film to give a fairly accurate, albeit romanticized, concept of life in the movie business was *What Price Hollywood?*, which was produced by David O. Selznick at RKO in 1932. Five years later Selznick developed the idea of that film into the more ambitious *A Star Is Born*, which was to be re-made in 1954 with further em-

75

A Star Is Born (1954): Exit Norman Maine.

Constance BENNETT
WHAT PRICE HOLLYWOOD

Constance Bennett with David O. Selznick at the time of making *What Price Hollywood?* (1932).

bellishments. Together, the three pictures make for an interesting study. It was Selznick's opinion prior to *What Price Hollywood?* that no movies about the place had been successful. There is some truth in this view, but there were exceptions. Years later he recalled, "I believe that the whole world was interested in Hollywood and that the trouble with most films about Hollywood was that they gave a false picture, that they burlesqued it, or that they over-sentimentalized it, but that they were not true reflections of what happened in Hollywood."

Selznick hired Adela Rogers St. Johns and told her, "It's time we made a really good picture about Hollywood, so why don't you go and find us a story?" Mrs. St. Johns had by this time been a writer for Hearst's *Cosmopolitan* magazine for ten years, with some screen stories and Hollywood-oriented short stories and novels to her credit. The original title for the project was *The Truth About Hollywood*, and it was intended as a comeback vehicle for Clara Bow. But, according to Mrs. St. Johns, the unstable "It" girl had put on weight and was not prepared to lose it in time to start the picture, so the role was given to RKO contract star Constance Bennett.

Mrs. St. Johns says that the characterizations of a young, ambitious actress and her destruction-bent mentor and director were patterned in her original story on Colleen Moore and her husband John McCormick, although they had been divorced two years before this film went into production.

76

What Price Hollywood?: Lowell Sherman and Constance Bennett (as a waitress at the Brown Derby restaurant).

McCormick was Moore's producer, and an alcoholic. The role of the director in the film, played by Lowell Sherman, may also have been suggested by director Tom Forman, who put a bullet through his heart. Forman killed himself in 1926, following a nervous breakdown which had been brought on by a period of intense work. However, like most characters in films of this kind, the role was a composite of facts embroidered with fiction.

In *What Price Hollywood?* Constance Bennett appears at the beginning of the picture as a movie aspirant named Mary Evans. She is a waitress at the original Brown Derby on Wilshire Boulevard in Los Angeles across from the Ambassador Hotel and she obviously is not the only employee with an eye on the Hollywood scene. To a chef who wears his hair in a Valentino fashion she says, "I hear they're looking for Latin types this week." When movie director Max Carey (Sherman) enters, wearing full evening regalia and clearly under the influence of drink, Mary arranges with another waitress to attend his table. Carey is a dapper and amiable drunk, and one of the first pieces of advice he gives Mary when he realizes she is bent on cracking the picture business is, "Remember our motto—'It's all in fun.' Let me give you a tip about Hollywood. Always keep your sense of humor and you can't miss."

He invites her to a premiere at Grauman's Chinese Theatre and demonstrates his own bizarre sense of humor by driving up to the swank affair in a bat-

Colleen Moore and her producer-husband, John McCormick.

tered old wreck of a car. The horrified attendent wonders what is to be done with the spluttering heap, and the cavalier Carey hands him the keys, advising him he can keep the car as a tip. According to Adela Rogers St. Johns, the incident was based on an actual occurrence, when writer Wilson Mizner did this at a premiere.

At the theatre Carey introduces Mary to producer Julius Saxe (Gregory Ratoff). She makes it known that "All I need is a break." Carey takes her home with him and awakens the next morning with little recall of the previous evening, but when his guest reminds him of his offer to get her a screen test, he proves as good as his word.

Carey is a single man, but there is nothing lecherous about him in his attitude toward Mary. He appears blithe in his loneliness, and when Mary tries to persuade him to give up drinking, he cocks an eyebrow and retorts, "And be bored all the time?" He is a man whose career is in jeopardy due to his drinking, and, replying to a remark that whiskey is his ruin, he quips, "You're right. What the picture business needs is light wines and beer." Carey directs Mary in her test and discovers, as he had expected, that despite her confidence she is devoid of any knowledge about acting. He dismisses her, but she later rehearses her scene alone until she masters it and begs for another chance. This time Saxe happens to see the footage and immediately decides she has a certain quality. He puts her under contract and her progress is rapid.

There is no romance between Mary and Max Carey, mostly because he is a man convinced of his decline and unwilling to hurt her. He submerges his personal feelings and she remains grateful to him. Now a star, she goes on location to Santa Barbara and there meets handsome, wealthy, polo-playboy Lonny Borden (Neil Hamilton). He courts her, but she is cavalier in her behavior toward him. She accepts a supper engagement, for which he hires an orchestra, and when Mary doesn't bother to turn up, he proceeds to her bedroom, drags her out of bed and carries her to the lavishly catered midnight meal. A conquered woman, she agrees to marry him. When she reports this to her boss, producer Saxe remarks, "Who is going to be foolish enough to marry a picture star?" Carey chimes in, "It won't last," and when Mary asks what it is that won't last he informs her, "My liver—and a movie star's marriage." After the wedding ceremony Saxe exclaims, "It was a marvelous wedding—we've broken all records for this church."

The strain of being married to Mary Evans soon begins to tell on Lonny Borden. Their honeymoon is curtailed because of her filming schedule, and he is forced to wait for hours on sets while she finishes her work. As time goes by he becomes more and more impatient with the lack of privacy and the demands made upon his wife: "Everything you do is reported and discussed and exaggerated." Lonny is particularly disgusted when a magazine writer appears to interview them in her series about "Great Lovers of Today." After some months of this sort of thing Lonny informs her that he is leaving and getting as far away from Hollywood as possible. "You live in a world where people are cheap and vulgar without knowing it." Carey tells the distraught Mary, "I made you what you are today—I hope you're satisfied."

Carey's career now starts to fall apart as his drinking undermines his ability. Mary is divorced from Borden and shortly afterwards discovers that she is pregnant. But her career continues to soar and she receives an Academy Award as the best actress of the year. Carey disappears and when Mary finds him he has been jailed as a drunken driver. She takes Carey home and nurses him, but to her advice to pull himself together, he matter of factly tells her, "I'm washed up. It's all gone." Some time later Carey gets up to look for a drink. At a dressing table mirror he peers at his dismal reflection and compares the sad sight with a nearby photograph of himself, in which he appears suave and elegant. Discovering a revolver in a drawer, Max Carey ponders his predicament, puts the gun to his chest and pulls the trigger.

The suicide of Carey is one of the most believable incidents in *What Price Hollywood?*, thanks to the skill of Lowell Sherman and the good taste of George Cukor. In less adept hands the scene could easily have become mawkish. Sherman played his role amusingly, but behind the quips and the offhand manner was a subdued quality of despondency and a faint air of self-mockery, which at no point called for pity. The decision to kill himself seems suddenly arrived at, as if a wall has collapsed inside the man. The death is filmed with tilted angles and fast cuts—flashing bits from Carey's past—in a manner quite advanced for a 1932 picture. The moment of death is shot in slow motion, and it was someone's stroke of genius to accompany the entire scene with a disturbing whirring noise on the sound track. Slavko Vorkapich, the montage specialist, apparently contributed strongly to this sequence.

The death of Carey increases the anguish of Mary Evans. Scandal implies that his death at her home is in some way due to her, and the public turns against

her. Explains Saxe, "If you were an ordinary girl it
wouldn't matter, but you're a picture star. They
make you and they break you." When a reporter asks
Mary if her ex-husband is likely to get custody of
their young son, she panics and leaves Hollywood.
Mary makes a home for herself in France, but Lonny
discovers the address and arrives to see his son.
However, this is a greatly changed Lonny, no longer
arrogant but sympathetic toward Mary and now
realizing how badly he had behaved in leaving her.
He asks to be forgiven, and he also asks to be taken
back. When Mary senses his sincerity, she happily
agrees to a reunion.

Of the more than fifty films in which she appeared
between 1922 and 1951, Constance Bennett considered her role as a movie star in *What Price
Hollywood?* to be her best performance. Never
highly regarded by the critics as anything more than
a competent actress, Bennett nevertheless achieved
great public popularity and by 1932 she drew top
money for her work. She was also the epitome of a
movie star of that era, living stylishly, spending large
sums of money on clothes and acquiring a title by her
marriage to the Marquis de la Falaise de la Coudraye
(Gloria Swanson's ex-husband). She divorced the
marquis in 1940, claiming desertion, and a year later
married Gilbert Roland, a marriage which also
ended in divorce. At the time of her death in 1965 she
was the wife of Brigadier General John Theron
Coulter, her fourth husband. Always noted for her
keen sense of business, the beautiful and shrewd Miss
Bennett ran various cosmetic and clothing enterprises in the last twenty years of her life and
enjoyed herself on a fairly high social plateau. She
was also a woman with humor. When writer Gene
Ringgold approached her with the idea of doing a
career profile for *Films in Review*, she agreed but
advised him, ". . . keep it light. And be truthful
about my screen career. After all, I was no Sarah
Bernhardt. . . ."

What Price Hollywood? remains the film by
which Lowell Sherman is best remembered,
although it was not his final work as an actor despite
his announcement to that effect. He appeared in two
other films and directed several more before his
death in 1934 at the age of forty-nine. Sherman had
been a popular actor all through the twenties and
had given it up for directing. Selznick particularly
wanted him to play Max Carey and sent Adela
Rogers St. Johns to try and change his mind about
turning his back on acting. She recalls: "I knew it
was a part no actor could resist, but I approached
Lowell with the idea that I was seeking out his help

What Price Hollywood?: Constance Bennett barging into
the screening room of the producer played by Gregory
Ratoff.

What Price Hollywood?: Constance Bennett, Lowell
Sherman and Gregory Ratoff.

What Price Hollywood?: Neil Hamilton and Constance
Bennett.

Constance Bennett, at the time of making *What Price Hollywood?* with her husband, the Marquis de la Falaise de la Coudraye.

John Barrymore.

and advice on the script. Well, before I could finish telling him about it, he was on the phone to David saying he thought it would be a good final role for him." Sherman played the part of the director with a John Barrymore-ish flourish, as a mordantly humorous fellow, covering up inner despair with bravado. Sherman had had ample opportunity to study Barrymore—he was married to a sister of Dolores Costello, then Barrymore's wife.

About Selznick, Mrs. St. Johns says, "He was very young to be in charge of a studio. He was then thirty and a lot of fun. I loved working for him, but we fought, because he was dictatorial right from the start, and I was the kind of person who liked to have my say." However, no one had final say with Selznick, and he hired Gene Fowler and Rowland Brown to prepare an adaptation based on the St. Johns story, and then Jane Murfin and Ben Markson to do the screenplay. The original prototypes of Colleen Moore and John McCormick were changed considerably during the evolution of the script.

For director George Cukor *What Price Hollywood?* was his first major film, and his career ascended from this point. Oddly, it was Cukor who would direct the second version of *A Star Is Born* and come back to the kind of material he had dealt with in *What Price Hollywood?* All three films are interesting as illustrations—both real and romantic—of the film business during the periods in which they were made. The differences are less than the similarities.

David O. Selznick was not immediately enthusiastic about the idea of filming *It Happened in Hollywood*, the original title of *A Star Is Born*, but his astute wife, Irene, one of the daughters of Louis B. Mayer, liked it and he respected her opinions. Selznick, ever the romantic, challenged himself to make in early three-color Technicolor what he considered would be a really first-class picture on the subject. The original concept was that of director William Wellman, who had begun his career in 1923 and by this time had directed more than forty films. Wellman claims that the story and its characters are based on his own observations and experiences and that he prepared the written outline with scenarist Robert Carson. This claim is somewhat at variance with Selznick's stand that the actual original ideas and story lines *eventually* used were primarily his, although he admitted that Wellman came to him with the suggestion of doing a Hollywood picture.

Years later, Selznick said, "We started without anything more than a vague idea of where we were going, and it was really a relatively easy script to write. We had two sets of writers on it, curiously, and Dorothy Parker and her husband Alan Campbell did the final dialogue and some amendments in the scenes. But I can say that ninety-five percent of the dialogue in that picture was actually straight out of life and was straight 'reportage,' so to speak."

Selznick himself was a man with an ability to write, as his voluminous memos prove, and at no time in his career was he ever content with the first draft of a script, no matter how good it may have been. When Wellman and Carson completed their screenplay, Selznick asked Rowland Brown, who had co-authored the adaptation of *What Price Hollywood?* to prepare his own treatment of *A Star Is Born.* Brown declined, feeling that the Wellman-Carson script needed no further work. Selznick then hired Parker and Campbell, and after they had handed in their script, he persuaded Robert Carson to do some additional rewriting. While all of this was going on, Selznick called in a pair of young writers who were under contract, Ring Lardner, Jr., and Budd Schulberg, and instructed them to prepare their version of the Wellman-Carson-Parker-Campbell material, warning them to keep their work secret.

But Wellman discovered what was going on and complained to his agent, who happened to be Selznick's brother Myron. Fraternal sentiment played no part in the singularly tough, shrewd mind of Myron Selznick, and he supported his client, forcing Selznick to restore some of the Wellman-Carson material that had been revised. *A Star Is Born* was nominated for several Academy Awards, but the only Oscar it won went to Wellman and Carson as authors of the original story, although Wellman reportedly admitted to Selznick at the ceremony, "You ought to get this—you wrote more of it than I did." As for all the effort that went into writing and screenplay, Selznick stated his whole philosophy as a film-maker in these words: "I have learned that nothing matters but the final picture."

To play the leading roles in *A Star Is Born* Selznick chose two stars whose circumstances were almost the opposite of the characters they were to play. As Esther Blodgett—renamed Vicki Lester—the young girl who goes to Hollywood and eventually becomes a star, Selznick picked Janet Gaynor, then thirty and regarded in the industry as a star in decline. Miss Gaynor had won an Oscar for the 1927 *Seventh Heaven,* but by the mid-1930s her appearances on the screen were relatively infrequent. In an interview during this period she was quoted as saying: "Once I thought that success, stardom, an insured

John Gilbert with Greta Garbo in *Queen Christina* (1933).

income were happiness. I find that the struggle is not in attaining success but in staying there. And for what success gives you with one hand, it takes away with the other. I have no personal life at all."

To portray Norman Maine, an actor whose hedonism and lack of stamina caused his career to dissolve and lead him to suicide, Selznick chose a man whose own career bore no similarity—Fredric March. March was in high gear all through the thirties. He had won an Oscar for the 1932 version of *Dr. Jekyll and Mr. Hyde,* and he had achieved the rare balance of being admired by both the public and the critics. His agent happened to be Myron Selznick, who forced his brother to pay dearly for the actor's services.

The characterization of Norman Maine is a composite based mostly on actors John Barrymore, John Gilbert and John Bowers, in addition to producer John McCormick, who had been Colleen Moore's husband. By the time *A Star Is Born* went into production, Barrymore had already slipped from a high level of artistic integrity to an alcoholic parody of himself. He would continue to work until his death in 1942, but his performances were an ever-increasing caricature that lampooned his drinking, his love life and his former glory as a classical actor.

A little of the Barrymore flamboyance is apparent in Norman Maine, but the chief characteristic borrowed for the part is the mysterious tendency toward self-destruction. One scene in *A Star Is Born,*

John Bowers in the mid 1920s.

and used almost verbatim in the 1954 remake, is entirely Barrymore-inspired. This is the one in which the drunken actor retreats to a sanitarium to cure himself of drinking, and is seen in the company of a male nurse as his friend and employer Oliver Niles visits him. This is exactly what Barrymore had done in 1936 in order to be able to play Mercutio in MGM's *Romeo and Juliet*. Among his visitors at that time was George Cukor, who was hoping to use Barrymore as De Varville in *Camille*, but he was not well enough and the part went to Henry Daniell. Cukor reported the visit to Selznick, who decided to use it in *A Star Is Born*. Ironically, Cukor was to direct James Mason in this poignant scene eighteen years later.

John Gilbert is one of the many tragic figures in the history of Hollywood. He had become an MGM matinee idol in the mid-twenties, starring in films like *The Big Parade*, *The Merry Widow*, and *Flesh and the Devil*. In the latter Gilbert was co-starred with Greta Garbo, resulting in what was then called "a torrid romance." The two were paired again in *Love* and *A Woman of Affairs*, and Gilbert was idolized by hordes of female fans, who heard his voice only in their imaginations. Unfortunately, Gilbert drew snickers from the audience when he actually spoke "I love you," in his first talkie.

Colleen Moore told the authors of this book that "when his first talking picture was seen in the projection room by Mayer, Thalberg and other bosses they said, 'we have a new star in Jack Gilbert.' What happened was that the words 'I love you' had never been heard by a movie audience from the screen. Before this, the audience put words in the mouths of the actors. When Jack Gilbert spoke the first love words ever heard on the screen, the audience was embarrassed and giggled, and this was the start of all the stories about Gilbert's voice. King Vidor will tell you the same thing. If you see Jack in *Queen Christina*, you will hear nothing extraordinary about his voice other than perhaps a little too much enthusiasm."

A contributing factor was that Gilbert's type of leading man suddenly went out of vogue with the Depression and the coming of sound. The change in his career was swift and painful, and it could only have been more painful when his actress wife Ina Claire forged ahead with her own career. They were divorced in 1931 and a year later Gilbert married a starlet named Virginia Bruce, his fourth wife.

Gilbert is generally regarded as the first major casualty in the coming of sound to the movies, but he did not, as is often supposed, immediately leave the

82

A Star Is Born (1937): Andy Devine, Janet Gaynor and Edgar Kennedy.

A Star Is Born (1937): Janet Gaynor with make-up men Eddie Voight and Paul Stanhope.

screen. Later, in an effort to restore him to favor MGM co-starred him with Greta Garbo in *Queen Christina* (1933), but not even that ploy could save his career. He had become reclusive and alcoholic, and Virginia Bruce divorced him. Her career bloomed as his collapsed, and it is fair to assume that she was at least a part of the concept of Vicki Lester. Gilbert suddenly died of a heart attack on January 9, 1936, a mere forty years of age. Unlike Norman Maine, who let his career carelessly slip from his fingers, Gilbert's had been torn away from him by a shift in styles and the introduction of the microphone.

The actual suicide of Norman Maine is, as William Wellman makes clear, patterned after the tragic fate of John Bowers. Bowers had been a New York actor before coming to Hollywood in 1915, and he enjoyed substantial employment as a leading man—although never as a major star—up to the coming of sound. Bowers married actress Marguerite de la Motte after he had co-starred with her in *When a Man's a Man* in 1924. He also appeared to advantage in such pictures as *Lorna Doone* (1922), *Richard, the Lion-Hearted* (1923), *So Big* (1924), *Laddie* (1926), *Whispering Smith* (1926), and *Three Hours* (1927). Bowers was forty-five and separated from his wife at the time of his death. It had been several years since he had worked in a film. Morose and depressed, he announced to a friend his intention of getting into a little boat and sailing away

A Star Is Born (1937): Janet Gaynor and Guinn (Big Boy) Williams.

A Star Is Born (1937): Fredric March, Joseph Schildkraut and Janet Gaynor. This sequence was deleted from the film, thereby eliminating Schildkraut's role as a dress designer.

into the sunset, never to be seen again. He was as good as his word. On November 15, 1936, he hired a small sailboat and put out to sea. The next day a lobster fisherman came across the sailboat drifting aimlessly about a mile off the shore at Santa Monica. The boat was empty. A day later the tide washed up the body of John Bowers. Also, Adela Rogers St. Johns tells of witnessing John McCormick's attempt to drown himself by swimming out to sea, after his separation from Colleen Moore.

This then was Norman Maine—a touch of John Barrymore, a bit of John Gilbert and a little more of John Bowers and John McCormick. As for Vicki Lester, she could be any one of the thousands of girls who have beat a path to Hollywood in the hopes of getting into the movies, and one of that small percentage who actually succeed.

Other than *What Price Hollywood?*, the only previous film that used some of the basic ideas found in *A Star is Born* was a relatively obscure picture of 1923 called *The World's a Stage*. In this Elinor Glyn story, a screen star (Dorothy Phillips) marries an irresponsible youth who becomes a shiftless alcoholic (Kenneth Harlan). Her former suitor (Bruce McRae) tries to straighten out the husband and comfort the star. The accidental death by drowning of the husband allows him to marry her.

As *A Star Is Born* (1937) begins, the camera moves in on a snow-covered house somewhere in the Rocky Mountains. Esther Blodgett (Gaynor) arrives home after having been to the movies and her family chides her, "You and your movies. That's all you think about." The determined young lady informs them, "I want to be somebody." Only her gruff but kindly grandmother (May Robson) believes in Esther and her dreams, and she gives her the money to get to Los Angeles. Esther takes a room in an inexpensive hotel and is befriended by a young assistant director named Danny McGuire (Andy Devine). One evening at a concert at the Hollywood Bowl they spot the famous star Norman Maine making a drunken fool of himself scuffling with newspaper men who want his photo. She next sees Maine when Danny gets her a job as a waitress at a party given by studio head Oliver Niles (Adolphe Menjou) at his home. Again, Maine is drunk. He enters the kitchen as Esther is washing dishes and offers to help her. In doing so he breaks a number of plates, and to escape the attention the noise creates, he suggests they slip away together. His charm and persuasiveness overwhelm her, and when Esther admits she hopes to get into pictures, he offers to help, sensing that she

A Star Is Born (1937): Director William Wellman talking to March and Gaynor during the filming.

has a quality that might register on film. He browbeats Niles into giving her a screen test, the results of which are good enough to get her a contract. Niles and his brash publicity man Matt Libby (Lionel Stander) invent a name for Esther—Vicki Lester. Soon she appears with Maine in a film, "The Enchanted Hour", and after the preview they overhear comments that will shape their future—Vicki Lester is a bright, exciting new star and Maine is now considered lackluster and on the way to becoming a has-been.

Earlier in the film Esther had tried to register with Central Casting as an extra, but had been turned away with the advice that the chances of success are one in a hundred thousand. To this Esther had replied, "Maybe I'm that one." And now she has proved to be just that. Vicki Lester becomes a major box-office attraction, but it does nothing to diminish her love and devotion to Maine. They announce to Niles and Libby their plans to get married, but to avoid the glittering, glaring ceremony the studio plans for the occasion, they slip away to a small town and get married under their real names—Alfred Henkel and Esther Blodgett.

Maine's career completely collapses and he becomes dependent on his wife. On the evening when she is to receive an Academy Award—the ceremony is staged at the Biltmore Bowl in the Biltmore Hotel in downtown Los Angeles—he arrives during the presentation and drunkenly takes a stance beside her and berates the audience. Inadvertently, he hits Vicki in the face with a wild swing of his arm, the embarrassment of which brings him to his senses, and she quietly leads him back to her table.

A Star Is Born (1937): Adolphe Menjou, Lionel Stander, Fredric March and Janet Gaynor.

A Star Is Born (1937): Mr. and Mrs. Norman Maine at their Beverly Hills paradise.

A Star Is Born (1937): Janet Gaynor.

A Star Is Born (1937): Pat Flaherty, Fredric March and Adolphe Menjou.

86

A Star Is Born (1937): Janet Gaynor and Fredric March.

Maine later submits to a "drying-out session" in a small sanitarium, and one of his few visitors is the sympathetic Niles, who tells him, "I hate to see you going the way of so many others." Weeks later, in a bar at the Santa Anita race track Maine, sober and drinking ginger ale, greets Libby pleasantly. But Libby, no longer having to contain his contempt in the line of duty, sees no reason to be either polite or sympathetic. Instead, he points out that Maine has no problems: "You can live off your wife." Maine strikes out at Libby, but Libby knocks him to the ground. After this humiliation, Maine orders a double Scotch.

After Maine has been missing for several days, Vicki and Niles locate him in a police station, where he is one of a number of drunks lined up to receive sentence. The judge recognizes Maine and gives him no pity, telling him that he has received every advantage and opportunity the other men have not. The judge is about to impose a sentence when Vicki intercedes and begs for Maine to be released in her custody.

At their Malibu Beach home Maine sleeps for some time and then awakens during a conversation between Vicki and Niles. He hears himself being described as "a shell of what he once was," and after listening to her tell Niles she is going to give up her career to take care of him, he realizes the burden he

is to his wife. He gets up and joins Vicki, pretending to feel better and to be in good spirits. He announces his new regime of physical fitness and says he is going for a swim. As she leaves the room he stops her—she turns and smiles—and he asks, "Do you mind if I take just one more look?"

Maine then goes through the door leading to the beach and walks down to the ocean. He slips off his sandals and his bathrobe and walks into the sea.

Maine's death is publicized as an accident, and at his funeral mobs of noisy fans crowd around the grief-stricken Vicki. She screams as a souvenir hunter yanks the black veil from her face. She wants to retire and retreat from the public, but later, when she is asked to appear at a premiere, her friends, including Grandma, persuade her that she should do so, that her husband sacrificed himself so that she could continue her career without his being a burden to her. At the premiere a radio announcer asks her if she will step to the microphone to say a few words to the audience. Vicki hesitates for a moment, then quietly and proudly announces, "This is Mrs. Norman Maine. . . ."

The re-make of *A Star Is Born* came into being through the enterprise of Judy Garland and her husband, Sid Luft, both of whom considered it an ideal comeback vehicle for her. Judy both knew and liked the material, having played Vicki Lester in the

A Star Is Born (1937): Adolphe Menjou, Janet Gaynor and Andy Devine.

Lux Radio Theatre version on December 28, 1942, directed by Cecil B. DeMille. Her contract with MGM, in effect since 1936, was terminated in 1950 following several years of problems and difficulties between the star and the studio. By the time she made *The Pirate* with Gene Kelly in 1948, the twenty-six-year-old Garland was already a disturbed woman, increasingly temperamental and unreliable. Her marriage to Vincente Minnelli became strained, and *The Pirate* was her last film under his direction. MGM followed the not very commericially successful *Pirate* with *Easter Parade*, co-starring Judy with Fred Astaire in a light, bright piece of entertainment. This called for a follow-up, *The Barkleys of Broadway*, but she withdrew from that picture, claiming nervous exhaustion. There were also many delays in the filming of Garland's next picture, *In the Good Old Summertime*.

MGM acquired the film rights to *Annie Get Your Gun* as a Garland attraction, but after weeks of spotty work and many delays, the studio suspended her and hired Betty Hutton to play the part. After three months of suspension she returned to work to make what would be her last MGM picture, *Summer Stock*, a modestly conceived musical which required six months of production, again due to

Garland's tardiness and sicknesses. She was next scheduled to do *Royal Wedding*, but Jane Powell had to be brought in when the by-now-familiar behavior pattern made dismissal necessary. By 1950, the studio was tightening its operations in face of the diminishing box-office returns caused by the rise of television and other factors.

Judy Garland's personal plight became vividly apparent in June of 1950, when she tried to commit suicide by slashing her throat. Her mother, from whom she had been frequently estranged, moved in with her and little was heard for a year. Late in 1951 she met Sid Luft, who became her manager and arranged for her to appear at the Palladium in London. The success of that engagement restored Garland to popularity. It was followed by a record-breaking nineteen weeks at the Palace Theatre in New York and a resolve to make a comeback in Hollywood. Luft and Garland formed their own production company, Transcona, and with *A Star Is Born* in mind, approached producer Edward L. Alperson, who had bought the rights to the screenplay from David O. Selznick. They were unable to interest any studio in their plans until Alperson managed to arrange a deal for them with Warner Bros. The star and the manager, now

A Star Is Born (1937): May Robson,
Andy Devine, Janet Gaynor and
Adolphe Menjou.

married, decided that the only person to write their
script was playwright and occasional screenwriter
Moss Hart, who asked for a fee of $100,000 and
expenses, which included a beach house in Los
Angeles and another home in Palm Springs.

Having set up production, Warners then
discovered that the rights to *A Star Is Born* were not
entirely free and clear. The canny Selznick had
reserved distribution rights in foreign countries. But
it so happened that Warners had negotiated for the
rights to Hemingway's *A Farewell to Arms* from
Paramount, and Selznick had long been trying to get
Warners to release the property. After the necessary
proposals and counterproposals, Selznick agreed to
pay $25,000 for a mutually agreeable settlement. He
was free to film the Hemingway story, which
regrettably turned out to be less than a major hit and
ended Selznick's career as a producer, and Warners
proceeded with *A Star Is Born*, which also failed to
become quite the commericial winner they hoped
for.

In this version, Esther Blodgett is not a starry-eyed
hopeful, she is already a professional entertainer
making a living as a singer with a touring dance
band. A more important difference is the fact that
she is not driven by the desire to become a famous

film star. It is Norman Maine who charges her with
ambition and instills in her the necessary confidence,
convincing her that she has the unusual quality that
separates certain rare individuals from the general
run of entertainers.

This version opens with a gala star-studded
benefit show staged for the Motion Picture Relief
Fund at the Shrine Auditorium in Los Angeles. In
this well-executed sequence searchlights flash across
the sky and crowds mill around the celebrities as they
arrive at the theatre and are interviewed for radio
upon entering. Backstage a large number of
costumed chorus girls, sundry performers and stage
hands frantically prepare, and among them are
Danny McGuire (Tommy Noonan), the pianist in
the Glenn Williams band, and Esther, the band's
singer. The part of the pianist is a transference of the
role of the assistant director played by Andy Devine
in the Selznick version. Also very much on hand is
publicist Matt Libby (Jack Carson), who is there to
watch out for his problem star, Norman Maine
(James Mason). Libby, who personally despises
Maine, has every reason to be worried about the
alcoholic, capricious and unreliable actor.

Maine turns up drunk, weaving his way through
the chorus girls and at one point jumping up on a

89

A Star Is Born (1954): Judy singing "That Man that Got Away." Wally Ruth portraying saxophonist (but not actually playing).

A Star Is Born (1954): Tommy Noonan and Judy Garland.

90

cowboy's horse as it is about to go on stage. He mingles with a group of Cockney singers, persuading one of them to let him have his pearly jacket and cap. Esther looks toward the commotion and remarks to Danny, "Mr. Maine is feeling no pain." She and the musicians then go on stage and perform "Gotta Have Me Go With You," during the course of which Maine takes an interest in them and moves to go on stage. He breaks away from those trying to restrain him, and it quickly occurs to Esther to work him into the act, getting him to join in the dance steps. The amused audience assumes this is the planned appearance of Maine and responds heartily.

Afterwards Maine, much more sober, thanks Esther for saving his face and asks her to join him for the evening. She explains that she and the band have to leave immediately for another job, and with some difficulty manages to get away from him. But Maine finds out where she is performing and goes to the Cocoanut Grove, which happens to be a nightspot frequented by Maine. As he enters, the headwaiter greets him and assuming that he is looking for companionship, points to a young girl. Maine replies, "Too young. . . I had a very young week last week." Then Maine's eye fixes upon a girl dancing some distance from where he and the headwaiter

A Star Is Born (1954): James Mason.

stand. The latter follows the actor's gaze and quickly shakes his head. "That's Pasadena," he whispers, "Leave it alone."

Esther has already left, but later he finds her in a small jazz joint on the Sunset Strip. He listens intently as she sings "The Man That Got Away." Maine tells Esther that her singing is extraordinary. "You've got that little something extra Ellen Terry talked about. . . . She said star quality was 'that little something extra.' " The dumbfounded Esther is then persuaded by Maine to come with him to her apartment, where she tells him her background. Genuinely impressed with her talent and her personality, Maine forces his studio boss Oliver Niles (Charles Bickford) to give Esther a screen test. The warm-hearted, intelligent Niles—a none-too-plausible characterization in the actual Hollywood scheme of things—agrees in order to placate his mercurial star, but he eventually discovers that the girl does indeed have a rare quality.

Esther's introduction to studio life is coldly impersonal. Make-up men discuss her as if she were a cosmetic dummy: "Do you think maybe the Dietrich eyebrow . . . the Crawford mouth . . . to take attention away from the nose?" She emerges from the make-up building so hideously transformed that

A Star Is Born (1954): Judy as a drive-in car-hop in a sequence cut from the picture. Chick Chandler is the customer.

A Star Is Born (1954): Jack Carson, James Mason, Judy Garland and Charles Bickford.

A Star Is Born (1954): James Mason and Judy Garland.

Maine doesn't recognize her. Employed as an extra, she ruins a take in her confusion as she plays a girl at a train station leaving in a snowstorm. Everywhere she goes in the studio she is told "Glad to have you with us," but the words are hollow. Libby informs her that they will have a new name invented for her by the end of the week, and when she lines up for her paycheck she discovers she is now Vicki Lester. Through Maine's pushing she gets a part in a musical, the highlight of which is her performance of the long narrative musical number, "Born in a Trunk," in which an established song-and-dance star tells the story of her career.

Vicki's movie is given its preview on a double bill with a Norman Maine picture. The audience makes it clear that Vicki is a smash hit and that Maine is no longer an attraction. Afterwards at a party he points to the brightly lit sky above Hollywood and says, "It's all yours, Esther. You're going to be a great star. Don't let it take over your life." Her concern is not with stardom but with her love for him. He shakes his head, "It's too late. It is, I tell you. I destroy everything I touch. You've come too late."

But Esther convinces him that they should be together. They marry in a quiet civil ceremony far from Hollywood, to the chagrin of Libby who has arranged extensive press coverage, and Maine uses his real name, here given as Ernest Sidney Gubbins. Libby arrives as they leave the office of a Justice of the Peace. He makes light of the elopement by referring to the invisible knife in his back, and tries to persuade them to go along with the rest of his publicity plans. Maine brushes him off and drives away. The bitter Libby turns to Danny and spitefully says, "Well, I wish them luck. Just wait your turn, I always say."

The marriage becomes difficult when Maine loses his contract with the studio, his drinking and unreliable habits having sapped his vitality as an actor. Unable to get work, Maine squanders his time at home while his wife's career takes her to the heights of popularity. The loving Vicki does her best to entertain him when they are together, but minor incidents disturb Maine, such as having to explain on the telephone that he is not the butler, having a messenger boy address him as "Mr. Lester," and putting up with a columnist asking for his help in getting an interview with Vicki.

On the evening on which she receives an Oscar—this time the ceremonies are conducted at the Cocoanut Grove with television coverage—he turns up drunk, applauding as she gives her speech of gratitude. He mounts the steps to the dais and sits on the floor. Up to this point the scene closely resembles the situation in the Selznick version of *A Star Is Born*. But now the tone is entirely different. Whereas March's Maine behaved arrogantly, Mason's Maine is pitifully humble. He waves a hand toward the audience, "I know most of you out there by your first names, don't I? . . . well, I need a job." He lurches to his feet and claims, "I can play comedy," and as he flings his left arm wide in a bravura gesture Vicki steps toward him to help. The audience gasps as Maine's hand hits her face, and then in a mixture of regret and embarrassment the two cling to each other.

Several of the most touching scenes in the earlier version were used almost literally in the Cukor version—including the scene in which Niles visits Maine in the sanitarium, and the harrowing incident at the racetrack bar in which the vicious Libby vents his contempt on the actor. The two films run parallel from this point, with Maine being arraigned in court as a drunken driver and his wife assuming custody of him. Cukor duplicates the scene in which Maine awakens to hear Niles and Vicki discussing him, the poignant moments being played in a dimly lit closeup of the pathetic actor. Maine's line, "Do you mind if I take just one more look?" becomes in this version, "I just wanted to look at you again." Again the sandals and the bathrobe lapping in the surf as Maine goes for his final swim.

The Cukor version makes much more of Matt Libby's response to Maine's death. Lionel Stander's playing of Libby was unpleasant in a grating, obvious way. Jack Carson, a good actor mostly squandered as a buffoonish comic, played Libby as a bitter, resentful man and created an excellent characterization. In his office he answers calls from newspaper writers and proffers false words of sympathy for the tragedy of Maine, but to a colleague he says, quoting T. S. Eliot, "This is the way the world ends, Not with a bang, but a whimper." It remains for Oliver Niles to point out to Libby, "You missed a lot not knowing Norman Maine." The closing scene returns us to another benefit at the Shrine Auditorium, where Vicki delivers the obligatory line: "Hello, everybody. This is Mrs. Norman Maine. . . ."

Judy Garland was nominated for an Oscar for her fine performance as Vicki Lester, but the 1954 Best Actress award went to Grace Kelly for *The Country Girl*. Time has proved the failure to win the award rather poignant. This was a highlight of Garland's career, and *A Star Is Born* along with *The Wizard of Oz* and *Meet Me in St. Louis* are the three films by

A Star Is Born (1954): James Mason and Judy Garland.

which she can best be remembered. Sadly, the facts in Judy Garland's life were much closer to those of Norman Maine than to Vicki Lester. During the making of *A Star Is Born* her insecurity, temperamental tantrums and long periods of sulking caused the film to run far beyond its schedule. The final cost of five million dollars was more than twice the original estimate. James Mason was hired for a twelve-week period at a fee of $125,000, but he had to be retained for an additional ten weeks, for which he received another $125,000. Fredric March had played his Maine for a higher weekly salary of $15,000, but he had no Garland to stretch the shooting schedule.

While Cukor's *A Star Is Born* is clearly a showcase for the talents of Judy Garland, it is also a high point in the career of James Mason. The British actor had been in Hollywood since 1949, following several years of popularity on the British screen, and he appeared in more than twenty pictures during the 1950s. In that respect his situation was quite the reverse of the actor he here so subtly played.

Fredric March's Maine had been a rather soft gentleman, undermined by a lack of purpose, but Mason's Maine is a deeper and more devious man, flawed by a streak of cruelty. At one point, while drunk, he warns someone, "I know myself extremely well. I'm just near the fighting stage at the moment, and if I don't get my way, I begin to break up people and things." The character is pitiable, but Mason does not play him for pity; he is merely a sensitive, intelligent man who has brought about his downfall by self-indulgence and lack of regard for others—a not-uncommon occurrence in the film industry. Mason admits he was fearful of making the film, mostly because it was to be produced by Sid Luft, a man with no experience in handling films of such scope and expense.

The original released version ran three hours. After opening to disappointing business, the film was cut down by twenty-seven minutes. In an interview with Rui Nogueira for the magazine *Focus on Film* Mason claimed that some of the best dramatic scenes were deleted, and that in his opinion the long musical sequences were a liability. "I think Wellman's *A Star Is Born* is a much better picture because it tells the story more simply and correctly, because really the emphasis should be on the man rather than the girl. It's more his story and to tell it correctly the balance should be in his favor, and that's the way it was in the original film."

Mason also explained that Judy Garland, whom he considered to be a "magical girl," lost some poignant scenes in the editing to make room for the songs. "I think that Judy's particular talent as an actress had seldom been properly exploited, but in some of her films at MGM, like *The Clock*, she showed talent which was very comic and touching. Touching because she played with a bright smile and a great spirit, while the situation was rather dramatic, even tragic perhaps. She had in fact a quality which can only be compared to Chaplin's heartbreaking quality."

Warners' *A Star Is Born* rates as one of the most unfortunately edited major films in the history of the industry, and a particularly sad case in view of the excellent material deleted. Harold Arlen and Ira Gershwin supplied the songs, of which "Gotta Have Me Go With You," "It's a New World," "Someone at Last" and "The Man That Got Away" remain. Despite the abundant musical material a decision was later made, doubtless by Judy Garland and her producer husband, to add another number. This was the acclaimed "Born in a Trunk," which, despite its entertainment value as a separate piece of material, severely upsets the balance of the picture. It was composed by Leonard Gershe and not directed by Cukor but by Richard Barstow, who also did the choreography for the whole picture. Running more than a quarter of an hour, it badly disrupts the flow of the story and caused other sequences of the film to be drastically cut.

A Star Is Born (1954): Tommy Noonan, Judy Garland and Charles Bickford.

According to George Cukor: "It's very sad the way Warners cut this picture. Moss Hart and I offered to edit it and sweat out twenty minutes in a way they wouldn't have noticed. But all the important decision makers were away on vacation and other people—the 'they' one can never discover—decided to hack pieces out of it, including charming scenes that conveyed the growth of the romance between Judy and Mason. There was a wonderful moment with the two of them on a sound stage, when Mason proposed to her before an open microphone, and everybody heard them. The editing fragmented the story and that's the reason, in my opinion, it lessened Judy's chances of winning the Academy Award."

The lack of sensitivity shown by Warners in the editing of Cukor's *A Star Is Born* is just one factor in a complex, baffling business peopled by all kinds of artists and all kinds of businessmen, none of whom can be entirely sure that what they do will meet the approval of the public. And whether movies turn out to be claptrap or masterpieces, they are made only because it is in someone's interest to make them—the effort exists only within a framework of profit-making. As for the old adage about giving the public what it wants, the late Samuel Goldwyn shook his head and said, "I don't believe the public itself knows what it wants. They only know after they've seen a picture on the screen whether they like it or not. No one is enough of a genius to know the answers in advance."

A Star Is Born (1954): James Mason, Timothy Farrell, Charles Bickford and Judy Garland.

CHAPTER FOUR

VITAGRAPH ROMANCES

The fascination with films dealing with behind-the-scenes aspects of movie making goes back almost as far as the beginnings of motion pictures. In December of 1908 Vitagraph released what was, as far as can be determined, the first film in this genre, *Making Motion Pictures: A Day in the Vitagraph Studio.* This significant film opens in the executive office of Vitagraph, where a script is being carefully considered. A director and supervisors enter, receive their instructions, and proceed to the studio in the Flatbush section of Brooklyn. Preparations begin, actors and actresses are made up, and performers and crew are shuttled in the studio cars to the location—in this case, a busy city thoroughfare.

After the scene is shot, everyone returns to the studio where, following a quick meal at the Vitagraph lunch counter, the studio scenes are rehearsed and photographed. All the necessary equipment for the different effects required are shown, as well as the rapidity with which scenes are set up, made ready by the stagehands and dismantled. During all of this a good deal of slapstick comedy is inserted, obviously to give some entertainment value to the offbeat production. After the picture is finished, it is projected, and the audience sees *Love Is Better than Riches*, the story within a story, in its entirety.

Although *The New York Dramatic Mirror* and

The Film Index agreed that the picture was a novel subject that would doubtless attract much attention, it was not immediately followed by a deluge of imitators. Other than a fifteen-minute Edison production of early 1912 called *How Motion Pictures Are Made and Shown* ("the most comprehensive motion picture description of the way films are produced," according to *The New York Dramatic Mirror*), which was handled in a straight, non-fictional, informative manner, the next behind-the-scenes picture was again produced by Vitagraph and called, appropriately enough, *A Vitagraph Romance* (1912).

This one-reel drama is the first purely fictional production to use actual studio atmosphere and personalities mixed with performers who portrayed actors, actresses, script writers, and directors. The story is about the daughter (Clara Kimball Young) of a senator (Edward Kimball) eloping with an author (James Morrison) against the wishes of her father. The boy starts writing scenarios for moving pictures, but is not particularly successful. While out walking, he and his wife see a film company photographing a sequence. He recognizes the director (James Young)*
as an old friend, and during their conversation the

* In real life, Clara Kimball Young was the wife of actor-director James Young and the daughter of actor Edward Kimball.

97

We Can't Have Everything: Elliott Dexter, Wanda Hawley (far left), Tully Marshall, Theodore Roberts and members of the harem.

A VITAGRAPH ROMANCE.

Elopement--Parents'
Anger — Scenario
Writing — Picture
Artists - Happiness.

Evolved round the Vita-
graph Studios and intro-
ducing, for the first time
in pictures, the

**THREE HEADS
OF THE
VITAGRAPH Co.**

Released Dec. 19th
Length 994 ft. approx.

A Vitagraph Romance: Advertisement in *The Moving Picture World* (1912).

Mabel's Dramatic Career (1913): Mack Sennett concerned about Mabel Normand's predicament in a movie within a movie. That's Fatty Arbuckle clutching Sennett's coat.

director tells him to call at the Vitagraph Company. The next day they are employed by Vitagraph, and soon the girl becomes one of their leading actresses.

The Senator, passing a moving picture theatre, sees a photograph of his daughter among the Vitagraph players and goes in to watch her on the screen in a melodrama. Father hastens to the studios in Brooklyn. He is introduced to the heads of the company (Albert E. Smith, J. Stuart Blackton, and William T. Rock, played by themselves) and conducted through the plant. The Senator finds his daughter in the midst of filming a sentimental scene. Her eyes suddenly meet his, and, overcome with joy at finding her, he readily forgives her and the husband and offers the young man a position to take charge of his business and political affairs.

The response to *A Vitagraph Romance* encouraged other studios to construct fictional stories around the making of motion pictures. *Mabel's Dramatic Career*, a 1913 Keystone production scripted, directed and featuring Mack Sennett, apparently was one of the first films, if not the first, with studio life as a backdrop to be filmed in or near Hollywood. In the summer of 1912 Sennett began producing and directing his Keystone comedies at 1712 Allesandro Street (now called Glendale Boulevard) in what was then the Los Angeles suburb of Edendale. Keystone's leading lady was Mabel Normand, and *Mabel's Dramatic Career* contained the usual partially improvised, hilariously absurd Sennett ingredients.

During the relatively brief screen time, Mabel is established as a kitchen maid on a farm who is fired when she becomes extremely jealous of her boy friend's (Sennett) attention to another girl. Mabel then is "driven out into the cruel world" and goes to "the city." With remarkable swiftness she gets a job as an actress at the Keystone studios.

Some time later, Sennett, realizing that he loves Mabel, leaves the farm to find her. While passing a nickelodeon, he sees her picture on a poster outside and goes in to watch the now glamorous Mabel on the screen portraying a girl in great difficulties. When the villain (Ford Sterling) of the film within a film has her tied to a post, with gunpowder about to go off, Sennett—forgetting it is a movie he is watching—loses control and fires a pistol at the screen. The audience escapes into the street pursued by the enraged Sennett. Determined to find the "villain," Sennett discovers that in reality the actor is married to Mabel and is the father of her children. While peering into their window, he is doused with water from above and then leaves dejectedly.

Mabel's Dramatic Career and a somewhat abridged reissued version of *A Vitagraph Romance* are preserved at the Museum of Modern Art in New York.

Over the years, Sennett made numerous comedies, both shorts and features, with the movie studio as a background. Charlie Chaplin was featured in two one-reelers for Sennett in 1914. In *A Film Johnnie* Charlie follows some actors going into the Keystone studio and creates havoc by ruining several scenes and spoiling a thrilling rescue staged at a real fire. In *The Masquerader* Charlie is an actor in a movie studio who misses his cue and ruins a scene. Fired, he returns to the studio disguised as a woman. Finally, the ruse is discovered and the inevitable chase is on!

Chaplin's first two-reel film for Essanay in Chicago, *His New Job* (1915), also has a studio background. Starting as a prop man, Charlie becomes a movie hero following a series of comic circumstances which includes ruining several sequences of the film in production. In the two-reeler *Behind the Screen* (Mutual—1916) Charlie is discovered working on the set as a stagehand. Eventually, he is selected for a leading part in a comedy in which he ducks a barrage of custard pies. But his boss and some "dignified" actors are soon covered in custard. These Chaplin subjects are still available.

Meanwhile, other production companies were making movies about movies. The hearts-and-flowers plot of Excelsior's *The Moving Picture Girl* (1913) had to do with an actress deserting her wealthy husband and taking their child with her. The daughter grows up and becomes the star of a moving picture company. While the company is on location in front of a beautiful mansion, the owner of the house recognizes the girl as his daughter by a birthmark, and they are happily reunited.

Edison's *Peg O' the Movies* (1913) was a two-reel

The Mack Sennett Keystone Studio in Edendale circa 1916.

The Christie Film Company at Sunset Boulevard and Gower Street in 1914. The site of the first studio in Hollywood.

Charlie Chaplin in *His New Job* (1915).

drama about a girl joining the Edison film company and going west, where she eventually is found and whisked away by her old suitor. Edison also made *Joey and His Trombone* in 1915, a one-reel comedy centering around the Edison Studio in the Bronx and featuring Gladys Hulette.

The Movie Queen, a Warners film of 1914 in three reels, used the Cinderella formula as the basis of its plot. Through the efforts of a wealthy woman, a poor seamstress becomes a leading lady with a film company. While photographing *"Cinderella"* on location at a nobleman's estate, she leaves behind her slipper. Later, after an attempt at seduction by her director, she decides to leave the studio—apparently disenchanted—and then takes up her old occupation of seamstress. In the meantime, the count has returned to his estate, discovered the slipper, and after a search, finds the girl.

Mutual's *Film Favorite's Finish* (1915) told of the arrival of a handsome leading man into the ranks of "The Climax Film Company" players. He refuses to talk to anyone except other leading players, takes an interest only in those portions of the film in which he dominates, and of course takes advantage of the women who regard him as a "motion picture idol." Eventually, he gets his comeuppance.

Using a dream as a device to project the ordinary person into the realm of motion pictures was used several times in the early years. In Selig's *Movin' Pitchers* (1913), some children are watching a Western being filmed through a knothole in the fence surrounding the yard of a studio. Suddenly, in the minds of the children, the scenes being photographed begin again and are re-created by the boys and girls.

A clerk and a stenographer in Falstaff's *Movie Fans* (1915) sit side by side in a movie theatre daydreaming. When a scene comes on showing "a famous author completing a masterpiece," it seems to the clerk that the author is himself. The girl sees the "Movie Queen" performing a scene, and in her imagination the girl becomes the "Movie Queen." After the show, mutual friends introduce them and it is love at first sight. The attraction grows stronger when the two confess their ambitious and romantic dreams. In fancy, they see themselves the brilliant attractions of a great studio. They marry, but their dreams of fame do not come true. Instead, they find domestic happiness.

Ignatz, the leading character in *A Movie Nut*, a Banner two-reeler of 1915, studies night and day to become a movie actor. After applying for a position at every studio, he finally gets his chance, but bungles it by trying to show the director how to direct. Later he dreams that he has at last reached the pinnacle of fame, and is the only rival of Charlie Chaplin for the crown of the King of Comedy. He is rudely awakened by the landlady, who demands the rent or the room.

Vitagraph produced a five-reel feature in 1916 called *Movie Money* which made novel use of the dream motif. Graham Baker's script told of a man falling asleep while sitting in a movie theatre. He dreams of the time he acted in a film and stole the director's wallet, but during a chase scene, dropped the wallet. At this point, the man wakes up and sees the film he was in projected on the screen. He sees the exact spot where the wallet was dropped. Leaving the theatre, he rushes to the location and finds the wallet. The O. Henry ending: The wallet is filled with stage money.

In 1918 Cecil B. DeMille directed one of his popular features dealing with "the restless spirit of the times" called *We Can't Have Everything*. Rupert Hughes's novel (scripted by brother William de Mille) concerned itself with marriage and divorce problems in the New York society of the period. One aspect of some complicated triangles in the story line concentrated on a young millionaire (Elliott Dexter) who falls in love with a movie actress (Wanda Hawley). This allowed for some sequences depicting the making of a movie. Tully Marshall played the director of the film-within-a-film and later said that his mannered interpretation was a deliberately exaggerated composite of D. W. Griffith (Marshall's first film was *Intolerance*) and DeMille. The character was shown trying to tackle the problems facing a director in a second-rate studio while guiding a sequence taking place in a harem. The budget plainly allowed for little opulence in the set. Theodore Roberts played the part of the actor who was cast as a sultan in these amusingly satirized scenes.

Hughes, in his novel, had the studio burn down when the sultan epic was only half-completed. Because of the expense involved in creating a studio fire, it was decided to eliminate the spectacle from the final shooting script. But when the picture was being shot a real fire broke out on the original Famous Players-Lasky (Paramount) lot at Vine Street and Selma Avenue in Hollywood. Cecil DeMille, coming back from location in Griffith Park, saw the flames from a distance. DeMille recalled the situation in his autobiography: "I found our studio . . . going up in flames. Bill [DeMille's brother] was already on the scene. Our minds had a single thought. We would get our 'fire stuff' after all. Cameras were set up. Players leaped into costumes. Grand old Theodore Roberts agreed to be photographed coming out of a burning dressing room on my assurance that he would not catch fire and, if he did, we would extinguish the flames when he came out. All the players were magnificent. Only the Fire Department was puzzled. The firemen had never seen the victims of a conflagration enjoying it so much before. After they had finally put out the blaze, they did not wait around long enough to see me start another little fire in the ruins, in order to get closeups."

By the time DeMille's *We Can't Have Everything* was released in the summer of 1918, feature films dealing with Hollywood, movie personalities, studios and film making were still sporadic and tended to fit no specific pattern. But in the 1920s a cycle began on a very simple but exceptionally effective formula that would be repeated with minor variations over and over into the 1940s and beyond.

We Can't Have Everything (1918): Theodore Roberts (far left), Wanda Hawley and Tully Marshall (far right).

CHAPTER FIVE

MERTONS AND MARYS OF THE MOVIES

By 1920 the romance of the movies was in full bloom. The star system, fan magazines, worldwide publicity, the glamour of the film capital and its inhabitants, the enormous salaries—all encouraged vicarious living on the part of young men and women (and many not so young) seated "spellbound in darkness" in the thousands of movie palaces all over the world. Glamour, riches, and hedonism—long the hallmarks of nobility, society and theatre people—were now to be found in movie personalities. Shopgirls would watch the ingenues of the screen marry handsome and wealthy young men, and immediately in their imaginations project themselves into the situation. Housewives, bored with the routine and reality of domesticity, could escape for a short while and identify with women being swept off their feet by storybook lovers who would deluge them with adoration and passion. The working man and the rising middle-class male would see and identify with the handsome "go-getter" who meets and successfully pursues that pert, attractive symbol of the modern woman "liberated" by post-World War I attitudes.

Since getting into the movies and becoming a star was considered the ultimate goal of innumerable patrons of the movies beginning in the early years of the century and hitting a high point in the 1920s and 1930s, it was only natural that pictures centering on this theme would begin to appear on a regular basis. In June of 1922 a novel by Harry Leon Wilson was published which immediately captured the imagination of the general public. Called *Merton of the Movies*, it originally ran serially in *The Saturday Evening Post*. The author was a popular dispenser of fiction of the time (*Ruggles of Red Gap*, etc.) who had gone to Hollywood for three months in 1921 to soak up background for his new story. His mentor was Nat Deverich, a pioneer actor, director, producer, and agent, who arranged for Wilson to go into the studios. Wilson hung around—watching, listening, and taking notes. Deverich also made sure that Wilson was invited to Hollywood parties, where he observed everything and continued to take notes.

A naïve and far from great novel, *Merton* was a satiric, disillusioned Midwestern view of movie-making. The reviews at the time commented that the

Merton of the Movies (1924): Glenn Hunter leaving the Midwest for Lotus Land.

This warning appeared in newspapers in 1921.

movie atmosphere was well done and there were compliments about its "different treatment of Hollywood." George S. Kaufman and Marc Connelly immediately turned the successful novel into an even more successful play. Then, almost two years after the play opened on Broadway, Paramount released its version of *Merton* with Glenn Hunter repeating his stage role.

The plot had to do with Merton Gill, a serious young grocery clerk in Simsbury, Illinois, who has studied "movie art" through a correspondence course and saved enough money to go to Hollywood in hopes of becoming a great movie actor. He is unable to find work until bit player-extra-stunt girl "Flips" Montague (Viola Dana) takes him under her wing and gets him on the lot. Merton wants nothing to do with comedies; he sees himself as a dramatic artist who desires to do something "bigger and finer." When Flips arranges to have him appear in a comedy, Merton believes he is uplifting screen art, but his imitation of a serious actor he much admires (Elliott Roth) appears to others as uproarious burlesque, and Merton becomes a sensation without knowing that he is funny. Believing himself a failure, he is surprised to get a contract for comedy parts and finds that Flips is in love with him. (Similarly, in the 1927 *Polly of the Movies* a plain little girl, played by Gertrude Short, makes her first picture which is intended as a melodrama, but turns out to be a comedy hit. Naturally, she is humiliated.)

104

Merton of the Movies (1924): Glenn Hunter.

Merton of the Movies (1924): Merton gazes at the chair of his idol.

Merton of the Movies (1924): Glenn Hunter and Viola Dana.

Make Me a Star (1932): Stuart Erwin as Merton.

Make Me a Star: Ben Turpin giving Stuart Erwin a lesson in the art of pie throwing.

Make Me a Star: Joan Blondell comforting poor Merton. Sam Hardy on the left.

The film version of *Merton*, directed by James Cruze, minimized the pointed satire and concentrated instead on the pathos and burlesque. Merton's various dreams of success as an actor were cleverly depicted. The introductory sequence shows Merton as a cowboy high on a cliff, watching a young woman in the clutches of desperadoes. Heroically, he descends by a rope and faces the outlaws rolling a cigarette with one hand. One of the men prods him with a pistol. Merton smiles, and with a William S. Hart movement he suddenly grabs the weapon from the startled villain. The scene then dissolves into reality, showing Merton in the rear room of the town grocery store in Illinois with his arm around the neck of a store dummy.

It was photographed in and around the Famous Players-Lasky (Paramount) lot on Vine Street and Selma Avenue, and the Hollywood atmosphere was in evidence throughout the film. However, no "guest stars," "cameos," or "celebrity flashes" were used. The previously released *Souls for Sale, Hollywood, Mary of the Movies,* and *Night Life in Hollywood* had recently milked that gimmick. In fact, those pictures in general dissipated *Merton*'s impact as a film. The success of *Merton* as a novel and a play inspired the production of the above films, but by the time *Merton* could be brought to the screen, the idea had been played out, and, despite good reviews, *Merton* was not an unqualified commercial success.

In 1932, following the stage success of Kaufman and Hart's *Once in a Lifetime,* Paramount re-made *Merton* as *Make Me a Star.* The story line remained the same; Stuart Erwin was Merton and Joan Blondell was Flips. There was some updating to bring in gags about a sound man's artful modifications to Merton's voice. Ben Turpin was cast as himself, the slapstick comedian of the films Merton despised. Studio cameos of contract players Maurice Chevalier, Clive Brook, Tallulah Bankhead, Sylvia Sidney, Frederic March, Claudette Colbert, Gary Cooper, Jack Oakie, and Charlie Ruggles were featured. The mixture of gags and pathos was retained.

The property was sold to MGM and refashioned as a vehicle for Red Skelton in 1947. This time it was done as a period piece of the early silent movie days, with the accent on broad slapstick. Buster Keaton was employed by MGM during this time as a gag man and trouble-shooter. He gave Skelton many pointers on the techniques of silent movie-making and worked on the construction of some of the comedy sequences. Virginia O'Brien was the girl. Hugo Haas as "von Strutt" presented the inevitable caricature of the tyrannical German director.

Make Me a Star: Gary Cooper and Tallulah Bankhead, then appearing together in *Devil and the Deep,* putting in cameo service with Stuart Erwin.

Merton was still the small-town boy, but this time around he starts as a movie-struck usher before going to Hollywood.

Back to the early 1920s: Obviously inspired by the book and play of *Merton of the Movies*, Columbia's *Mary of the Movies* (1923) was an uneventful and inexpensive working over of the new formula. To earn money needed by her family, Mary (Marion Mack) goes to Hollywood to break into the movies. She has no luck and takes a job as a waitress in a studio restaurant (a device used again many years later in *It's a Great Feeling*). Finally, through her resemblance to a star who has been taken ill, she gets the lead in a picture. The celebrities viewed along the way included Barbara La Marr, J. Warren Kerrigan, Herbert Rawlinson, Bryant Washburn, Louise Fazenda, Douglas MacLean, Anita Stewart, Estelle Taylor, Bessie Love, Elliott Dexter, Wanda Hawley, ZaSu Pitts, Carmel Myers, and directors Rex Ingram, Maurice Tourneur and John McDermott.

Within the next few years the Merton theme was repeated with little variation. In *Drug Store Cowboy* (1925) Franklyn Farnum played a clerk in a drug store who wanted to get into the movies. He is given a chance, and winds up marrying a leading lady, played by young Jean Arthur. In First National's *Bluebeard's Seven Lives* (1926), a plodding bank clerk (Ben Lyon) becomes an extra and then a star.

The year-old comic strip *Ella Cinders* became a starring vehicle for the extremely popular Colleen Moore in 1926. Ella, who slaves in the Cinders household to insure the comfort of her stepsisters and "Ma" Cinders, wins a movie contest and is sent to Hollywood. There she finds that she has been the victim of a hoax and is jobless. Finally, Ella gains entrance to a studio and disrupts productions. Caught in a fire scene being filmed and thinking it is real, Ella is awarded a contract for her splendid acting. One amusing sequence has Ella taking a screen test, during which an escaped lion makes her register the proper expressions of terror. Alfred E. Green, the director of *Ella Cinders*, appears as himself, and Harry Langdon does a cameo. *Ella Cinders* is a modest production which deviates considerably from the popular comic strip. Gone in the screen version are "Pa" Cinders, Blackie (Ella's brother), and her husband, Patches. Waite Lifter, the local iceman (who is really a millionaire's son) and Ella's boy friend, is a new character played by Lloyd Hughes.

One of the best of the silent films about the movies is *Show People*, produced in 1928 by Metro-

Merton of the Movies (1947): Hugo Haas as the director giving directions to Red Skelton and others.

Merton of the Movies (1947): Tom Dugan, Red Skelton and Alan Mowbray.

107

Ella Cinders (1926): Colleen Moore and Harry Allen.

Ella Cinders.

Show People (1928): Dell Henderson and Marion Davies.

Goldwyn-Mayer. There is much style, humor, and nostalgia in this end-of-an-era delight. Released just as sound was coming in, it is indeed a capsule roundup of what was best about the small-town-to-film-capital epics. Glimpses of the studios, film personalities, landmarks, and old-time slapstick comedy techniques abound. Marion Davies, in one of her best performances, plays Peggy Pepper, a Georgia girl who wants to be a dramatic actress and goes to Hollywood with her father, Colonel Pepper (Dell Henderson).

At the opening of the film they are seen driving down Hollywood Boulevard and, in some fancy and considerable geographic reshuffling, going by the Paramount, Fox, First National and MGM lots. At first she can only find work at "Comet Studios" as a patsy for a young slapstick comic, Billy Boone (William Haines), but later with his help she becomes a serious dramatic actress and a star at "High Arts Studio." She changes her name to Patricia Peppoire, and fame and wealth go to her head. She becomes insufferable—snubbing Billy in favor of Andre (Paul Ralli), her romantic leading man who looks, dresses, and acts like John Gilbert. He tells her that she has "the temperament of Nazimova, the appeal of Garbo, the sweetness of Mary Pickford and the lure of Pola Negri." In these scenes Davies mimicked the peculiar pucker of the lips identified with Mae Murray, and the protruding front teeth affected by Miss Murray and other grand

Show People: The director (Sidney Bracy) implores his heroine to cry, abetted by a violinist and an onion wielding assistant (Ray Cooke).

Show People: William Haines and Marion Davies.

109

Show People: William Haines, Marion Davies and guest star Charlie Chaplin.

Show People: Marion Davies and Paul Ralli.

Show People: Marion Davies and William Haines.

ladies of the cinema at the time. The character was faintly reminiscent of Gloria Swanson, who had been a Mack Sennett slapstick comedienne and went on to become a "serious artist" and the wife of the Marquis de la Falaise de la Coudraye. In *Show People* Patricia Peppoire almost marries Andre, her leading man, who calls himself "Le Comte D'Avignon." Peggy eventually comes down to earth and gets together with lovable, patient Billy Boone.

The guest stars include John Gilbert, Norma Talmadge, Estelle Taylor, Lew Cody, Renee Adoree, Charlie Chaplin (who asks Peggy for her autograph after the preview of her first film), Doug Fairbanks, Mae Murray, William S. Hart, Rod La Rocque, columnist Louella O. Parsons, and author Elinor Glyn. At one point Marion Davies as Peggy Pepper sees Marion Davies as Marion Davies at the studio and shrugs as if to say, "She's not so much." King Vidor, *Show People*'s director, appears in the final sequence as himself directing a World War I epic starring the characters played by Davies and Haines. (Three years earlier, Vidor's *Big Parade* had been released by MGM). Other inside material includes a six-piece string ensemble accompanying Patricia Peppoire, which was actually Miss Davies' own ensemble, hired to play for all her films; the "Comet Studios" are in reality the old Mack Sennett Studios in Edendale; the policemen were ex-Keystone Cops; and the man who squirts Marion Davies with seltzer was Kalla Pasha, Mack Sennett's masseur and a onetime member of the Sennett stock company. The staging of a typical two-reel comedy was a distinctive touch, and so was Harry Gribbon, another Sennett regular, as a director, grimacing as he watches his comedy film at a preview.

Fortunately, unlike many of the Hollywood films of the twenties, *Show People* is still with us. Negatives and prints are in reasonably good condition.

Another late 1920s MGM behind-the-scenes romp in the *Merton* lineage (and also still available) is *Free and Easy*, Buster Keaton's first sound comedy, released in early 1930. Although uneven and lacking the sustained charm and style of *Show People*, this combination farce, musical comedy, sentimental drama, and burlesque has some marvelous moments and contains a generous amount of material relating to the filming of early sound films.

Keaton is the befuddled manager of a Kansas beauty contest winner, "Miss Gopher City," who arrives in Hollywood, along with her mother (Trixie Friganza), to break into the movies. He crashes the studio gate, which sets off a chase through sound stages where several films are in progress. Lionel Barrymore is discovered directing a bedroom scene in a melodrama with John Miljan and Gwen Lee. (Barrymore the year before played himself directing John Gilbert and Norma Shearer in the filming of the balcony scene—both legitimate and burlesqued—from *Romeo and Juliet* in MGM's *Hollywood Revue of 1929*). In another scene on the lot, Buster listens in while Cecil B. DeMille is conversing with music arranger and conductor Arthur Lange and writer Joe Farnham, trying to decide which leading lady to use in his next film: "Garbo? Norma Shearer? Joan Crawford?" Director Fred Niblo (*The Mark of Zorro, Ben-Hur*) playing himself, is featured in considerable footage. He is seen directing the picture in which Keaton works as a bit player. Naturally, Keaton fouls things up, but through his unconscious clowning, he eventually gains a studio contract as a comedy star (sound familiar?). In addition to those personalities previously mentioned, William Haines, William Collier, Sr., Dorothy Sebastian, Karl Dane, Jackie Coogan and director David Burton can be seen.

The film ends on a Pagliacci note: Buster must go on and be funny after learning that his girl (Anita Page) is going to marry the leading man (Robert Montgomery), an old boyhood friend of Buster's.

Mack Sennett's 1921 comedy feature, *A Small-Town Idol*, while not strictly speaking in the *Merton of the Movies* formula, was a forerunner of *Merton* and those that followed. Ben Turpin played a church sexton engaged to the village belle, until he is falsely accused of stealing and driven from town. In Hollywood, he is contemplating suicide and just happens to be on the scene when the leading actor in a melodrama declines to risk his life by jumping from a high bridge. Turpin, with nothing to lose, does the jump for the actor, but is forced to do it again because it is discovered that the director's cap covered the lens of the camera. A success, Turpin is given the leading role and becomes a star!

Did anyone ever *not* make it in pictures after coming from a small town with stars in his or her eyes? Ah, yes; many. In *Sophie of the Films*, a Nestor Universal comedy in series form back in 1914, Sophie, played by Victoria Forde, leaves her old homestead to become a motion picture heroine. Fortified with a diploma from "The Bunkem School of Dramatic Art," she presents herself at "The Uneeda Feature Film Company" where she makes a hit with the leading man (Eddie Lyons). When the leading lady (Carmen Phillips) quits because she is

The MGM Studios in Culver City (1929).

Buster Keaton and Trixie Friganza in *Free and Easy* (1930).

Free and Easy: Buster Keaton, standing between directors Edward Sedgwick, Cecil B. DeMille and Fred Niblo.

Free and Easy: Director Fred Niblo showing bit player Keaton how to act like a cavalier.

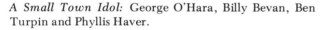

A Small Town Idol: George O'Hara, Billy Bevan, Ben Turpin and Phyllis Haver.

not allowed to take a bath during working hours(!), Sophie is given her big chance. But she spoils every scene, is fired, goes back to the homestead, and takes her old job in a laundry.

On a more serious level, *A Girl's Folly*, a feature film directed by Maurice Tourneur and released by World in 1917, explored some of the pitfalls inherent in the lure of the movies. The girl's folly in this instance is getting romantically involved with the handsome leading man of a movie company—Ken Driscoll, "a motion picture idol." The actor (Robert Warwick) meets the young lady (Doris Kenyon) while shooting on location in rural New Jersey. He suggests that she go to the World studios in Fort Lee, New Jersey, and try her luck in the movies.

Ben Turpin in *A Small Town Idol* (1921).

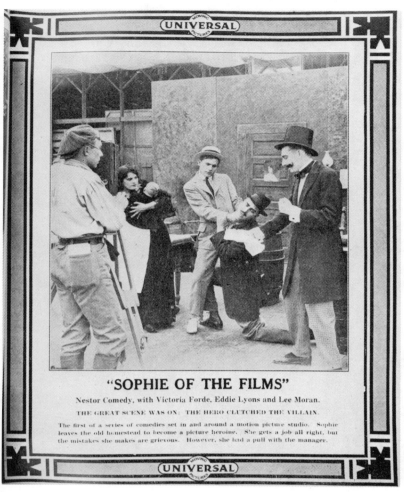

Sophie of the Films (1914): *Universal Weekly*—July 4, 1914.

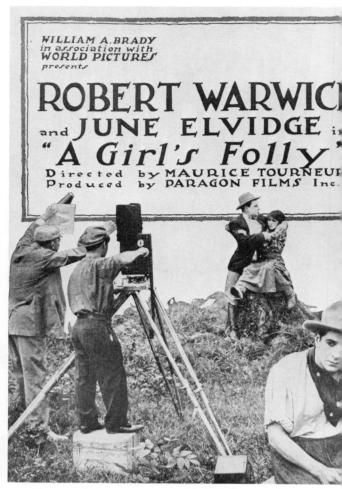

A Girl's Folly (1917): Robert Warwick, looking rather forlorn, in the foreground.

This title card from *A Girl's Folly* almost sums up the entire chapter (and then some).

"I think the girl's a find --- anyhow, I'm going to take a chance and give her the ingenue role in our next picture."

The girl leaves for "the city" the next day and arrives at the studio with the "movie idol." A test is quickly arranged after the studio manager takes one look at her and enthusiastically exclaims, "I think the girl's a find—anyhow, I'm going to take a chance and give her the ingenue role in our next picture." Unfortunately, her test turns out to be poor, but rather than go home, she consents to letting the leading man "take care of her." He has become bored with his long-time romance (June Elvidge). During a party at which the girl is being introduced to the actor's show biz friends (and a profusion of alcohol via the drinking out of the slipper routine), Mama (Jane Adair) arrives, apparently having sensed disaster, and takes daughter back home, where she marries her country sweetheart. Then the idol decides that his old flame is not so bad after all.

The screenplay by Frances Marion and Maurice Tourneur originally was titled *A Movie Romance*. *Variety* thought that "the public should be greatly interested in seeing how moving pictures are made—it is all here—but whether it is good for the picture business or not to show these things is another matter."

The documentary-like view of film making as practiced at the World Film Corporation during that period is fascinating to view today. Considerable footage is taken up by studio atmosphere, color and detail. The interior set used for the Western Ken Driscoll is shooting is on a turntable for easy adjustment to the changing sun. On the way to see the girl's test, the characters walk by the large film-drying drums, the editing room and the projection booth. The lighting, composition and overall direction by the stylish Tourneur are still impressive.

In Samuel Goldwyn's 1921 production of *Doubling for Romeo*, Will Rogers played an Arizona cowboy in love with Lulu (Sylvia Breamer). In order to win her, she decides he must learn to make love as they do in the movies. So the cowboy gets work as a double for the villain and the hero on the Goldwyn lot in Culver City (now MGM). He resigns at the mention of a retake after being battered in a fight before the cameras. Then, given the part of a lover, he fails and is dismissed. Back in Arizona, the cowboy has nothing to show for the trip. After a dream in which he imagines himself as Shakespeare's Romeo, he uses different tactics and sweeps Lulu off her feet.

There was a good deal of fun poked at temperamental stars and directors, film cowboys, and the Hollywood scene in general. At the time, *Doubling for Romeo* was considered the best and funniest of Rogers' early features. Briskly paced and inventive, it still plays quite well.

Mack Sennett's 1923 version of the small-town girl coming to Hollywood and not making good in pictures was *The Extra Girl*, starring Mabel Normand. After winning a beauty contest by a fluke, Mabel cannot find any work in Hollywood except as an assistant in the wardrobe department. Later she returns to Illinois and marries a garage mechanic. One memorable scene shows her leading a lion around the lot by a rope, under the impression that she is taking a Great Dane for a walk. She finally discovers her mistake, and is petrified with fear. Miss Normand did not use a double for this scene—in

Doubling for Romeo (1921): Will Rogers emoting.

115

Doubling for Romeo: Will Rogers in an unorthodox fencing position. (Raymond Hatton on far right.)

Doubling for Romeo: Rogers cavorting a la Fairbanks.

fact, according to Mack Sennett, she never used a double in her career. The incident was borrowed in part for the Betty Hutton 1947 fictionalized version of Pearl White's life, *The Perils of Pauline.*

In *Stranded* (1927), an Anita Loos story, another small-town girl (Shirley Mason) goes to Hollywood, fails miserably in an acting job, goes to work in a beanery, and finally gives up her career ambitions for her boy friend from back home (William Collier, Jr.).

James Cruze directed *A Man's Man* in 1929, a cynical depiction of Hollywood, in which William Haines is a soda jerk who comes to Hollywood because his wife (Josephine Dunn) thinks she looks enough like Garbo to interest film producers. The soda jerk buys some worthless oil stock from a discredited sometime assistant director (Sam Hardy), who makes a play for the wife, persuading her that he will make her a star. They discover the truth and realize that fame and fortune are not for them. Garbo and John Gilbert, playing themselves, and at the height of their much-publicized romance, are seen attending a premiere at Grauman's Chinese Theatre.

In January, 1923, *Photoplay* published a short story by a young Hollywood writer, Frank Condon, telling of a girl who went to California and found neither fame nor fortune. Jesse L. Lasky bought the story, called simply "Hollywood," for Paramount and it was assigned to director James Cruze who had just completed *The Covered Wagon.* The resulting 1923 film, *Hollywood,* is one of the most important and interesting of the early films in this genre.

The carefully-wrought adaptation related the adventures of Angela Whitaker, who, ambitious to be a movie actress, takes her grandfather (Luke Cosgrave) from a Middle Western town to Hollywood for his health. After arriving, Angela sees a number of movie stars, but does not recognize any of them. At the Hollywood Hotel she encounters more, but still doesn't recognize them. While at the Famous Players-Lasky Studio looking for a job, she again meets numerous celebrities without knowing who they are. Angela makes the rounds of all the studios, meeting the most prominent people in the industry, recognizing nobody, and getting nowhere in her quest. Meanwhile, her grandfather, basking in the sunlight, is discovered by director William de Mille and hired as a "type" in spite of his protests. Angela delivers a package to Pickfair, and, of course, does not recognize Hollywood's nobility.

Grandfather is given a contract, taken up by the movie crowd (he plays golf with Leatrice Joy), and

116

Mabel Normand in *The Extra Girl*
(1923).

The Extra Girl: Mabel Normand as
an assistant in the wardrobe department.

The Extra Girl: Mabel Normand,
Mack Sennett and director F.
Richard Jones.

his health improves markedly. Then the rest of the
family comes to Hollywood, and each one, including
Angela's boy friend (George K. Arthur), becomes a
performer in the movies without half trying. Angela
and her boy friend marry. Later, their twins—Mary
and Doug—and even their parrot, are borrowed by
a casting director. Everyone makes it but Angela.

Hollywood included more celebrity cameos than
any of the behind-the-scenes in the movie colony
films. Some of the eighty-odd celebrities glimpsed
during the film were Mary Astor, Agnes Ayres, Baby
Peggy, Noah Beery, Charlie Chaplin, Betty
Compson, Ricardo Cortez, Viola Dana, Cecil B.
DeMille, William de Mille, Douglas Fairbanks, Julia
Faye, James Finlayson, Sid Grauman, Alfred E.
Green, Alan Hale, William S. Hart, Jack Holt,
Leatrice Joy, J. Warren Kerrigan, Jacqueline
Logan, Jeanie Macpherson, Thomas Meighan,
Owen Moore, Nita Naldi, Pola Negri, Anna Q.
Nilsson, Jack Pickford, Mary Pickford, Chuck
Reisner, Will Rogers, Ford Sterling, Anita Stewart,
Gloria Swanson, Estelle Taylor, Ben Turpin and
Lois Wilson.

In order to avoid confusion with the real actors
playing themselves, it was decided that the leading
players in the story would be virtual unknowns who
had little or no previous exposure in films. Hope
Drown, who played the heroine, came from a stock
company in San Diego; Luke Cosgrave ("Grandpa")
was discovered by Cruze in a Salt Lake City stock
company; George K. Arthur, who played Angela's
boy friend, was from England. Both Cosgrave and
Arthur went on to appear in many other films;
ironically, Hope Drown faded into obscurity
following this one picture.

Since *Hollywood* is, unfortunately, as of this
writing, among the multitude of "lost" films, with no
known print or negative extant, we can only
speculate on its quality. The eminent Robert E.
Sherwood included it in his book *The Best Moving
Pictures of 1922-1923*, and his comments are worth
noting:

Cruze treated *Hollywood* as a fantasy rather than as a
grimly realistic drama. Together with [scenarist] Tom
Geraghty, he kidded his subject from start to finish, introducing elements of the wildest absurdity. In this way he
avoided the semblance of propaganda; he never attempted to defend Hollywood, or the art of the motion
picture; he never preached or moralized or drew con-
clusions.

In one episode he visualized a dream in which the [girl's
sweetheart] . . . imagined himself a knight errant who had

117

Hollywood: The beach at Santa Monica in 1923: Pola Negri, left; Lila Lee, George K. Arthur.

Hollywood: Luke Cosgrave greeting Nita Naldi.

Hollywood (1923): Director James Cruze and Julia Faye.

journeyed to the Twentieth Century Babylon to rescue his girl from the clutches of that dread dragon, the Cinema. It was utter insanity. The various stars, garbed as sheiks, licentious clubmen, aristocratic roués, bathing girls, apaches, and the like, moved about in weird confusion through a distorted nightmare. There was slow motion photography, reverse action and double exposure; no sense was made at any given point.

In another scene, Angela was shown making a futile application for work at the Christie Comedies studio. When she joined the line before the casting director's window, a corpulent gentleman stepped aside and politely gave her his place. When she had been firmly refused, the fat man walked up to make his plea but the window was slammed in his face and the word "Closed" displayed before his eyes. The camera was moved into a closeup, and Fatty Arbuckle was shown gazing at that one final word.

This topical allusion referred to the barring of comedian Roscoe "Fatty" Arbuckle from the screen after the court trials which resulted from the death in 1921 of Virginia Rappe, an actress who died after a party (an "orgy" according to newspaper accounts of the time) in Arbuckle's hotel suite in San Francisco.

The Hollywood scandals of the early 1920s were a major factor in precipitating the cycle of films centering about the movie colony. In addition to the Arbuckle *cause celébrè* there was the strange suicide of actress Olive Thomas and the never satisfactorily explained death of actor Bobby Harron in September of 1920, the still officially unsolved murder in early 1922 of director William Desmond Taylor (which implicated Mabel Normand and Mary Miles Minter), the death of actor Wally Reid from morphine addiction in January of 1923, and other events that were played up and sensationalized in the press. Hollywood was pictured as a capital of sin, where every known vice and depravity were in rich abundance.

Taking advantage of this attitude, a cheap exploitation picture of 1922, *Night Life in Hollywood*, promised lurid revelations, but instead delivered an idealized picture of the film community. A brother and sister set out from Arkansas for the modern Babylon they believe Hollywood to be. Their attempts to lead a wild life backfire, for they soon realize that "Hollywood people are no different from the folks back home." On hand to illustrate the "just folks" motif were Wally Reid and his family, J. Warren Kerrigan and his mother, Sessue Hayakawa and his wife, Bryant Washburn and family, etc. To press further, Will Rogers' home and an Easter service at the Hollywood Bowl were shown.

While *Hollywood* was in production, Rupert Hughes was preparing the screen version of his own novel, *Souls for Sale*, at the Samuel Goldwyn studio in Culver City. Purporting to be another revelation of life in the film capital, the book and film were propaganda hokum which attempted to whitewash the film industry and all who worked in it.

The plot was merely a framework upon which to build a series of melodramatic and self-congratulatory incidents. It begins with the heroine, bearing the intriguing name "Remember Steddon" (Eleanor Boardman)—a small-town girl and daughter of a minister—marrying an affable stranger (Lew Cody). On their honeymoon train heading west, she realizes she has made a mistake and gets off during a water stop in the desert. The husband is revealed as a wanted Bluebeard, who marries, insures, then kills off his wives. The girl is found by a movie company shooting a *Sheik*-like desert epic on location and she becomes an extra. Later, in Hollywood, because she has heard bad things about movie people, "Remember," or "Mem," as she is called, at first rejects the urgings of director Frank Claymore (Richard Dix) and star Tom Holby (Frank Mayo) to work in motion pictures, but she eventually makes the rounds of the studios (Famous Players-Lasky, Metro, Fox, Robertson-Cole, Pickford-Fairbanks, Goldwyn) in search of a job and sees well-known directors at work, including Erich von Stroheim directing *Greed*, Fred Niblo directing *The Famous Mrs. Fair* and Charlie Chaplin directing *A Woman of Paris*.

Mem finally gets her chance from Claymore, works hard, and steadily rises to fame. Her leading man and her director are both in love with her, but

Hollywood: Luke Cosgrave, Cecil B. DeMille and DeMille's scenarist, Jeanie Macpherson.

119

Mem's husband appears on the scene and she cannot get rid of him. The company is filming a lavish circus sequence when a storm wrecks the big top and sets fire to it. During the confusion, the husband, trying to get rid of the director, starts a large airplane propeller used as a wind machine, but he himself accidentally runs in front of it and is killed. Mem then chooses the director over the actor, and presumably all is well.

Hughes decided as an afterthought to emulate what Cruze was doing with *Hollywood* (shooting concurrently on another lot); that is, sprinkle a generous assortment of Hollywood personalities at random throughout the melodramatics. In *Hollywood* the stars were rather artfully worked in, but in *Souls for Sale* they were arbitrarily dragged in by the gross. The line-up consisted of, among many others, Barbara Bedford, Hobart Bosworth, Chester Conklin, Elaine Hammerstein, Patsy Ruth Miller, Anna Q. Nilsson, ZaSu Pitts, Milton Sills, Blanche Sweet, Florence Vidor, George Walsh, Kathlyn Williams, Claire Windsor, writer June Mathis, and directors Fred Niblo, Erich von Stroheim, Charlie Chaplin, and directors Marshal Neilan and King Vidor.

Souls for Sale seemed to be dedicated to the proposition that nowhere in the world could one find a more serious, dedicated and artistic group of workers than those inhabiting the film colony. Everyone—with the exception of Bluebeard, who is not of the movies—is noble, dutiful, sober, self-sacrificing. In this respect it is as ridiculous as those films which present Hollywood in the opposite terms.

In the novel, Holby, the leading man, pontificates on the subject at the drop of a hat:

"Is there any part of the country where booze parties are unknown? The dope fiends aren't all in Hollywood. Every other town has about the same quota . . . . I tell you the average morality is just as high in Hollywood or Culver City as anywhere else in the world. We've a bunch of hard workers and the women work as hard as the men. They're respected and given every opportunity for wealth and fame and freedom. The public has been fed on a lot of crazy stories. A few producers kept up the idea.

"A lot of bad women are at large in the movies, but most of 'em were bad before they came in and they'd have been a lot worse if they had stayed at home. The moving picture did more to keep girls and boys off the streets than all the prayer meetings ever held. They drove the saloon out of business more than any other power. The screen is the biggest educational and moral force ever discovered and it hasn't got a

Souls for Sale (1923): Richard Dix as the director.

fault that is all its own. I tell you it's a cowardly shame to throw dirt on it. I hold my head just a little higher than ever, and I am shouting just a little louder than before that I'm a movie man."

Mae Busch, playing the star of the company for whom Mem substitutes when she is injured, is shown as compassionate, unselfish and dedicated. Barbara La Marr, cast as the vamp, is revealed to be a good down-to-earth worker and not at all like her image.

The author in a newspaper interview in 1923 was quoted as saying—presumably with a straight face—that "my characters are composite types. They are just like other folks, except that for cooperation, kindness, and charity, I think they are perhaps a little superior to the general run of mankind. I have known all classes of men—soldiers, writers, lawyers, storekeepers—and I think that for real nobility the actor beats them all."

One thing is certain: according to this film, the movie people at that time were probably the most accident-prone group in the world, and everyone was constantly in danger. The character portrayed by Barbara La Marr is struck by lightning while working on the circus set—her husband having been killed in an airplane crash during a stunt scene; Mem almost falls from the catwalk between scenes; a

120

Souls for Sale: Making the girl's
(Eleanor Boardman) test.

Souls for Sale: Directing the circus
climax.

Souls for Sale: Richard Dix, Barbara La Marr, Eleanor Boardman
and Frank Mayo watching the test.

121

Souls for Sale: Mae Busch.

three-hundred-pound lamp in the studio falls on the actress played by Mae Busch. The propeller accident, according to Rupert Hughes, was based on an actual occurrence during the filming of Hughes' *The Remembrance* in 1922. Actress Patsy Ruth Miller was almost killed on the set of that film when she accidentally came dangerously close to the whirling prop, which in those days was not enclosed in a protective covering. The story seemed to be designed specifically to show the frightful risk that movie stars must make for the sake of their art—and it was all presented in a deadly serious manner.

For years *Souls for Sale* was considered a lost film, but recently a somewhat abridged version was found in Czechoslovakia (with Czech titles) by Eileen Bowser of the Museum of Modern Art, and is now at the Museum in New York. It is a fascinating relic of the real and romanticized Hollywood of 1922.

Souls for Sale: The circus fire, staged on the Goldwyn lot.

123

CHAPTER SIX

MOVIE CRAZY

One of the most frequently stated requisites for a life in the motion picture industry is a sense of humor. In a business made hazardous by rapid changes of fortune and shifting tides of taste, those who make their living producing, directing, writing and acting in films most certainly need humor to offset the insecurities and the absurdities of their often bizarre trade. Hollywood's tendency to mock itself is most acceptably presented in its comedies about picture people. If the dramas contain situations too searing to be convincing, and the musicals are too trivial to matter, then the comedies at least allow Hollywood folk to let off steam ribbing themselves. And truth is best hidden in jest.

Of the thirty-five or so movie comedies about Hollywood most are minor items. A few stand out, such as *Once in a Lifetime*, from the Kaufman and Hart play, and Preston Sturges' *Sullivan's Travels*. Others have served as platforms for the likes of W. C. Fields, Olsen and Johnson, Jerry Lewis and Harold Lloyd. Some series "B" pictures placed at least one episode in the movie capital, and this was also the case with various comedy teams. Ma and Pa Kettle never made the Hollywood scene, but the Jones Family did, as did the Cohens and Kellys and Abbott and Costello. This device was first used in 1924 when Samuel Goldwyn presented *In Hollywood with*

Potash and Perlmutter. The screenplay for this ephemeral nonsense was by the esteemed Frances Marion, who had done the first Potash and Perlmutter picture the year before. The material was adapted from the play *Business Before Pleasure*, with Alexander Carr and George Sidney playing the wild-scheming business partners. The story revolved around the antics of Potash and Perlmutter trying to break into the movie business as producers, and the footage included shots of Norma Talmadge being directed by Sidney Franklin, and Constance Talmadge being directed by David Butler.

The next film to place a comedy team in the midst of movie-making was Universal's *The Cohens and Kellys in Hollywood*. Made in 1932, this was the sixth in the series with George Sidney as Cohen and Charlie Murray as Kelly. Here Kelly's wife Kitty (June Clyde) is a waitress who sends a photo of herself to a studio asking for a chance in the movies. Within a week she receives a telegram instructing her to report as soon as possible. Kitty becomes a star of silent pictures, with her husband as manager, but when the talkies come in, they are out. However, Cohen now gets a job writing film theme songs—until the demand for theme songs dries up and then they all go home. *The Cohens and Kellys in Hollywood* included a wild caricature of a Russian

125

The Errand Boy (1962): Jerry Lewis adds a charge to a birthday party at the studio.

The Jones Family in Hollywood (1939).

Abbott and Costello in Hollywood (1945).

Abbott and Costello in Hollywood, with guest stars Lucille Ball and Preston Foster.

director by Luis Alberni. It also contained a sequence at the Cocoanut Grove in the Ambassador Hotel with glimpses of Tom Mix, Boris Karloff and Lew Ayres, all under contract to Universal at that time.

The Jones Family was a series produced by 20th Century-Fox. The studio made fifteen of them between 1936 and 1940. These comic adventures of a supposedly typical Midwestern family had Jed Prouty as John Jones, Spring Byington as his wife, and a brood of five children. The screenplay for *The Jones Family in Hollywood* (1939) was based on a story by Joseph Hoffman and Buster Keaton, at a time when Keaton was tackling anything in order to make a living.

In this episode the family makes the trek to Hollywood when father attends an American Legion convention held there. While he plays in the Legion band, the kids do all the usual landmarks and manage to get mixed up with film people. Lucy (June Carlson) falls for a flippant juvenile star (William Tracy) and Jack (Ken Howell) comes under the spell of a vamp (June Gale). Lucy gets a screen test, but when her father visits the studio, he stumbles over equipment and creates havoc. The young star compromises Lucy, but Jack comes to the rescue and by the end of the picture the Jones Family is happy to leave for home.

The device of letting a comedy team loose in the movie studios didn't turn up again until 1945, with *Abbott and Costello in Hollywood*. It has the comedians as a pair of studio barbers who become agents—Abbott seeing this as a chance to get rich. Their only client is a young country singer (Robert Stanton, the younger brother of Dick Haymes) and they chaotically romp around "Mammoth Studios" (actually MGM) trying to get him a job, driving directors and producers crazy with their antics. They succeed in spite of themselves, and the singer gets his break, playing opposite Frances Rafferty. Lucille Ball, Butch Jenkins and Preston Foster put in service as guest stars. But the comedy is too wild to have much point as satire, and only an agent could be offended.

Ten years later came Universal-International's *Abbott and Costello Meet the Keystone Kops*, which took the pair back to the Hollywood of 1914. The result was moderately amusing, with Fred Clark as a rival comic making things difficult for Bud and Lou. He swindles them and sells them to the Edison Studios in New York and then takes off for California, followed by Abbott and Costello, who by accident become a comedy team in pictures. When

Abbott and Costello Meet the Keystone Kops (1955), plus Lynn Bari and Fred Clark.

the larcenous Clark absconds with production money, they again take off in pursuit of him, this time enlisting the services and the vehicles of Mack Sennett's police force. The best thing about this picture is the appearance of Mack Sennett himself as the chief of the Keystone Kops. Sennett was by now seventy-five years of age. Heinie Conklin and Hank Mann were also on hand to play in the dizzy chase finale. What is wrong with this film is the conflict of style between Abbott and Costello and the veterans of the silent screen, with neither the script nor the direction helping to meld the disparities. Director Charles Lamont might well have borne in mind one of the fundamentals of master comedy-architect Mack Sennett: "When mystified, they do not laugh."

Satire without dialogue is difficult, but there were several attempts during the last years of the silent era to gibe the industry. *My Neighbor's Wife* (1925) was based on a story by James Oliver Curwood, "The Other Man's Wife," although neither title seems relevant to the plot. This is about a young fellow (E. K. Lincoln), the son of a millionaire, who wants to become a film producer and spends what little he has on buying a script, and then borrows $40,000 from the father of his sweetheart (Helen Ferguson) to make the picture. He hires a German director, Eric von Greed (William Russell), and, to the surprise of everyone, their product turns out to be a success, getting him the career he wants and the blessing of his sweetheart's father for their marriage. From this distance the only amusing thing about *My Neighbor's Wife* is the lampoon of Erich von Stroheim, who the year previously had directed his magnum opus, *Greed.*

In 1926 Laura La Plante played the dual role of a movie star and her look-alike in *Her Big Night.* The look-alike is offered a thousand dollars to double for the star at a personal appearance because the star is off gallivanting with a millionaire on his yacht. The resulting complications involve a suspicious news-

127

The Talk of Hollywood (1929).

paperman, a worried producer, a conniving publicist, the look-alike's boy friend and the millionaire's wife.

The look-alike gimmick also was used in *Honolulu* (1940), in which a screen star (Robert Young) is tired of the unceasing attention of his fans. He talks his double, a pineapple planter from Hawaii (also Young), into letting the star vacation in Hawaii while the planter makes the actor's personal appearance tour. The 1925 *Scandal Street* carried the idea into heavy melodrama by having a star (Niles Welch) killed in an automobile accident during production on a film. The dead actor's double takes his place, and the picture is completed with the public unaware of the actor's death. The deception succeeds, and the look-alike gracefully assumes another man's wife and fame.

Throughout the 1920s Bebe Daniels was one of Paramount's highest paid stars. A versatile lady, she played all kinds of roles, but appeared to best advantage in light comedies. One of the best was *Miss Brewster's Millions* in 1926. Here Bebe was a penniless Hollywood extra who inherits a million dollars, with the provision that it must be invested and not spent. But her Uncle Ned (Ford Sterling) arrives on the scene, and, to spite his late brother, he offers Bebe five million dollars if she can get through the inherited one million within thirty days. With the help of her lawyer (Warner Baxter) she squanders the money and then discovers that Uncle Ned is penniless. However, it turns out that the money she thought she had frittered away by backing a motion picture company has paid off handsomely with the success of the company. In this one the last laugh was Hollywood's.

Bebe Daniels' husband, Ben Lyon, appeared in a Hollywood-based comedy in 1927, *High Hat*, written and directed by James Ashmore Creelman for First National. The setting for this silly yarn is a studio called "Superba-Prettygood" and Ben is an extra in love with Millie, the wardrobe mistress (Mary Brian), who is also loved by another extra, Tony (Sam Hardy). They are all working for a temperamental German director named von Strogoff—another send-up of von Stroheim—who is making a picture about the Russian Revolution. The shifty Tony steals some jewels entrusted to Millie and turns them over to crooks. Ben pursues Tony, and their long chase ends up on the set of von Strogoff's picture. The fight is filmed by von Strogoff, and Ben's victory advances both his career and his love life.

Hollywood's first sound comedy about itself was

The Talk of Hollywood in 1929 and dealt, not surprisingly, with the problems of switching from silent film-making to sound. Mark Sandrich, who was soon to make a name for himself directing several of the Fred Astaire-Ginger Rogers musicals, staged this pioneer effort and also wrote the story in collaboration with Nat Carr, who played the leading role of J. Pierpont Ginsburg, a movie producer unable to raise the money to make his first talkie. The producer is eager to make a success of the picture in order to give his daughter Ruth (Hope Sutherland) and his lawyer, Sherline Oliver (John Applegate), a good send-off for their marriage. One of Ginsburg's biggest problems is his expensive star, Adore Renée (Fay Marbe)—a rather simpleminded spoof on the French actress, Renée Adorée, who starred in Hollywood silents during the twenties (*The Big Parade*) and whose career was wiped out by the coming of sound. Adoree would die three years later, at the age of thirty-five.

The fun in *The Talk of Hollywood* arises from Ginsburg's attempts to make a talking picture with the help of his lawyer, who has put all his money into it. Adore fails to turn up on time, his casting director brings in the wrong actors, and singers and dancers stand around while the harried producer tries to straighten out his mess. At the end of what he thought was a good day's shooting, he finds that the microphones did not record properly. After the picture is completed, a drunken projectionist mixes up the reels and the distributors leave in disgust, except one who interprets all this as deliberate burlesque and orders more of the same. Exaggerated though all this may appear today, the agonies and anxieties of *The Talk of Hollywood* were derived from the problems producers went through during this trying period.

The best of Harold Lloyd's sound pictures is *Movie Crazy*, made in 1932, although there are those who prefer *The Milky Way*, made three years later. The incredible thing about Lloyd was his lack of the out-landishness that generally marks comedians. He was not grotesque or wistful. Instead he was a fairly good-looking, decent, rather timid, ordinary fellow in the image in which he chose to present his comedy. All through the twenties, in pictures like *Grandma's Boy*, *Safety Last*, *The Freshman* and *The Kid Brother* he had revealed this nice young man in bizarre and dangerous situations, and by making these films for his own production company Lloyd became one of Hollywood's richest citizens. The coming of sound did not alter his style, but it did gradually diminish his popularity.

Movie Crazy (1932): Harold's screen test, with Harold Goodwin not too impressed.

129

Movie Crazy: Harold Lloyd and Constance Cummings.

Movie Crazy: Kenneth Thomson, Constance Cummings and Harold Lloyd.

His *Movie Crazy* is yet another saga of a dreamy hopeful trying to break into the movies. It is simply about a young Kansan who writes to a film studio for work as an actor and encloses a photograph. By mistake he slips into his envelope a photo not of himself but of a handsome actor, and within days he receives a telegram instructing him to appear at the studio. The naïve Harold enters the world of motion pictures the instant he steps off the train in Los Angeles, since the company to which he applied happens to be filming a location sequence at the station with a glamorous actress, Constance Cummings, and her rather unpleasant alcoholic leading man, Kenneth Thomson. Then and there Harold gets his first work in the movies as an extra, but he mistakes instructions and in his confusion upsets props and equipment, and ruins take after take. He also ruins the straw hat of producer Robert McWade, which becomes a running gag all through the picture. McWade, seemingly in a perpetual state

of exasperation, orders a screen test for Harold, believing him to be the actor in the photograph, but the test turns out to be a protracted disaster, with the director (Sidney Jarvis) laboring through dozens and dozens of takes. Harold is confused and depressed, but Constance finds him strangely appealing, mostly because he is the only man she has ever met who didn't make a pass at her. She nicknames him "Trouble," and she cannot resist the temptation to have a little fun at his expense. Made up as a Spanish senorita in a black wig she flirts with the guileless, open-hearted Harold who gives her his college pin. When next she sees him as herself Constance pretends to be jealous of the senorita and tells him to get the pin back. Then, as the senorita, she refuses to return it and poor Harold hardly knows what to do.

He gets a note from Constance saying she is through with him, but she writes it on the back of an invitation to a party, and that, of course, is the side he reads. At the party he accidentally swaps jackets

with a magician in the washroom and returns to the
guests with eggs, mice and rabbits emerging from his
clothes. To make matters worse for him, the wife of
the producer gets a squirt of water in her eye from his
lapel flower while dancing with him. This sequence,
one of the highlights of Lloyd's career, is hilariously
developed for almost ten minutes and harks back to
his brilliance with purely visual comedy.

Harold tackles his rival for Constance during the
making of a picture, but the actor knocks him out
and pushes him into a wicker basket. Prop men carry
the basket onto the set (a sinking ship, with water
pouring into the hold) and Harold regains con-
sciousness as Thomson is molesting Constance.

Not realizing that the action is part of the script,
Harold gallantly rescues Constance and engages
Thomson in a long and antic scrap, all of which is
captured on film because the director has been
knocked out accidentally and has given no order to
stop the cameras. When the footage is screened in a
projection room, the producer realizes Harold, in his
innocence, has a great flair for slapstick comedy and
offers him a contract. *Movie Crazy* retains much of
its appeal and its humor, thanks to the genial quality
of Lloyd's playing. At the time of making this picture, he was thirty-nine years old, and still convincing as a young rube.

In 1930 twenty-six-year-old Moss Hart wrote a
play satirizing Hollywood and called it *Once in a
Lifetime.* On the advice of Broadway producer Jed
Harris he took it to George S. Kaufman, who liked it
enough to agree to become Hart's collaborator in the
revision and improvement of the material. The play
opened on Broadway in September of that year and
became one of the major successes of the season. Hart
had never been to Hollywood and admitted that his
entire knowledge of the picture business had come
from reading *Variety.* He deduced that Hollywood
was "a wonderful absurdity" and set about tickling
its vulnerable ribs at the time of the Big Change from
silents to talkies. Despite its lack of mercy, Universal
bought the play and assigned Seton I. Miller to adapt
it into a screenplay. Miller made little alteration in
its structure and kept almost all the stringent
dialogue. However, the fact that it was now a movie
ribbing movie people softened the impact
somewhat.

Once in a Lifetime is mostly about a trio of undistinguished vaudevillians, George Lewis (Jack
Oakie) May Daniels (Aline MacMahon) and Jerry
Hyland (Russell Hopton), who astutely decide that
the film colony needs voice-culture experts, despite
the fact that the three of them know next to nothing

Once in a Lifetime (1932): Jack Oakie and Gregory
Ratoff.

Once in a Lifetime: Gregory Gaye, Gregory Ratoff and
Jack Oakie.

Once in a Lifetime: Jack Oakie, Mona Maris and Aline MacMahon.

Once in a Lifetime: Jack Oakie, Sidney Fox, Gregory Ratoff, Aline MacMahon and Russell Hopton.

about the subject. On the train to Hollywood they meet a powerful but vacuous critic-gossip columnist, Helen Hobart (Louise Fazenda), and con her into the necessary introductions. Through her they get to studio boss Herman Glogauer (Gregory Ratoff), who agrees to their setting up a school of elocution. The distraught Glogauer rants about the sound revolution: "And who have we got to thank for it? The Schlepkin Brothers. What did they have to go and make pictures talk for? Things were going along fine. You couldn't stop making money—even if you turned out a *good* picture you made money."

Among the characters hovering around Glogauer is playwright Lawrence Vail (Onslow Stevens —Kaufman himself played the part on Broadway), who, like everybody else at the studio, can never get to see the boss. After six months sitting in his office, doing nothing on full salary, he tells George, "I think Hollywood and this darling industry of yours is the most God-awful thing I've ever run into. Everybody behaving in the most fantastic fashion—nobody acting like a human being," and goes on to complain about the ridiculous waste of money.

When George finally gets to see Glogauer, he repeats the writer's sentiments word for word: "The whole business is in the hands of incompetents, that's what's the trouble!. . ." He adds, "And you turned the Vitaphone down! Yes, you did! They're all afraid to tell you. . ." Instead of feeling insulted Glogauer takes all this as a rare demonstration of courage: "By God, he's right! He's right . . . and to stand up there and tell me that—that's colossal!"

Glogauer now elevates George to the rank of supervising producer. He makes a movie called "Gingham and Orchids", and, among other things, occasionally forgets to have the lights turned on while shooting, causing portions of the picture to be badly underlit. Worst of all, Glogauer discovers that George has filmed the wrong picture. He has taken the script of a 1910 Biograph production and remade the whole thing. Glogauer's rage is moderated when the film is hailed as a critical success, with every absurd mistake taken as an inspiration or an innovation: "A return to the sweet simplicity and the tender wistfulness of yesteryear. . . . At last an actress who is not afraid to appear awkward or ungraceful. . . . The originality of the lighting, with the climaxes played in the dark. In the opening sequences the audience was puzzled by a constant knocking—then suddenly we realized it was what O'Neill did with the beating of the tom-tom in *The Emperor Jones*. It was the beat of hail on the roof." (Actually the beating was caused by George blithely cracking nuts all during the filming.)

Once in a Lifetime: Russell Hopton, Aline MacMahon and Jack Oakie.

135

Stand-In (1937): Leslie Howard and Joan Blondell.

Stand-In: Humphrey Bogart and Alan Mowbray.

The success of "Gingham and Orchids" causes the lucky but ignorant George to be hailed as "the wonderman of the talkies." He pointlessly buys two thousand airplanes, but before Glogauer can fly into a rage, other studios start calling to rent the machines because there are none available elsewhere. George, apparently, can do no wrong, and when workmen arrive to tear down the studio Glogauer doesn't fight the issue. "Tell them to go ahead! I don't know what it is, but it'll turn out all right!"

Once in a Lifetime chuckles at the illiteracy and the vanity of certain Hollywood types and clearly portrays success in such an insane business as more the result of chance than design. At one point the self-styled elocutionist, May, tries to control her indifference as columnist Helen Hobart gushes about the splendor of Herman Glogauer's life-style: "You must see his bathroom . . . it's the showplace of Hollywood! But they can see it some other time, can't they, Mr. Glogauer?" To which he replies with aplomb, "Any Wednesday. There is a guide there from two to five. Tell you what you do. Phone my secretary—I'll send my car for you."

It was thought that *Once in a Lifetime* was so severe in its lampooning of Hollywood that there was little chance of its being filmed. Kaufman and Hart pulled no punches in ribbing the "hangers-on" who flooded the town in its heyday, especially those who claimed to be voice-culture experts in the early days of sound. Aline MacMahon's clever portrayal of just such a shrewd type is one of the assets of this rollicking picture. So too is Jack Oakie's crude and not very bright George Lewis and Gregory Ratoff's harried, confused Glogauer. Ratoff, with his thick Russian accent, had played a similar part in *What Price Hollywood?*, but this time the portrait was even more wild. Improbable as Ratoff may have seemed in these roles, he did in fact divide his career between being an actor and a director, and therefore knew a good deal about studio administration. He obviously enjoyed playing Glogauer, particularly the scene when he finds his producer has made the wrong film: "Never in my life have I known such a thing! After this I make a ruling—every scenario we produce, somebody has got to read it!"

Perhaps *Once in a Lifetime* had been a little too acerbic in its humor; five years passed before Hollywood took to satirizing itself again. Two pictures of 1937 placed the industry's tongue in its cheek again, *Pick a Star* and *Stand-In*, the latter being the sharper. Hal Roach's *Pick a Star* was old-fashioned even for 1937, with Rosina Lawrence as a pretty young girl who wins an amateur contest in a small town, the prizes of which are a trip to Hollywood and two thousand dollars expenses. The promoter absconds with the money, but her boy friend (Jack Haley) sells his business and goes to Hollywood to try and arrange a screen test for her. In the meantime Rosita and her clownish sister (Patsy Kelly) receive a pair of free airline tickets from a nervous passenger who has just experienced a forced landing.

In Hollywood, Rosita takes up with a flamboyantly hammy actor (Mischa Auer), while her boy friend works as a waiter, still intent on getting her a screen test. She gets one of her own doing and dazzles the producers, and after realizing that the ham actor is an idiot, she takes up again with her faithful boy friend. All this is only mildly amusing, but the film does offer a few shots of movies in the making, including a musical sequence, and Laurel and Hardy make a guest appearance. Because of this bit by the famous comedy team, *Pick a Star* is often mistakenly listed as being one of their films.

Walter Wanger's production of *Stand-In* produced ripples of protest throughout the industry when it was released in 1937. It satirized as never before the Front Office manipulators of the studios, and once again it jabbed a wicked finger at the excesses of Hollywood's foreign-born directors. In this movie a director named Koslofski, broadly played by Alan Mowbray, was assumed to be another burlesque of Erich von Stroheim. 20th Century-Fox objected to Joan Blondell's doing a takeoff on Shirley Temple in the film. The title of the picture refers not so much to those workers who stand in for the stars while filming, but to a financial wizard who is sent by a New York banking concern to investigate the doubtful management of "Colossal Pictures," and thereby "stands in" for the stockholders.

Atterbury Dodd (Leslie Howard) must decide whether or not Colossal should continue or be written off as a bad investment. He knows nothing about picture-making and assumes that it is a business like any other, but quickly learns that it isn't. First he retreats from his plush hotel in order to escape an endless line of job-seekers and well-wishers, and takes up residence in a boardinghouse where he meets one of Colossal's workers, Lester Plum (Blondell), a stand-in. Ignorant of such a job, he asks her to explain. "Well, you wouldn't want a star to endure the heat of the lights while they set the cameras and microphones, would you? So they dig up a gal to stand in for the star while all this torture

Stand-In: Marla Shelton, Humphrey Bogart and a vintage Moviola.

Boy Meets Girl (1938): Pat O'Brien and James Cagney.

137

Boy Meets Girl: Dick Foran, Pat O'Brien, James Cagney, Ralph Bellamy and Marie Wilson.

goes on. When everything's set the star, cool and immaculate, puts her dainty little feet on the chalk marks. The stand-in, worn and wilted, fades out of the picture."

The innocent efficiency expert gradually has his eyes opened to a number of film facts of life, with the guidance of Lester, who is a stand-in for Colossal's temperamental star Thelma Cheri (Marla Shelton). It dawns on Dodd that Thelma isn't a very good actress and that it is costing the studio a lot of money to make her work presentable. Her new picture, "Sex and Satan", is being directed by the self-indulgent eccentric Koslofski, whose excesses include sending to Switzerland for edelweiss, even though the flowers are not likely to be seen in the blizzard sequence for which he wants them. Koslofski boasts that for his film "From the Cradle to the Grave" he used a real cradle and a real grave. Dodd also notices that the studio's top producer, Douglas Quintain (Humphrey Bogart), seldom does any work because

he is always drinking, because of his frustrated love for Thelma. Worst of all, he discovers that Ivor Nassau (C. Henry Gordon), a producer at another studio, is in league with Koslofski and Thelma to make "Sex and Satan" an expensive flop and ruin Colossal. With Lester as his assistant, Dodd takes action.

Dodd manages to get rid of Thelma by getting her publicly drunk and breaking her contract on a moral turpitude charge and, with the jiujitsu he has learned from Lester, he slings Ivor Nassau out of the studio when Nassau takes over as the new boss.

Despite all this, his New York employers decide to get rid of Colossal. Now imbued with the spirit of the picture business Dodd takes a stand against the bankers and rallies the workers for a period of forty-eight hours in order to turn "Sex and Satan" into a hit. Quintain, whom Dodd manages to pull out of his alcoholic daze, edits most of Thelma's scenes out of the Dorothy Lamour-like jungle epic and cuts the

138

Boy Meets Girl: Marie Wilson, Pat O'Brien, James Cagney and Ralph Bellamy.

remaining footage so that a gorilla becomes the star of the picture. In this form it is a comic gem and saves Colossal. Atterbury Dodd learns that his slide-rule theories and mathematical formulas have little bearing upon the making of movies.

Hollywood managed to take *Stand-In* in stride. It could have offended only its more sensitive executives and not the main body of workers. The script by Gene Towne and Graham Baker, based on a story by Clarence Buddington Kelland, made it clear that squads of skilled technicians and hard working laborers are more important to the making of films than the overpublicized officers in all the front offices. *Stand-In*, it might be noticed, was an independent production of Wanger's, released through United Artists, and not the product of any of the major studios. Bogart and Blondell, both Warner employees at that time, were hired to support Leslie Howard, and for Bogart it was a welcome relief from playing humorless heavies at Warners. He also was

pleased to be able to make another picture with his friend Leslie Howard, who had been responsible for Bogart's getting the role of Duke Mantee in the film version of *The Petrified Forest* the year before. The spirit with which actors played their parts in *Stand-In* suggests that they enjoyed poking fun at Hollywood life.

Boy Meets Girl was the film that brought James Cagney back to Warners in 1938 after a two-year absence from the studio, during which time he made a pair of films for Grand National. It bore some resemblance to *Once in a Lifetime* in that it was also a tremendously successful Broadway satire dealing with seemingly mad movie makers. It was written by Sam and Bella Spewack, and when Warners purchased the property they hired the Spewacks to do the screenplay. Warners initially intended it as a vehicle for Marion Davies, but she and/or William Randolph Hearst wanted changes in the story line, feeling that since it was really about a pair of male

139

The Carthay Circle Theatre, one of the favorite premiere houses in Los Angeles.

140

writers her role would have to be built up in order to take star billing. Warners resisted because it would endanger the nature of the script, and by the time the project had been delayed a year or so, Davies' appeal to the public had slipped to the point where she did not have the power to make demands. She wisely decided to retire from films.

Cagney, whose own battles with Warner Bros. over money might well have been turned into a comedy, agreed to return to the studio when they finally brought their price up to $150,000 per film, plus a share in the profits. The shrewd Cagney had fought with them from the start of his association with the studio in 1930. George Abbott, who had directed the stage version, was supposed to have directed the film, but Cagney insisted on Lloyd Bacon, with whom he had worked on seven pictures. Warners then teamed Cagney with his friend Pat O'Brien for the fifth time, and Bacon directed them at breakneck pace.

The Spewacks had worked in Hollywood before *Boy Meets Girl*, and it was assumed that they had patterned their antic pair of writers, Robert Law (Cagney) and J. C. Benson (O'Brien)—Allyn Joslyn and Jerome Cowan played the roles on Broadway—somewhat after Ben Hecht and Charles MacArthur, although they denied this. The film is set in Warners' Burbank studio and shows shots of frantic picture-making activities. Most frantic of all are Benson and Law, who claim that the theme of "boy meets girl—boy loses girl—boy gets girl" is the basis for every story, particularly when they are at a loss to think of a plot for producers immediately in need of one. The wild pair is especially irksome to studio supervisor C. Elliott Friday (Ralph Bellamy) and to cowboy star Larry Toms (Dick Foran), who badly needs a story to save his sagging career. Dragged into a conference with Toms, Law admits he doesn't have a story, and his partner says, "Tell him one anyway." Law starts, "Once there was a princess . . ." The confused Toms finally interrupts him, "I've been listening to this story for two hours. Now, what's it about?" Law acts offended, "You didn't like our story?" Replies Toms, "I didn't say I didn't like it. I couldn't follow it," to which Benson snorts, "The only thing you could follow is the trail of a lonesome horse."

Law and Benson write a script for Larry Toms and as a gag they include a part for the infant son of a studio waitress Susie (Marie Wilson in the part that would have been expanded for Marion Davies). They become the godfathers of the baby and name him Happy. The baby's part in the picture gets

The Affairs of Annabel (1938): Lucille Ball and Edward Marr.

141

Annabel Takes a Tour (1938): Lucille Ball accompanied by Jack Oakie, Pepito and Ruth Donnelly.

Annabel Takes a Tour: Clare Verdera, Ralph Forbes, Lucille Ball and Jack Oakie.

bigger and bigger and he ends up stealing scenes from the desperate cowboy star.

Very little about *Boy Meets Girl* makes much sense, but it is a wicked spoof on screenwriters that could only have been written by those who know and understand their problems. Their Benson is a man who has worked his way up from studio painter and prop boy, and has become a writer by learning every formula and cliché in the trade. Law is a frustrated novelist, who, in his quieter moments admits: "We're not writers, we're hacks . . . My God, I wrote once. I wrote a book—a darn good book. I was a promising novelist. . . . And now I'm writing dialogue for a horse."

Producers are so unmercifully ribbed in pictures like *Boy Meets Girl* that it is a wonder the material gets on the screen. Here the pompous C. Elliott Friday announces to his writers: "Boys, we need a big picture. Not just a good story. I want to do something fine—with sweep, with scope—stark, honest, gripping, adult—but with plenty of laughs and a little hokum—something we'll be proud of. Not just another picture but the picture of the year. A sort of *Charge of the Light Brigade*, but as Kipling would have done it. Mind you, not that I think Kipling is a great writer. A story-teller, yes. But greatness? Give me Proust any time."

Among the scenes in *Boy Meets Girl* is an elaborate movie premiere at the Carthay Circle Theatre, with young Ronald Reagan as the radio announcer commentating in the forecourt. The movie being honored is *The White Rajah*, starring Errol Flynn. This is an inside gag. Flynn had written a story with that title and sold it to Warners, but it was never put into production.

In 1938 RKO decided to make a star of Lucille Ball, after having used her in small roles and as a featured player for three years. She was given the lead in a modestly budgeted program picture called *The Affairs of Annabel* as a movie actress badly in need of publicity to save her slipping career. The original title was *Menial Star*, but the studio wisely reconsidered. The screenplay took its inspiration from the exploits of fabled publicist Harry Reichenbach. Here Annabel is put in the hands of a wildly energetic publicity man, Lanny Morgan (Jack Oakie), who stops at nothing to get headlines, no matter how ridiculous or embarrassing his schemes turn out to be for his hapless client. Assigned to do a prison picture, Morgan manages to get Annabel involved with real crooks and sent to jail as a consequence. When she has to play a maid he gets her a job as such, but in a house terrorized by kidnappers—and so on.

The Affairs of Annabel did well enough for RKO to contemplate Annabel as a series for Lucille Ball. A few months later she appeared in *Annabel Takes a Tour*, again with Jack Oakie as the crazy publicist. Handling a promotional tour for Annabel, he invents a romance with an aristocratic writer of popular love novels—a bashful viscount (Ralph Forbes). She falls in love with him and announces that she plans to retire from the screen after their wedding. But the viscount's wife and children arrive on the scene, and Annabel dashes back to Hollywood to avoid a scandal. The sequel was less amusing than the previous picture, and RKO dropped the idea of continuing the series.

In his last film, *Playmates*, John Barrymore appeared, incredibly, in support of Kay Kyser, the bandleader, as a Shakespearean actor who takes a job with a dance band in order to catch up on back taxes. For Barrymore admirers, all his last films were sad spectacles. However, just before doing *Playmates* he made a film which qualifies for consideration here, *World Premiere* (1941), in which he played the role of an eccentric movie producer.

Paramount's *World Premiere* has Barrymore as the producer of a film called "The Earth's on Fire", which deals with the Axis powers in Europe. To drum up publicity, the producer has his picture premiered in Washington, D.C., and instructs his publicists to send him threatening letters from spies. But real spies are assigned to steal Barrymore's movie before it can be shown and to substitute reels of Nazi propaganda in its place. Eventually the picture is recovered and the spies captured, not that it makes much difference to producer Barrymore, who can hardly recognize his own picture when he sees it. *World Premiere* is a not very good knockabout satire on harebrained publicists and scatterbrained producers, with Ricardo Cortez as an amorous actor, Frances Farmer as his jealous co-star and an amusing characterization by Eugene Pallette as a rich backer completely befuddled by the picture business.

Preston Sturges carved himself a lasting place in the history of Hollywood with a series of sharp, brilliant comedies all made in one four-year segment of his life. He had been a screen writer all through the 1930s, and after years of pleading finally got a chance to direct his own material. His first picture was *The Great McGinty*, which satirized small-time American politics, followed by *Christmas in July*, which poked fun at advertising contests. These were minor masterpieces but successful enough to let Paramount give him a bigger budget and major stars like Henry Fonda and Barbara Stanwyck for *The Lady Eve*, a devastating dig at the foibles of the idle rich.

Then came Sturges' movie about Hollywood, and for the first time the industry felt the sting of a true satirizer. The film was *Sullivan's Travels*. Sturges, who later broadened his stroke to gibe at the whole American way of life in films like *The Palm Beach Story*, *The Miracle of Morgan's Creek* and *Hail the Conquering Hero*, was not a cruel man, and his satire was always compassionate. *Sullivan's Travels* has lost its initial impact with the passing of time and with the appearance of more brutal pictures about film people, but what Sturges had to say about his own kind still has some validity.

John L. Sullivan (Joel McCrea) is an established director, but troubled because he feels films have been used too much for trivial entertainment and not enough as a means to convey socially conscious comments on life. When first seen he is in a screening room discussing his newest picture with studio executives Labrand (Robert Warwick) and Hadrian (Porter Hall). He points out that his picture is a moral lesson on the fight between capitalism and labor, and Hadrian responds: "Who wants to see that stuff? It gives me the creeps." Hadrian suggests a musical ("Ants in Your Plants of 1941") and Sullivan explodes: "How can you talk about musicals at a time like this, with the world committing suicide, with corpses piling up in the streets, with grim death gargling at you from every corner, with people slughtered like sheep . . ." Hadrian interrupts to point out, "Maybe they'd like to forget that." Sullivan realizes the hopelessness of trying to convince his bosses and decides the best thing for him to do is go out on the road and take a close look at reality for himself.

Borrowing a tramp's outfit from the costume department, Sullivan has his chauffeur drop him off in a run-down district and he roams around with only

World Premiere (1941): Don Castle, Luis Alberni, Virginia Dale, Sig Rumann, Ricardo Cortez, Frances Farmer, John Barrymore and Fritz Feld.

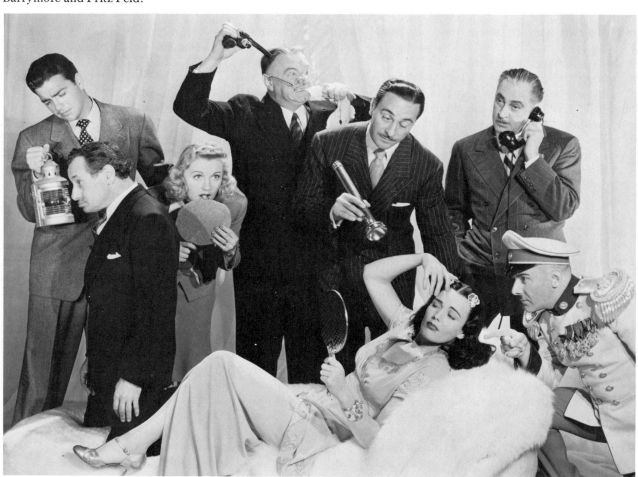

Sullivan's Travels (1941): Joel McCrea and Veronica Lake.

Sullivan's Travels: Standing —Byron Foulger, Margaret Hayes and Porter Hall. Seated —William Demarest, Franklin Pangborn, Veronica Lake, Joel McCrea and Robert Warwick.

Sullivan's Travels: Veronica Lake and Joel McCrea.

a dime in his pocket. His adventures turn out to be more harrowing and more enlightening than he had imagined, including being arrested as a vagrant and set to work on a chain gang at a prison farm. He makes the acquaintance of a penniless starlet (Veronica Lake) and together they travel the country, hopping trains, sleeping in missions, and scavenging for food. Whenever he speaks pompously about *Film* as the "Greatest educational medium the world has ever known," she deflates him.

Even his butler (Robert Greig), in a later scene, lets a little air out of Sullivan's lofty theorizing about poverty: "You see, sir, rich people and theorists, who are usually rich people, think of poverty in the negative—as the lack of riches—as disease might be called the lack of health. But it isn't, sir. Poverty is not the lack of anything, but a positive plague, virulent in itself, contagious as cholera—with filth, criminality, vice and despair as only a few of its symptoms. It is to be stayed away from, even for the purposes of study."

Sullivan learns another valuable lesson at the prison farm, when a Mickey Mouse cartoon is shown to the prisoners. He notices that anger and despair leave their faces as they laugh and become involved with the movie.

Back at the studio, Sullivan meets with his bosses, who have publicized his adventures on the road and are now eager to have him make a socially conscious picture to cash in on his experiences. But, to their astonishment, Sullivan has changed his mind. He doesn't want to make the proposed "O, Brother, Where Art Thou?" because he now considers it his job as a director to entertain: "There's a lot to be said for

146

making people laugh. Did you know that's all some people have? It isn't much, but it's better than nothing in this cockeyed caravan." Ironically, while Preston Sturges was true to Sullivan's words, he also managed to make trenchant comments on society and the human condition. And he said everything he had to say in just seven fine movies all made between 1940 and 1944. He died in 1959 without ever being able to equal that period in his life.

Ole Olsen and Chic Johnson were a team who had been in vaudeville since 1913. They appeared in a few early talkies, but made little impression on movie-goers until 1941 when they did *Hellzapoppin* for Universal. It was a screen version of their long-running New York show, which almost defied description—as does the film. On stage this loud, brash pair ad-libbed and broke all the rules of formal presentation, belting out songs and gags, combining the abstract with the vulgar, lacing it all with violent slapstick.

The point that *Hellzapoppin* couldn't be made into a movie is made soon after it starts, when the director stops the picture and frantically explains to Olsen and Johnson in a screening room that they must have a story. He brings in a writer, who outlines a plot and the pair jump into it, something about a party being given on an estate. As the story progresses shadows appear on the screen as people —supposedly in a movie theatre—get up and leave. Olsen and Johnson talk back to the projectionist, who gets tangled up in reels of film with his large usherette girl friend. Parts of other films are shown by mistake, and at one point Hugh Herbert steps out from behind the screen to talk directly to the audience.

Hellzapoppin amused audiences of 1941 by amazing them, and it did well enough for Universal to hire Olsen and Johnson for another picture two years later. *Crazy House* is better and funnier than its predecessor, and draws most of its humor from the pretended reluctance of Universal to make another film with Olsen and Johnson. It begins with New York Mayor Fiorello La Guardia bidding good-by to the pair as they leave for Hollywood, but news of their coming sends the workers at Universal into a panic and they barricade the entrances.

The resourceful pair have themselves shot over the studio walls by circus cannons, but the executives still refuse to back their picture. The boys decide to make their film independently, backed by Percy Kilbride, who thinks he has money but doesn't. Despite mishaps, they manage to get their picture amde and rush it into theatres before the company that has rented

Hellzapoppin (1941): Ole Olsen, Chic Johnson and Richard Lane.

Crazy House (1943): Franklin Pangborn looking horrified at this novel idea in hotel accessories by Olsen and Johnson.

147

them equipment can issue the attachment it had planned.

Crazy House moves at breakneck speed through a brief seventy-five minutes and manages, incredibly, to pack in more than a dozen musical numbers by five different bands and groups. Edward Cline, who directed W. C. Fields' lunacies for Universal, steered this mayhem through its course. One very good idea: Olsen and Johnson use the stand-ins of the stars they might have worked with at Universal to make their picture. Many of Universal's familiar players pop up in the course of *Crazy House*—Allan Jones, Johnny Mack Brown, Leo Carrillo, Andy Devine and Robert Paige.

This, such as it is, represents the best of Olsen and Johnson in the movies. They later appeared in *Ghost Catchers* and *See My Lawyer*, but after that it was a quick retreat to the stage. In fact, the whole plot of *See My Lawyer* was built around the pair trying to get out of a movie contract.

The last plateau in the film career of W. C. Fields consisted of four films he made for Universal between 1938 and 1941—*You Can't Cheat an Honest Man, My Little Chickadee, The Bank Dick,* and *Never Give a Sucker an Even Break.* He thereafter made guest appearances in a few films, but *Sucker* was his last major feature and his only film dealing with the film business. Fields wrote the original stories for all four films, co-scripting *Chickadee* with Mae West and inventing pseudonyms for the other three—Charles Bogle, Mahatma Kane Jeeves and Otis Criblecoblis. His own title for *Sucker* was *The Great Man,* but Universal didn't consider this sufficiently humorous. No title could have conveyed the scattered absurdity of the picture, which was purely a vehicle for Fields and nothing else. Its only point seems to be that it has none.

When first seen, Fields is standing in front of a huge billboard carrying the poster of himself in *The Bank Dick.* Despite the fact that he is thereby set up as a famous person, and using his own name, he nonetheless appears to be a hack writer trying to peddle a screenplay to "Esoteric Studios." His target is a harried, fluttery producer, played by Franklin Pangborn, also using his own name, and the poor man is driven wild by the idiocy of Fields' scenario.

In *Sucker* Fields is much as he was in many other films—a cheapskate, muttering sarcasm, who is nonchalantly ineffectual and pompously philosophical. In a small restaurant a plump waitress tells him, "You're about as funny as a cry for help," and when his niece, Gloria Jean, asks him if he was ever married, he replies, "No, I was in love

once with a beautiful blonde. She drove me to drink—the one thing I'm indebted to her for." Along the way he offers a cure for insomnia: "Get plenty of sleep." Finally getting to the producer's office to outline his new script Fields relates improbable situations, and the film cuts to enactments—such as Fields jumping from an airplane without a parachute when his whiskey bottle falls over the side of the observation deck—an open area at ten thousand feet! He lands on the mountaintop home of wealthy widow Margaret Dumont and recoils from her until he learns she is rich, and then he courts her. When he realizes she is just too monstrous to marry—even for money—he makes a hasty retreat down the sheer, two-thousand-foot cliffside. But the scene cuts back to the producer's office before it need be explained how Fields survived such a fall.

Never Give a Sucker an Even Break gives little insight into the picture business, but does include one scene in which Pangborn rehearses Gloria Jean in a ridiculously long aria on a sound stage full of noisy workmen. The picture ends with a wild car romp through the streets of Los Angeles as Fields volunteers to get a woman to a maternity hospital. He creates havoc, and as he clambers from the wreck of his car, Gloria Jean turns to the camera and says, "That's my Uncle Bill. But I love him." She might well have been speaking for any Fields addict seeing this picture. However, the picture does contain one apropos line, as Fields tells his wacky story to producer Pangborn, who explodes, "This script is an insult to a man's intelligence—even mine."

The Bank Dick, made just before *Sucker,* has Fields as a small-town character named Egbert Sousé, who, in an early sequence of the picture, cons a visiting movie producer, Mackley Q. Greene (Richard Purcell), into letting him take over the direction of the location company when A. Pismo Clam (Jack Norton) is too drunk to direct. Sousé spins a tale of having worked with D. W. Griffith and Mack Sennett, but once he gets to directing, it becomes apparent he is a fake—and A. Pismo Clam sobers up enough to reclaim his job.

Republic contributed a mildly amusing entry to the movies about the movies in 1942. *Yokel Boy* has Alan Mowbray as an executive producer dissatisfied with the publicity breaks "Mammoth Films" have been getting. The publicity director (Roscoe Karns) comes up with an idea: He has read about a fellow in the Midwest named Joe (Eddie Foy, Jr.) who is the world's champion movie-goer. There would be lots of publicity as a result of bringing Joe to Hollywood

Never Give a Sucker an Even Break (1941): Franklin Pangborn, W. C. Fields and Mona Barrie.

as a script consultant. Joe is promptly sent for. One of his first jobs is choosing a "Wow" girl. He picks the boss's cousin (Lynne Carver), a rank amateur. The star of "King of Crime", based on the life of a famous gangster, quits rather than work with the "Wow" girl.

Joe comes up with another suggestion: Why not hire the real gangster to play himself? But trouble and complications lasting until the end of the film begin after the arrival of the gangster (Albert Dekker), his torch-singing sister (Joan Davis), and their escort of musclemen. No such film would be complete without the eccentric foreign director—here played by Mikhail Rasumny.

Dreamboat, written and directed by Claude Binyon for 20th Century-Fox in 1952, contains a solid comic idea, well played. It tells of the indignation of a dignified college professor (Clifton Webb) when it is discovered that he was once a movie matinee idol of the Valentino-Fairbanks variety who ranked second in a nationwide popularity poll ("First was some stupid police dog") and the abrupt change his life undergoes when his old pictures are shown on television. The professor, who claims he became an actor only because he fell in love with a shrewd actress, Gloria Marlowe (Ginger Rogers), and did it to please her, wants no part of the commercial world of television, which he refers to as the "idiot's delight." Disgusted with the emergence of his past he snorts, "It's like exhuming a man from his grave." As for his pictures: "They were made to capitalize on the vicarious cravings of middle-aged glandular cases." Gloria, who is the hostess of the TV show featuring these silent pictures of twenty-five years earlier, is not about to let this profitable development in her career slip away. The professor, the former Bruce Blair, legally protests that all this is an invasion of privacy and detrimental to his prestige as an educator. When he finally gets his case to court, he asks for a television set to be placed on the witness stand, and in answer to the prosecutor's claim that this is the greatest educational force in the world, the professor flips the channels to show a string of commercials. He wins the case, but loses his job. His superior at the college, a lady dean (Elsa Lanchester), has been secretly in love with him for years and confesses she can no longer exist in the same building with Bruce Blair.

The film, amusing throughout its whole course, contains four excellent sequences depicting the triumphs of Bruce Blair in his heyday, each one of them a spoof on actual films of the past. First is a segment from a picture call "The Return of El Toro",

150

The Bank Dick (1940): Evelyn Del Rio voicing an opinion on Fields' direction of Reed Hadley and Heather Wilde. Cora Witherspoon and Jessie Ralph look on.

Yokel Boy (1942): Eddie Foy, Jr., Albert Dekker and Alan Mowbray.

Dreamboat (1952): Clifton Webb as "El Toro."

with Blair doing a Fairbanks, Sr., routine, a la *The Mark of Zorro*, leaping around athletically and dueling. Next, he is seen in a *Wings/Dawn Patrol*-type epic as a carousing air ace. When told that a certain German ace is overhead, he exclaims, "At last, Baron von Brickhofen has accepted my challenge." In a Foreign Legion picture, of the *Beau Geste* kind, he liquidates the Arab legions, and in a film that closely resembles *The Three Musketeers* he drives a coach at breakneck speed to save a lady from The Cardinal's Guards. Gloria Marlowe is the leading lady in each film, and Blair ends every segment kissing her hands, arms, shoulders and face. This old routine has now returned to plague the professor. The advent of television figured strongly as a plot device in two other films dealt with at length elsewhere in the text: *Callaway Went Thataway* and *What Ever Happened to Baby Jane?*

Dreamboat ends with a twist that might have pleased O. Henry. When Gloria Marlowe taunts the professor about the loss of both his job and her show, he blithely informs her that he has received an offer from Hollywood. Cut to the obligatory Carthay Circle Theatre and a movie audience laughing. Flash to the screen, showing a sequence from Clifton Webb's *Sitting Pretty*, in which he retaliates when a baby flicks Pablum at him. The professor seems smug at his new success, but quickly has the air let out of his balloon by Gloria: "We're going to do wonderful things together. I bought your contract."

Hollywood or Bust (1956) was the last of the comedies made by Dean Martin and Jerry Lewis as a team. Directed by Frank Tashlin, who had directed them before and would later direct some of Lewis' solo efforts, very little of the picture takes place in Hollywood. It begins in New York with the pair winning a red convertible and deciding to take off on a cross-country trip. Lewis badly wants to meet his favorite movie star, Anita Ekberg, and Martin needs to get away from irate bookies. On the way they pick up a lovely girl, played by Pat Crowley, who is making her way to Las Vegas to become a showgirl. When they get there, Martin wins $10,000 at the gambling tables. Another passenger on the trip is Lewis' huge Great Dane. This disdainful dog dominates the picture and justifiably becomes a hit once they arrive in Hollywood. The gentle monster falls in love with Ekberg's toy poodle and gains a contract in the process, but not until Lewis has reduced Paramount to a shambles in his quest to meet Anita.

Jerry Lewis set two of his own comedies in Hollywood, *The Errand Boy* in 1962 and *The Patsy*

Dreamboat: Clifton Webb as an air ace loved by Ginger Rogers.

Dreamboat: Clifton Webb, hero of the Foreign Legion, about to defend Ginger Rogers.

Dreamboat: Musketeer Clifton Webb assuring Ginger Rogers she has nothing to fear, with the possible exception of himself.

two years later. He also directed both films and, as has frequently been said about Lewis, if his considerable talent had been balanced with self-discipline, the results would have been funnier. *The Errand Boy* is much the better of the two and offers plenty of insight into the workings of Paramount (here called "Paramutuel"). In this Lewis is a genial but thick-headed mailroom clerk who spreads chaos through every department he visits. He lingers in a screening room and distracts a frantic director (Sig Ruman) with the disapproving look on his face. Another director (Fritz Feld—according to Hollywood comedies Germans make the zaniest directors) is driven apoplectic when Lewis is hired as an extra and gazes adoringly at the star (Pat Dahl). So smitten is Lewis that he leaves the set without realizing he has wrecked the scene. At a sound-dubbing session he innocently mixes tracks so that at a preview the star soprano sings with the squawk of a cockatoo (see *It's a Great Feeling*), and his passing through the secretarial pool results in all the typed scripts being scrambled. *The Errand Boy* is excellent in its first half, but sags in the second. Brian Donlevy is the tough studio head, Howard McNear is his cringing yes-man, and Iris Adrian is marvelous as a pompous star whose birthday party, held on a set, is wrecked by Lewis.

Like *The Errand Boy*, *The Patsy* was written by Jerry Lewis and Bill Richmond, but the premise is

154

Hollywood or Bust (1956): Pat Crowley, Jerry Lewis and Dean Martin.

The Patsy (1964): John Carradine, Keenan Wynn, Jerry Lewis, Phil Harris, Everett Sloane and Peter Lorre.

The Errand Boy: Jerry mixing up a Western.

Jayne Mansfield, Joan Blondell and Lili Gentle in *Will Success Spoil Rock Hunter?* (1957).

Tony Randall, as Rock Hunter, apparently spoiled by Jayne Mansfield as well as success.

too incredible to support the picture. Lewis is a hotel bellboy whose awkward manner catches the imagination of a team of movie people who have just lost their star comedian in a plane crash. The producer (Everett Sloane), the director (Peter Lorre), the writer (Phil Harris), the publicist (Keenan Wynn), and their secretary (Ina Balin) are desperate to carry through with their plans to make a picture, and seize upon Lewis as a trainable replacement. They bring in a voice coach (Hans Conried) to improve his diction, but nothing about him can be improved and they finally throw in the towel. Lewis then makes an appearance on the Ed Sullivan television show and delights the audience with comic bumbling. Now declared a winner, he contacts the group and persuades them to come back to him. *The Patsy* suffers from its weak core, and the abundant mugging and grimacing of Lewis only serve to make it more apparent. Hedda Hopper, Rhonda Fleming, Ed Wynn and George Raft pop up as guests, but to no avail.

George Axelrod's play *Will Success Spoil Rock Hunter?* was a spoof on Hollywood, but when 20th Century-Fox made their film version they chose to alter the target and make it a dig at the world of advertising, and in particular the business of huckstering on television. The entire credit—or blame—for the picture belongs to Frank Tashlin,

Peter Sellers doing "Gunga Din" duty in *The Party* (1968).

who wrote the screenplay, directed it, produced it and kept only the thread of the Axelrod original. Here Rock Hunter (Tony Randall) is an account executive in danger of losing his job if the agency loses their biggest client, Stay-Put Lipstick. Hunter saves the situation by enticing movie queen Rita Marlowe (Jayne Mansfield) to become identified with Stay-Put, but the price he pays for this is becoming identified with her. He is more or less adopted by Rita, to the annoyance of his girl friend (Betsy Drake) and Rita's boy friend, TV jungle star Bobo Branigansky (Mickey Hargitay—then married to Mansfield). The intimidated ad man agrees to marry Rita but faints before he gets to saying "I do." Life on the periphery of a movie celebrity, with its mobs of wild fans, proves too much for Hunter and he elects to retire to a chicken farm. *Will Success Spoil Rock Hunter?* is too obvious in its humor. But it has a sad, and possibly grotesque, nostalgic value because of the performance of Jayne Mansfield. She had come to prominence playing Rita Marlowe in the Broadway original, and her overblown burlesque of Marilyn Monroe could hardly be overlooked by Hollywood. And it was not a case of Mansfield *playing* Rita Marlowe—she *was* Rita Marlowe.

In 1968 Blake Edwards took it upon himself to direct and produce a film that would utilize the

The Party: The blonde is Carol Wayne; Peter Sellers is kneeling.

157

The Loved One (1965): Robert Morse and John Gielgud.

The Loved One: Robert Morley, Robert Morse, Jonathan Winters, Anjanette Comer, Rod Steiger, Roddy McDowall and John Gielgud.

techniques of the silent comedies but in a modern setting. *The Party* runs close to a hundred minutes, but its script is about half the size of the usual screenplay because Blake required Peter Sellers to perform as much physical comedy as possible, with a minimum of dialogue. The result was largely a failure. Edwards dragged out a simple situation, that of an awkward, clumsy actor making a shambles of a party at the home of a studio executive. By far the best part of this picture is the eight minutes which precede the credit titles. Here an Indian actor, Hrundi V. Bakshi (Sellers) appears in a Bengal Lancers-type epic on a location resembling the Khyber Pass. He has been imported from India to play a bugler, but he turns out to be less than

adequate. Bakshi plays the wrong calls and instead of falling dead, as per direction, he gets carried away with excitement and accidentally sets off the charge that blows up the fort—before the cameras and the company are ready to shoot the siege. The furious producer blackballs the nitwit Indian, but by another accident he gets invited to the party, resulting in scores of minor and major mishaps. If the bulk of the picture had been as good as its overture, *The Party* would be a milestone in screen comedy.

MGM's *The Loved One* in 1965 failed to win approval with the general public, despite a star-studded cast and its origin as a renowned piece of black humor. Evelyn Waugh's novel was, for its time, the most devastating spoof on certain aspects of Hollywood, such as the British colony in the movie industry and the lavish business built around death and funerals in Southern California. Waugh went to Los Angeles in 1946 to work on a film treatment of his novel *Brideshead Revisited*, but after weeks of painful conflict with studio executives and censors the project was scrapped and the disillusioned Waugh left, vowing never again to be associated with Hollywood and that no book of his would ever be sold for filming. However, the crippling British tax structure gradually caught up with him, and, desperate for money, he turned over his works to an estate, and thereby lost control of them.

He had written *The Loved One* immediately after his Hollywood experiences, and its screen rights were sold in 1950. Nothing came of the plans to turn it into a picture until 1961, when John Calley, Haskell Wexler and Martin Ransohoff bought the rights and arranged with MGM to make a film. Tony Richardson, then flushed with the success of *Tom Jones*, was hired to direct and English poet Christopher Isherwood and American satirist Terry Southern were contracted to write the screenplay.

What Richardson, Isherwood and Southern did to Waugh's book is what critics have wailed about since the beginning of the film industry: They drastically altered it and lost its flavor in the process. In its publicity MGM described it as a film "with something to offend everyone." *The Loved One* crudely flails away at—among other things—mother-love, lechery, avarice and nepotism, and for a picture made by a major American studio, it has a blatantly anti-American tone. "America the Beautiful" is used on the sound track to underline all that is ugly and grotesque about Los Angeles.

The best parts of the film are the opening sequences, which deal with the studios. Robert Morse, miscast as a young British poet, comes to visit

159

his uncle, Sir Francis Hinsley (Sir John Gielgud), an aging art director. The studio for which Sir Francis works, "Megalopitan," fires him, and he hangs himself from the diving board of his empty pool. It then becomes his nephew's task to arrange his funeral, which introduces him to the weird world of "Whispering Glades Memorial Park"—Waugh's dig at Forest Lawn.

The Loved One was a dubious subject for screen treatment, but better results could conceivably have been achieved with better taste and judgment. For film buffs it is amusing to see Roddy McDowall as a studio executive, a nervous son of a tycoon, who fully knows that his job comes with the family and not with ability. Robert Morley plays the head of Hollywood's British colony, a tribe Waugh satirized unmercifully. (It remains for someone to produce a good movie comedy about the legions of Britons who once made Hollywood one of the most colorful outposts of the British Empire.)

One of the less appealing facets of Hollywood has been its tendency to put its older talents to pasture and forget them. This was the theme of Columbia's *The Comic* in 1969, with Dick Van Dyke as a star of the silent era whose career is ended by sound and who is gradually reduced to impoverished obscurity.

The driving force behind this film is Carl Reiner, who wrote, directed and produced it. Reiner had worked with Van Dyke on his television series, and both men felt strongly about what had happened to certain old comics in the industry. Harry Langdon was a case in point, as was Buster Keaton, who had by this time recovered some of his former prominence after years of struggling to make a living in a business in which he had once been a giant. The case of Stan Laurel was less happy. He had lost all his wealth, and in the last dozen years of his life lived in a small apartment, supported by the charity of those who admired him. Both Van Dyke and Reiner idolized Laurel and discovered, to their anger, that Laurel had had to sell the rights to his own screen image in his need for money. *The Comic* was made, understandably, with a certain measure of bitterness, and is not, strictly speaking, a comedy.

The story is told in flashback form, beginning with the funeral of Billy Bright (Van Dyke) and the voice of the deceased telling the story from the sound track. It is the voice of a bitter man, who sneers at the cheap funeral and the meager turnout, recalling the days when he was the top man in movie comedy. Billy is a vaudevillian who makes good in the early days of Hollywood. His two-reelers elevate him to

The Comic (1969): Dick Van Dyke and Michele Lee.

Myra Breckinridge (1974): John Huston and Raquel Welch.

stardom, and he marries his pretty co-star, Mary Gibson (Michele Lee). The marriage is a good one until he dallies with the wife of a producer and, despite his protestations, Mary leaves him and takes their young son with her. When sound comes, Billy refuses to change his style, and his career rapidly runs downhill. Years later, as a grumpy old man he keeps company with his fellow veteran of silent fame, Cockeye (Mickey Rooney, in a role clearly based on the cross-eyed Ben Turpin), and together they visit an old movie theatre playing their pictures. Billy's fortunes pick up a little after an appearance on the Steve Allen television show and he gets work doing commercials, but he is no longer really a funny man but a whining relic.

The best bits of *The Comic* are those depicting the early days of movie comedy, with Cornel Wilde as a director putting Billy and Cockeye and Keystone Cops and Bathing Beauties through Sennett-like slapstick paces. These sequences are a good accounting of the period. The tone of the picture alters with Billy's decline, becoming decidedly downbeat. Columbia did not regard the film highly enough to give it major distribution, and it did poorly on the market. Perhaps the public, like the industry itself, did not like to be reminded that great entertainers sometimes fall by the wayside and receive little help.

To date (1975), the only other film comedy set in Hollywood has been *Myra Breckinridge*, made by 20th Century-Fox in 1970 at a cost of five million dollars. Gore Vidal's novel, a salty tale of transsexualism, proved difficult to translate to the screen, and the accounts of the making of the picture kept gossip columnists happy for months. Ten different versions of the screenplay were written, with producer Robert Fryer and director-scenarist Michael Sarne in constant battle and much bickering between the confused and angry actors. Mae West, for a fee of $40,000, chose to make this a vehicle for her return to the screen and wrote her own material, with the result being that her scenes are totally unrelated to the rest of the proceedings. Miss West, already the better part of eighty, here seems a pale travesty of her former self.

Myra Breckinridge, a monument of tastelessness, nevertheless has much to interest film students, partly because of numerous clips from old Fox pictures. The film was so severely edited that the studio decided to pump it up with old footage in order to bring it to feature length. The clips were used to punctuate and comment upon Myra's adventures, but they were intercut in such a way as to alter the tone of the original. A clip of Laurel and Hardy in this context makes them appear homosexual. Several stars objected to the use of their likeness. Loretta Young was successful in having her clip (from *Call of the Wild*) removed because it was intercut with a sodomy sequence. The United States Government forced Fox to excise a clip of Shirley Temple in *Heidi* because of its place in a masturbation episode. (Shirley Temple Black was at this time a United Nations delegate.)

Myra Breckinridge is the story of a lad named Myron (Rex Reed) who undergoes a sex operation and emerges as a girl named Myra (Raquel Welch). She goes to Hollywood to claim an inheritance from Buck Loner (John Huston), an old cowboy star who now runs a talent school for movie hopefuls. Myra learns to expect nothing from this crooked roué. Leticia Van Allen (West) operates an agency handling well-built young men, and it appears to be mostly a business for her own gratification. Aside from waging sexual warfare Myra achieves little in the course of this confusing fantasy, and at the end suffers an injury in a car crash which somehow restores her to being Myron. Myron also appears from time to time in the course of the picture as a droll, invisible (to all but Myra) alter-ego. In both the opening and closing the two of them dance together down Hollywood Boulevard to the accompaniment of Shirley Temple singing "You Gotta S-M-I-L-E to be H-A-Double P-Y" from *Stowaway* (1936).

The same week it released *Myra Breckinridge*, Fox issued Russ Meyer's semi-porno *Beyond the Valley of the Dolls*, which was also set in Los Angeles and dealt with a group of young people somewhat involved with the entertainment industry—mainly pop singing. Both films received X ratings, the first in the history of 20th Century-Fox.

Myra Breckinridge: John Huston and Mae West.

CHAPTER SEVEN

HOLLYWOOD CAVALCADE

Although the public prefers its movies about the movies to deal with famous actresses or actors (real or fictional), other less glamorous figures such as directors, writers, stunt men, talent scouts and various film industry types are occasionally the subjects of Hollywood on Hollywood films.

20th Century-Fox's *Hollywood Cavalcade* (1939), a major production in Technicolor, attempts to compress in an entertaining fashion a good deal of Hollywood history, lore and legend from the year 1913, when film-making started to take a firm hold in Hollywood, to 1927 when sound was introduced. Through the experiences of Michael Linnett Connors, a fictional director played by Don Ameche, appear a variety of achievements: Mack Sennett's Keystone Cops, bathing beauty and custard pie slapstick comedies, the Griffith and DeMille spectacles, the sentimental love stories, Adolph Zukor's bringing of stage plays and stage stars to Hollywood, Samuel Goldwyn's glorification of the established author and the use of important stories for films, the advent of dog hero movies with Rin-Tin-Tin, the *Madame X* courtroom dramas, and

Al Jolson in the first part-talking feature film, *The Jazz Singer*.

Hollywood Cavalcade is of particular importance to this survey, because it represents the first attempt by the motion picture industry to look at itself in retrospect in a feature film. Heretofore all Hollywood films about films—whether comedy, drama or romance—dealt with the then contemporary picture business. There had been no attempt to do a period piece about early moviemaking, a study of a famous film personality of yesteryear, or a panorama of any kind. Although *Hollywood Cavalcade* made use of the typical 20th Century-Fox simplistic formula in the characterizations of the leading players, it did present a certain amount of the flavor and charm of moviemaking of years past.

The story itself relates the rise, fall, and rise again of an enthusiastic young director (Ameche). At a New York theatrical performance in 1913 he sees a promising understudy, Molly Adair (Alice Faye), who is substituting for the leading woman. He persuades her to make the trip to the West Coast and

163

A premiere at Grauman's Chinese Theatre in 1930.

the movies, promising her a brilliant future. Upon arriving, Molly is furious when she discovers that Connors is only a prop boy. However he persuades the head of "Globe Pictures" (Donald Meek) to let him direct a test of his find on a rooftop. When her test turns out well, Connors directs Molly in a comedy with Buster Keaton (played by himself). During one scene Keaton just happens to pick up a pie in a moment of frustration and throws it at Molly. More pies are thrown, and at the screening of the rushes everyone is convulsed with laughter and enthusiastic about the new type of comedy. Molly is soon referred to as "The Queen of the Custard Pies."

Connors, hard-working, filled with ideas, lives and breathes film. He comes up with the bathing beauty comedies, followed by a series of pictures with comic cops. Connors, in a moment of inspiration exclaims: "I've got the greatest idea in the history of the world—bar none! Who are you the most afraid of? Burglars? Bandits? No! You're most afriad of cops! Cops! Because they are a symbol of authority—they can boss you around, and you all hate the boss! So I'm going to put a bunch of cops on the screen, and they're always going to get the worst of it. . . . And when they do, the whole world will laugh."

We then see "Help, Murder, Police!", a re-creation of a typical Mack Sennett Keystone Cop comedy circa 1914, involving chases in vintage cars, motorcycles and trains with wildly improbable actions in defiance of all physical laws. The cops, of course, are an instantaneous success.

Wanting full control, Connors and his old friend Dave Spingold (J. Edward Bromberg) start their own company with Molly and her romantic leading man, Nicky Hayden (Alan Curtis), billed as "The Lovers of the World." Molly, secretly in love with Connors and loyal to him, feels that he does not care for her and secretly marries Hayden while they are making a film. When Connors, directing a lavish spectacle, hears about the marriage, he is brokenhearted and refuses to direct "The Lovers of the World" anymore.

Deep in despair, Connors loses his spirit and soon gets a bad reputation for walking off pictures at Fox and Paramount and indulging in expensive, elaborate failures. He even turns down an opportunity to discover Rin-Tin-Tin. A has-been, no company will hire him.

Molly and her husband have signed with Metro and gone on to even greater fame. In 1927 Mack Sennett salutes them during their fifth wedding anniversary party at the Cocoanut Grove. But Molly

Hollywood Cavalcade (1939): Stuart Erwin, Don Ameche and Alice Faye.

sees a dejected, boozy Michael Connors seated at a nearby table. She later suggests to Dave Spingold that he sign Mike to direct her new silent film, a courtroom drama called *Common Clay*.* Connors accepts, and after a tense beginning on the set, his old skill and imagination return.

During the filming, Molly's husband is killed in an automobile accident, and Molly, seriously injured, is taken to a hospital. The backers want the film finished with a double. Connors refuses and steals the negative. Then he notices throngs of people outside the theatre where *The Jazz Singer* has opened and is creating a sensation. Connors goes in and listens to Al Jolson singing "Kol Nidre" on the screen (in a re-created sequence played by Jolson) to an electrified audience. Although before this, Connors has said that "people don't want to hear their idols talk," he now sees that talking pictures are inevitable and filled with exciting possibilities. He notes that about ninety percent of *The Jazz Singer* is silent, with no dialogue or singing, and tells Molly at the hospital that they will finish *Common Clay* with some sound sequences when she is well enough. The resulting part-talking picture is a big hit, and Molly and Connors are back together.

* A peculiar anachronism. Fox made an all-talking picture in 1930 with Constance Bennett called *Common Clay*. Victor Fleming was the director.

Hollywood Cavalcade: Alice Faye taking the pie hard and fast.

Hollywood Cavalcade: Buster Keaton, Stuart Erwin and Don Ameche.

Hollywood Cavalcade: Alice Faye as a Sennett-like Bathing Beauty.

Threaded throughout *Hollywood Cavalcade* is a nostalgic score consisting entirely of older, evocative songs such as "Whispering," "Just a Memory," "I Love You, California," "My Blue Heaven" and "Memories."

In addition to a brief personal appearance, Mack Sennett supervised the re-created scenes of his own Keystone Cop, custard pie and bathing beauty comedies, which were based on his Keystone comedies of the silent years. Sennett and Mal St. Clair, the director of the interpolated material and a Sennett director from the early days, gathered some of the old Keystone regulars—Hank Mann, Chester Conklin, James Finlayson, Heinie Conklin and Ben Turpin—to lend authenticity to the proceedings. Rin-Tin-Tin's great grandson was on hand to play his illustrious predecessor, and Lee Duncan, Rin-Tin-Tin's owner and trainer, appeared briefly as himself.

Although primarily fictional, the Ameche and Faye roles suggested certain aspects of the careers and personal relationships of Mack Sennett and Mabel Normand. Mabel, of course, was Sennett's leading lady (and his first "Bathing Beauty") during the early years depicted in *Hollywood Cavalcade*. They also were linked romantically for a long period and came close to marrying in 1915. Years later, after her death in 1930, he referred to her more than once as "the most important thing in my life." A few

Hollywood Cavalcade: Stuart Erwin and Don Ameche above; Chick Chandler below.

Hollywood Cavalcade: The party at the Cocoanut Grove—standing is Mack Sennett, to the left is Buster Keaton and to the right Alan Curtis, Alice Faye, J. Edward Bromberg, unidentified player and Stuart Erwin at far right.

Hollywood Cavalcade

months before he died in 1960 at the age of eighty, he mentioned Mabel in an interview and said that he "always regretted not marrying her." Sennett was a lifelong bachelor.

A director from Russia making films in Hollywood is one of the leading characters in *The Last Command* (1928), an exceptional silent film directed by Josef von Sternberg with a controlled, striking style. Holding up extremely well, it can still be shown to almost any audience and produce a remarkable effect. The basic idea, supposedly suggested by producer-director Ernst Lubitsch, is intriguing and based partially on a true situation.

After the opening credits, a card flashes on the screen: "The Magic Empire of the Twentieth Century! The Mecca of the World!", followed by a second card: "Hollywood—1928!" We are introduced to Leo Andreiev, a onetime revolutionary leader in Russia and director of the Kiev Imperial Theatre, now respectably established as a top Hollywood film director (William Powell). Andreiev is having difficulty in selecting the right type for the small role of a Russian general in a new film he is making. Going through scores of photographs, he recognizes a man who was at one time a cousin to the Czar and the commanding general of the Russian army (Emil Jannings). He tells his assistant (Jack Raymond) to have the extra report to the studio in the morning. The old, broken recluse, with a facial tic, is reached in a seedy rooming house.

The next morning at the "Eureka Studio" (the then-new Paramount lot, off Melrose Avenue) the old man joins the hordes of extra players waiting to enter the studio. This scene is titled "The Bread Line of Hollywood" and places the ex-general in the midst of a wild mob being doled out portions of the uniforms they are to wear as extras ("One corporal! One general!"). In the make-up room the old man takes out of his wallet his own star of the Order of Alexander Nevsky and attaches it to his studio uniform, but the cigar-chewing assistant director, referring to the old man as "Pop," tells him in a patronizing manner that the director has an important part for him and the uniform must be correct. The assistant then places the decoration on the opposite side of the jacket. The old man moves it back. "In Russia that was worn on the left side. I know because I was a general." The assistant changes the medal once again. "I've made twenty Russian pictures. I should know about Russia!"

While waiting along with the other extras to be called to the stage, the old man stares at himself in the make-up mirror. This cues a lengthy flashback which comprises the bulk of the picture: It is Imperial Russia in 1917. Here we meet the antithesis of the dejected, vague old man. The general is an imposing figure: brilliant, authoritative, courrageous, shrewd—with a generous overlay of European sophistication. Andreiev, who later becomes the director, is brought before the general as a revolutionary in wartime Russia. The general has him jailed, but takes his actress-companion, Natacha (Evelyn Brent), as hostage and mistress. Much later the general's staff is executed by a revolutionary mob, but he is spared for the moment and forced to serve as fireman on the train heading for Petrograd. Natacha has desperately arranged this short reprieve, and then maneuvers his escape from the train seconds before it plunges into a river with her still on board.

We are now back in the Hollywood studio. The old man is confronted by Andreiev, the director, on the set. "I have waited ten years for this moment, Your Highness. The same coat, the same uniform, the same man—only the times have changed." He corrects the positioning of the medal and puts the general "in command" of a group of soldiers in an artificial snow-covered battlefront on the stage. During the scene the old man, caught up by the uniform, the soldiers, snow, trenches, and the strains of the old Russian national anthem played by the set musicians, is oblivious to camera and crew. He is back in Russia, facing his troops in revolt, giving his last command. He then collapses and dies.

Although Lubitsch supposedly suggested the germinal idea, many assumed the script was an elaborate and fanciful embellishment of what happened to some refugee aristocrats from Russia and elsewhere in the 1920s. According to film historian Kevin Brownlow, General Lodijenski of the Imperial Russian Army, who played extra parts and bit roles in Hollywood and ran a Russian restaurant at the same time, was the specific inspiration. Lodijenski, who in the late 1920s used the name Theodore Lodi, appeared as generals, captains, grand dukes, ministers of war, and masters of the hunt in several Russian and Graustarkian romances of the late silent years (e.g., *The Cossacks, The Swan, General Crack*, etc.).

The performances in *The Last Command* are excellent. It is certainly by far Emil Jannings' finest American role, having been designed from the pattern laid down by his two international successes made in Germany, *The Last Laugh* (1925), and *Variety* (1926), in which he played degraded and pitiable middle-aged men in humiliating cir-

The Last Command (1928).

The Last Command:

The Last Command: The director
(William Powell) and flunkies.

The Last Command: Emil Jannings
and Jack Raymond.

169

cumstances. Evelyn Brent, von Sternberg's pre-Dietrich *femme fatale* and lady of mystery, projected a complex, intelligent, and yet sensual woman.

The original design of the film did not include a flashback; the story was told in chronological order. Also, there was no train wreck or death of Natacha. In the earlier script she becomes a Hollywood actress reunited with Andreiev, and the general spends time in Amsterdam and New York before arriving in Hollywood to find her. On the set, Andreiev tells the general she is dead, when in reality she has merely changed her name. The structure of the script, apparently, was changed during the filming and editing stages.

Shortly after the release of *The Last Command* in 1928, Tiffany-Stahl Productions released the curiously titled *Clothes Make the Woman*, which undoubtedly was "inspired" by *The Last Command*. In this modest offering Princess Anastasia of Russia (Eve Southern) is saved from execution by a young revolutionary (Walter Pidgeon) who risks his life to help her escape. Years later they meet in Hollywood. Overnight he has become a popular movie star, and she, having been discovered among the extras, is hired to play the part she once lived. He accidentally shoots Anastasia in a re-enactment of the execution of the czar and his family, but she recovers and they marry.

In recent years, the director has been the subject of some films reflecting his revised role in contemporary film-making. *Targets* (1968), Peter Bogdanovich's first feature film, which he wrote, produced and directed, has two story lines running concurrently and then merging at the climax. The one is about a young sniper (Tim O'Kelly) and his innocent victims. The second features Boris Karloff as an aging, weary horror film star, Byron Orlok, who regards himself as a museum piece. He is bored with playing minor variations on a theme over and over again, and is concerned about the national obsession with youth and the abundance of youthful crimes. He walks out on his contract and refuses to make a scheduled personal appearance at a local drive-in. A young, low-budget director (Bogdanovich) hopes to dissuade Orlok from retiring and persuade him to star in a contemporary film he has written.

The stories converge at a San Fernando Valley drive-in movie. Orlok has reluctantly agreed to make the personal appearance, and the young psychotic sniper has hidden himself behind the screen, from which he will fire through a hole and

The Last Command: William Powell and Emil Jannings.

pick off families during the screening of Roger Corman's *The Terror* (1963). There follows a well-executed sequence involving theatre operation detail, brutally swift killings going unnoticed in the darkened lot, panic slowly building to hysteria and a mass exodus of colliding cars. Orlok, approaching in the flesh and as the giant shadow on the obliquely viewed screen, confronts the sniper from two sides. The young killer's lost mind reacts to this bizarre duplication by firing at both fantasy and reality. He is found curled up in a corner.

170

The Last Command: Emil Jannings and William Powell.

The Last Command: Emil Jannings
and William Powell.

171

The film opens with an extended period horror picture finale (lifted from Corman's *The Terror*). As it turns out, what we are watching is taking place in a screening room, with the producer, young director and Orlok in attendance. Roger Corman had stipulated to Bogdanovich when he let him make *Targets* that the picture must be brought in for around $100,000 and that a leading role must be created for Boris Karloff, who owned Corman five days of shooting.

In *Lions Love* (1969) the French film-maker Agnes Varda cast New York film-maker Shirley Clarke, who goes to Hollywood to join a *ménage à trois* in a rented house occupied by Jerome Ragni and James Rado (creators of *Hair*) and Viva. Their improvised dialogue consists almost entirely of non sequiturs. Miss Clarke is depicted as wanting to make a film about Los Angeles. The head of the studio (Max Laemmle) won't give her the right of final cut. In this Godard-Warhol-Clarke styled derivation, director Varda darts in and out of sequences, changing dialogue, make-up, and, in one instance—that of Clarke's suicide attempt, after being given a hard time by the producer—playing the scene herself because as Shirley Clarke says, "I sure as hell wouldn't kill myself over a lousy movie." As a picturization of the affluent hippie subculture of the 1960s, *Lions Love* wallows in that vapid, vain life style.

Targets (1968): Boris Karloff, Nancy Hsueh and director Peter Bogdanovich playing a director.

Alex in Wonderland (1970): The battle on Hollywood Boulevard.

172

A year later audiences were subjected to the American version of Fellini's 8½. In *Alex in Wonderland* (1970), Alex (Donald Sutherland) has just finished his first feature film directorial effort. Before it is even released, the Hollywood bush telegraph pronounces it a critical and commercial success—"an important film." But Alex finds himself in a dilemma: what does he do for an encore? What will that all-important second film be about? What, if anything, does he want to say? Haunted by the spectre of being a flash-in-the-pan success, Alex spends most of the picture searching for his identity and his second film. He discusses with his wife (Ellen Burstyn) the changes they can expect now that success has entered their lives, but he cannot decide on what form his new life style should take. He has difficulty "relating," sees a psychiatrist, engages in lengthy, pretentious talkathons with friends and associates at the beach, has troubles with his wife and experiments with LSD.

In a surrealistic manner he investigates contemporary social problems by fantasizing. In one such sequence he and his wife are dying from smog as they land at the Los Angeles International Airport; in another he is the sacrificial victim of an African tribal gathering; in the most elaborate of these interludes, Hollywood Boulevard is invaded by military troops. The action skips between "This is a fantasy but it is happening" to "This is how Alex would direct this fantasy if it were a movie." Two tap dancers do their number on burned-out taxi cabs to the sound track of Doris Day singing "Hooray for Hollywood."

Alex visits Fellini in his editing room and attempts to pay homage to his cinematic idol and in that way find part of his own film identity. He meets Jeanne Moreau at the Larry Edmunds Cinema Bookshop on Hollywood Boulevard. Continuing his search for the "right" material for his next project, he has a memorable encounter with Paul Mazursky, *Alex*'s director and co-writer, who portrays an MGM executive wooing Alex to do something "artistic" with material that the executive owns or will option:

Would you like to go to Paris and read a book? I'll give you a book I own. . . . Take your wife. . . . You want to do a love story?. . . . I have a book. . . . It's about a twenty-year-old who gets a heart transplant. . . . Read it in Paris. . . . She could be black. . . . And it might work well with a white doctor. . . . An Indian film? Could be a very important statement. . . . Relevant. . . . I have the American rights to Dostoevski's *The Idiot*. . . . You like my Chagall? Please take it.

Except for this gem of a sequence, *Alex in Wonderland* does not really come off. It is too self-indulgent, too self-consciously contemporary and —worst of all—dull.

Federico Fellini's Italian film, 8½ (1963), the

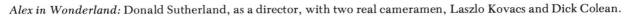

Alex in Wonderland: Donald Sutherland, as a director, with two real cameramen, Laszlo Kovacs and Dick Colean.

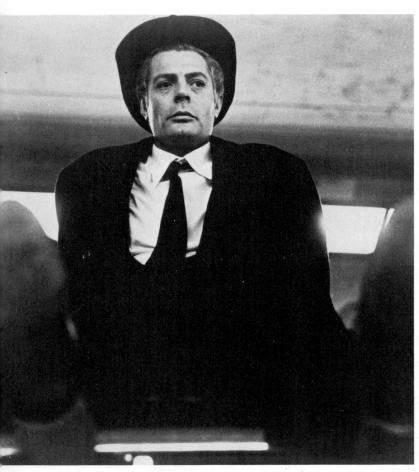

8½ (1963): Marcello Mastroianni.

obvious inspiration for *Alex in Wonderland*, recounts the artistic and moral crisis of a famous Italian motion picture director (Marcello Mastroianni), who, under pressure to begin a new work, finds himself bankrupt of ideas and concerned that his way of life is pointless.

Alex and 8½'s director were less fortunate than real-life director Mitchell Leisen playing director "Dwight Saxon" in the prologue and epilogue to *Hold Back the Dawn* (1941). This picture opens with Saxon directing a scene from *I Wanted Wings* at Paramount. The lunch hour arrives and the director is interrupted by a disheveled young man (Charles Boyer) who is in desperate need of $500. He has a story to sell but no time to write it. The director agrees to listen to a tale of a scoundrel's regeneration through the love of a beautiful and steadfast woman. At the conclusion of *Hold Back the Dawn*, the director is convinced that the story is worth many times the $500 and decides to make it as his next picture. Alas, Fellini's director in 8½ is not presented at a critical time with a ready-made narrative.

After Fellini had done *La Dolce Vita* in 1961 and enjoyed the applause and fame that it and he received, the director apparently found himself in a curious state of stagnation, unable to decide what his next film would be. He then analyzed himself and probed his memories, motivations and all that was in his mind. And from this self-examination he got the idea for 8½ (so called because Fellini had previously made six full-length features, plus three one-half

After the Fox (1966): Peter Sellers, left, as Fabrizi, greatest of all Italian directors.

174

segments of other motion pictures). In delineating the director's struggle to free himself from his problems, to find himself and bring some order and meaning to his career, Fellini in 8½ alternates between sequences of fantasy and reality—"All of them," according to Fellini, "taken, more or less, from my own life."

Peter Sellers does a take-off on Fellini in *After the Fox* (1966), a potentially good original screen comedy by Neil Simon, which misses. The plot: A master criminal (Akim Tamiroff) seeks to find a way to fence $3,000,000 in gold bars from a Cairo bank. The gold is on a Mediterranean steamer, and a spectacular cover must be found to mask its delivery. The master criminal recruits Aldo "The Fox" Vanucci (Sellers) to handle the difficult task. "The Fox" hits on the idea of pretending to make a film on an Italian beach. He raids camera and sound equipment belonging to director Vittorio De Sica during a sandstorm and marches into a little fishing town as the great avant-garde director Federico Fabrizi. Soon he has enlisted the entire population as extras—for free, naturally. The movie is to be called "The Gold of Cairo", and of course the gold is brought ashore as part of the script. Playing in the film are Victor Mature as a has-been actor trying for a comeback (with his security blankets, the slouch hat and trenchcoat) and The Fox's own sister, rechristened Gina Romantica (Britt Ekland). Fabrizi's explanation to his cast of what "The Gold of Cairo" is all about is hilariously vague, pretentious and nonsensical. It seems as though Antonioni as well as Fellini is being caricatured. "The Gold of Cairo" is directed and photographed in a mangled, chaotic manner—but a critic acclaims it a great work of art (à la *Once in a Lifetime*).

The director functioning realistically at his craft is believably shown in Francois Truffaut's highly entertaining French feature *Day for Night* (1973). Truffaut, playing a film director named Ferrand, is making a commercial French film at the Victorine Studios in Nice. He is besieged with problems: "Before starting, I hope to make a fine movie. Halfway through, I hope to make a movie," he says at one point. The laboratory ruins a whole day's work on an expensive crowd scene; one of the leading players threatens to abandon the picture when his girl takes off with a stunt man; a minor actress creates a crisis by revealing that she is pregnant, making it difficult to match her first and last scenes; an aging, insecure, champagne-sipping *grande dame* ruins innumerable takes because of her inability to remember lines and stage directions; a recalcitrant cat is uncooperative in a complicated scene; and the star dies before the completion of filming. When Ferrand learns of the death, he immediately absorbs the shock and begins redesigning the film around the actor.

Throughout *Day for Night* (a term meaning the filming in the daytime of scenes intended to be represented as taking place at night) Ferrand dreams of himself—in installments—as a little boy stealing still photographs from a movie theatre that is showing *Citizen Kane*.

After the Fox: Fabrizi introduces his stars, played by Britt Ekland and Victor Mature.

Day for Night (1973): Francois Truffaut.

Day for Night: Truffaut and his crew.

Day for Night: Jean-Pierre Leaud, Jacqueline Bisset and Francois Truffaut.

Although chiefly concerned with the surface of things, *Day for Night* is an instructive as well as absorbing film. Ferrand is coddling, consoling, enduring, decisive or prodding as the moment requires. The making of motion pictures is shown to be a frenetic and exasperating game, but it is also revealed as a passion and a creative compulsion. As the film runs its course, we realize that the relationships formed while making a movie are as artificial and transitory as the circumstances that brought the cast and crew together in the first place.

In René Clair's *Le Silence est d'Or* (or in America, *Man About Town*) 1947, Maurice Chevalier plays a middle-aged French motion picture director knocking out quickies in the French film industry of 1906. He shoots snow scenes in the boiling heat, beach sequences in dank winter, and his frequently lethargic crew plays cards through all emergencies.

An earlier French production, *Three Waltzes* (1939), devoted one section of a three-generation story to the filming of a picture with a French movie star played by Yvonne Printemps. The sequence is treated as a Gallic turn on *Once in a Lifetime*. Also, the cinema plays cupid and conciliator in uniting two lovers and a triple line of family history, all to waltz time.

If the contemporary director is reasonably presented in *Day for Night*, the old-time, autocratic European martinet is incredibly portrayed by Erich von Stroheim in a woefully dated but interesting RKO action film of 1932, *The Lost Squadron*. Based on an original story by stunt pilot Dick Grace, the plot deals with a group of World War I flyers who end up in Hollywood doing stunts for aviation films. The pathological director (von Stroheim) is jealous of his wife (Mary Astor) and one of the stunt flyers in his latest air epic (Richard Dix). He rubs corrosive acid on the control wires of a plane Dix intends to use in an upcoming stunt. After further complications, the flyer deliberately crashes his plane, which contains the body of the director whom another stunt pilot (Joel McCrea) has justifiably shot.

As contrasted with the quietly efficient and self-contained director played by Truffaut, the terrible-tempered, Teutonic director presented by director von Stroheim is something to behold. Before assuring his actors that they are addlebrained and totally incompetent, he had just twisted the wrists of his leading lady (who is also his wife) after seeing her in private conversation with the flyer. Impeccably tailored, moving with military precision, his bull head neatly shaven, a scar on his forehead, von Furst struts on the set surrounded by a battery of cameras and megaphones in various sizes with "Mr. von Furst" painted on each. His hands are covered with immaculately clean white gloves, and he handles his walking stick as though it were a sword.

Von Furst's directions for the upcoming scene are delivered pompously and drenched in sarcasm. Finally he cries, "Cameras!" and the action begins. Unhappy with what he sees, the director shortly yells "Cut!," takes off his topcoat and throws it to the ground and goes into a screaming, barely comprehensible rage. It is quite a scene, and yet professionals such as the distinguished documentarist John Grierson have stated that von Stroheim himself did on occasion reveal aspects of this manner when he was directing his silent epics. (Needless to say, this did not include the murdering of his cast and stunt men or twisting the wrists of his actresses.)

RKO, apparently not knowing quite how to handle this curious combination of war film, murder mystery, stunt drama, Hollywood satire, air spectacle, comedy and romance, came up with an advertising and publicity campaign that is probably

Le Silence est d'Or: Maurice Chevalier and Gaston Modot.

the ultimate of its kind. Here are excerpts from the 1932 press book:

Wingmen of the Hollywood skies courting death as they courted women—dangerously, glamorously! A wave of the hand . . . and off they streaked! . . . Plunging, zooming, climbing, crashing . . . that a madman below might create on film the supreme thrill to shock the world! And a story of romance tender as loving hands . . . dynamic as the thunderclap of destiny! Hollywood gave its magic soul to make this picture. Men dared death! Directors dreamt miracles! Cameramen risked all . . . to give you the supreme thrill . . .

177

The Lost Squadron (1932): Erich von Stroheim as the brilliant but mad film director.

And more—

Mortal eye never before witnessed its like! Skies torn asunder! Dazzle! Glitter! Thrill upon thrill! Whine and scream of wounded planes . . . Charge and wheel of flashing squadrons . . . An air show in the making . . . behind which you'll see the demoniac director who brought thrills at the price of death! Far flung genius of the studios . . .

And still more—

Batteries of cameras swung aloft against the skies where America's aces streak, plunge, soar, dive, crash at the command of a madman! Flaring panorama of sensation . . . A juggernaut lashing and tearing its way to the drumming heights of thrilldom . . . A love story that hits the vaulted heights of drama . . . Shatters the heavens! Rends the skies!

Von Stroheim, "The Man You Love to Hate," seemed to be an obvious target for caricature—to say the least—in several Hollywood looks at Hollywood films. The foreign director "Eric von Greed" in *My Neighbor's Wife* (1925), "Von Strogoff" in *High Hat* (1927), "Landau" in *Hollywood Speaks* (1932),

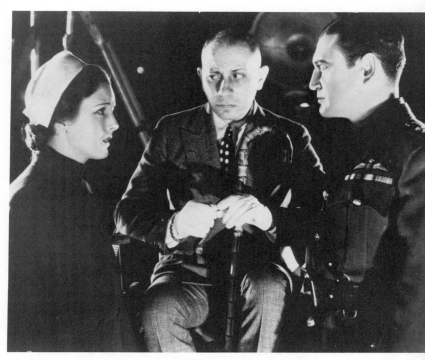

The Lost Squadron: Mary Astor, Erich von Stroheim and Richard Dix.

The Lost Squadron: von Stroheim, bottom left, observing the action.

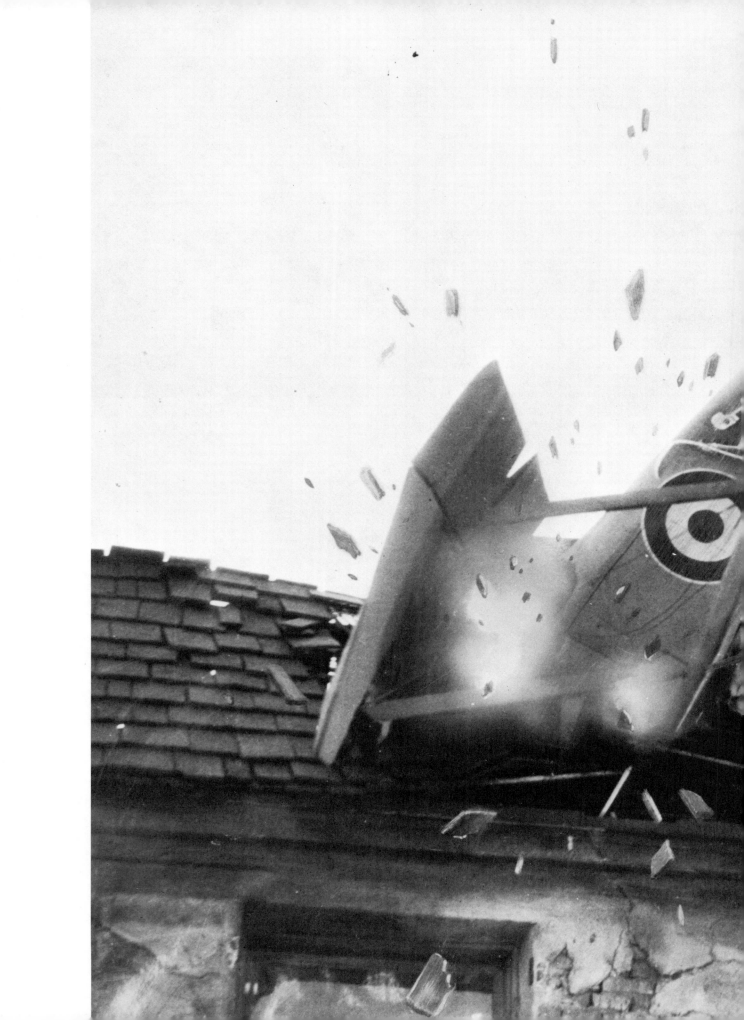

The Lost Squadron: Mary Astor and von Stroheim.

"Koslofski" in *Stand-In* (1937), "Von Strutt" in the Red Skelton edition of *Merton of the Movies* (1947), and to a slight degree, "Von Ellstein" in *The Bad and the Beautiful* (1952), were some of the entries, but *The Lost Squadron* is still the quintessence of von Stroheim on von Stroheim.

Most of Hollywood's feature films about stunt men, other than *The Lost Squadron*, have been low-budget quickies for the action market from the 1920s up through the 1950s. Their interest is only in the few stunt sequences rationed to each film. Ironically, the idea for this subject started promisingly with a novel Paramount film of 1918 called *The Goat*, which featured the acrobatic comic star of the stage, Fred Stone. Stone played an ironworker who is dissatisfied with the amount of money he is making. While working on a new studio lot one day, he catches the pet monkey of actress Bijou Lamour (Rhea Mitchell). Because of his athletic ability he starts doubling for her and becomes the official stunt man—"The Goat" of the studio. Then he is hurt while doubling in a battle scene; his horse stumbles and he is thrown to the ground. The star of the film, a matinee idol (Philo McCullough), is bandaged and quietly substituted in the hospital for The Goat, who is sneaked out the back door and paid off. When his loyal girl friend (Winifred Greenwood) goes to him, he realizes that he has been overly enchanted with Bijou and the movies.

Under Donald Crisp's direction, there was a good deal of studio atmosphere. Stone's athleticism was put to good use in the stunt sequences—he swings by his feet over a pool of water, walks up a flag pole, does some fancy roping and roller skating. One "human fly" bit is particularly effective. In the trade journal *Motion Picture News*, P. S. Harrison commented that the Frances Marion "story is a disclosure of picture-making as it actually is in the studio. I am afraid this will lessen the pleasure a spectator derives from watching a picture, as it will destroy some of the illusion due to the mystery surrounding picture production." Echoing this concern, *Motion Picture Magazine's* reviewer, Hazel Simpson Naylor, said: "I think that the exposure of the inside workings of a movie studio, even for farcical purposes, is bad judgment on the part of Lasky [Paramount] officials. Why take away the glamour even momentarily?"

In *The Speed Girl* (1921), Bebe Daniels played a film actress famous for doing her own movie stunts with airplanes and highpower roadsters. The script was quickly concocted to take advantage of the publicity surrounding Miss Daniels' real-life arrest and jail sentence for speeding in a Stutz roadster. Bebe Daniels' later husband, Ben Lyon, was the lead in *The Flying Marine* (1929). He is shown losing his hearing as a result of an injury received from some movie stunt work. An operation cures him, but he is killed after resuming his stunt flying.

Lucky Devils (1933), RKO's modest follow-up to *The Lost Squadron*, is built on the premise that a stunt man is in real trouble once he gets married. Bill Boyd plays the toughest of all the group of stunt specialists, who marries and—just as he had preached about others—loses his nerve and drops his friend (William Gargan) into a burning structure and almost kills him. Boyd, however, goes back for one especially dangerous stunt, makes it, and upholds the reputation of the stunt fraternity. Alan Roscoe injects a bit of satire into his role of the director, who, like "von Furst" in *The Lost Squadron*, doesn't care how many necks he breaks in his quest for screen thrills.

The primary characters from the aviation comic strip "Tailspin Tommy" appeared in *Stunt Pilot*, a low-budget Monogram release of 1939. The story takes Tommy (John Trent), Skeeter (Milburn Stone), and Betty Lou (Marjorie Reynolds) to Hollywood to make motion pictures. While a film company is shooting on location at an airport near Hollywood, someone puts real bullets instead of blanks in Tommy's gun to be used in a dogfight sequence

The Goat (1918): Fred Stone.

(footage through the courtesy of Howard Hughes' 1930 aviation spectacle, *Hell's Angels*). Tommy unknowingly riddles another flyer's (George Meeker) plane with bullets and is sought for murder, until it is discovered that the director (Pat O'Malley) switched the bullets.

A 1934 Universal serial called *Tailspin Tommy* included some chapters in which Tommy (Maurice Murphy) worked in a Hollywood air epic.

I'm Still Alive (1940), a cut above the usual cheap films in this genre, has Kent Taylor playing a stunt man married to a famous and temperamental film star (Linda Hayes). Their marriage is in jeopardy after she gets him a job acting rather than stunting in pictures and he is restrained from doing a stunt which results in a friend's (Don Dillaway) being killed. Then Taylor barnstorms the country in his plane and injures his sight, but heroically pinch-hits for his friend (Howard da Silva) when the latter is slated to do an unusually dangerous crack-up for a film. It's his grand finale as a stunt man, but the beginning of new domestic happiness.

In Republic's *Sons of Adventure* (1948) there are a good number of action sequences staged by Yakima Canutt and performed by stunt men—including street fights, shootings, stagecoach holdups, catching runaway horses and other situations in this vein. Russ Hayden and Gordon Jones become friends while serving in the South Pacific during the Second World War. Hayden secures a job for his pal, a circus stunt man, and they go to work on the set of a Western film. In a gun-firing scene the hero of the film is accidentally killed when a real bullet is put in the place of the usual blank. (Sound familiar?) Hayden eventually outsmarts the killer, discovered

Lucky Devils (1933): Creighton Chaney—later called Lon Chaney, Jr. (left sitting); William Bakewell (rear sitting); Julie Haydon (center sitting); Roscoe Ates, William Gargan and Bill Boyd standing.

183

Sons of Adventure (1948): Russell Hayden, Lynne Roberts, Roy Barcroft, George Chandler and John Newland.

The Last Movie (1971): Dennis Hopper, hand raised, directing a sequence on location in Peru. Laszlo Kovacs on camera.

to be the assistant director (George Chandler), who dies in a fall from a catwalk at the top of a sound stage.

The crudely made and inept *Hollywood Thrill Makers* (1953)—also called *Movie Stunt Men* and *Hollywood Sunt Man*—consists, to a large degree, of clips from old Richard Talmadge stunts sandwiched in with new footage designed to give the impression that William Henry (as a stunt man) is performing the feats. Henry has retired from stunting after a bad airplane accident and because of his wife's fear of his profession. After a friend is killed executing a stunt first offered to Henry, he emerges from retirement long enough to do the difficult job so that the friend's widow can get a check for $5,000.

The substitution of real bullets for blanks, the death during the performance of a stunt of one of the hero's close buddies, a stunt man's newly acquired wife's drawing the curtain on further stunt activities, a last-minute substitution by the hero for a dangerous stunt, and of course the homicidal director who risks his stunt men's lives in his demoniacal quest for more spectacular thrills —without these formula ingredients the stunt man movie apparently would have been doomed.

Although *The Last Movie* (1971) could hardly be called a film in the traditional stunt man category, the primary plot line centers on a stunt man (Dennis Hopper) who stays behind in Peru after the Hollywood company for which he works finishes a blood-bath Western—shown being directed by Samuel Fuller. The stunt man has visions of making the village a permanent location for other Westerns. But the natives re-enact the movie as a religious rite,

with the stunt man being the victim of the sacrificial ceremony. Intercut with this material in a seemingly senseless manner are other ideas and plots. The surrealistic, schizophrenic *Last Movie* gives every indication of being another tedious exercise in self-indulgence.

In *The Great Waldo Pepper* (1975), Robert Redford plays a flyer unable to cope with the transition from pioneer barnstorming to big-time aviation. Near the conclusion of the film Waldo turns to stunt flying in Hollywood's aerial epics of the early 1930s (*The Lost Squadron* revisited). There is to be a re-enactment of a crucial World War I air battle between Waldo, playing a man he wished he had been, and Ernst Kessler (Bo Brundin), a debt-ridden former Imperial German ace hired to be a technical adviser on a phony film about his exploits. Kessler, like Waldo, is a true romantic, and given a chance to relive as closely as possible that heightened, idealized moment of his glory, accepts Waldo's challenge really to fight in the air. They demolish each other's planes and eventually crash. Fortunately, we are spared the von Stroheim-like character; this time the director is presented as a straightforward fellow of the let's-get-the-job-done-properly-and-efficiently school.

Few major films have dealt in any depth with the screenwriter. He figures strongly as a down on his luck hack in *Sunset Boulevard*, a psychopath in *In a Lonely Place*, a college professor-Pulitzer Prize winning novelist and screen writer in *The Bad and the Beautiful* and as seemingly mad and outrageous studio contract scribes in *Boy Meets Girl*—all of which are discussed elsewhere in this book. Even one

184

The Last Movie.

of the leading characters in the 1912 *A Vitagraph Romance* is a scenarist. But most film-goers do not find Hollywood writers of particular interest, nor do they find them glamorous. The process of writing a script is difficult to infuse with drama for an audience.

In a trifle of 1921 called *Her Face Value*, T. Roy Barnes played a press agent and husband of a film star (Wanda Hawley) who becomes a successful scenarist after his wife is injured while performing in a dangerous scene. An idealistic scenario writer (Percy Marmont) comes to the film capital in *The Legend of Hollywood* (1924) to gain recognition. But his script is rejected by various film companies, and a young girl (ZaSu Pitts) saves him from suicide. In the inoffensive and forgettable PRC opus of 1945, *Hollywood and Vine*, James Ellison is a top screen

writer whose girl friend, a Hollywood hopeful (Wanda McKay), thinks is merely a soda jerk.

The entertaining *Without Reservations* (1946) has Claudette Colbert playing the intellectual authoress of a best-selling novel with more knowledge of literature than of the world. All of the exposition concerning her book is cleverly covered in a "March of Time"-like newsreel being shown a studio executive. He subsequently telegraphs the writer in New York that negotiations for the film version with Cary Grant to play the hero conflict with that star's heavy schedule, and someone else must be found —possibly a total unknown. The authoress doesn't think much of the idea until she sees two Marine flyers who are seating themselves in the train seat opposite her. One of these fellows, a captain (John Wayne), appears the personification of her fictional

185

character. The development of their romance supplies the balance of the plot.

Once in Hollywood, amusing use is made of movie personalities tied in by the radio program of Louella Parsons. She reports that the novelist has been seen lunching with a director, whereupon the fellow glimpsed with her is recognized as director Mervyn LeRoy. Cary Grant and Louella Parsons appear as themselves, but the best gag is one played by Jack Benny in the railway station when he approaches to ask the writer for an autograph.

An offbeat item of considerable interest is Paramount's *Hollywood Boulevard*, directed by Robert Florey in 1936. John Blakeford (John Halliday), an aging actor still seeking only leading roles, strolls down Hollywood Boulevard; he lunches at the Brown Derby, stops in for a drink alongside Jack Mulhall and Creighton Hale at the Trocadero bar, haunts the casting offices, and otherwise keeps up an elaborate pretense of greatness despite the ubiquitous "nothing today." Desperate for funds, he finally agrees to write his life story for a sensational

Hollywood Boulevard in 1937. The tall building at the right edge of the photo is the Hollywood Roosevelt Hotel and opposite is Grauman's Chinese Theatre.

Without Reservations (1946): John Wayne and Claudette Colbert

186

The Trocadero on Sunset Boulevard in 1937.

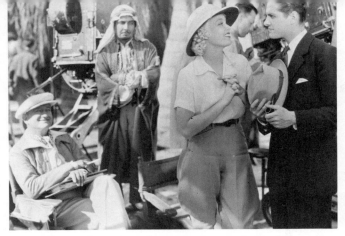

Hollywood Boulevard (1936): Francis X. Bushman, Roy D'Arcy, Esther Ralston and Robert Cummings.

Hollywood Boulevard: John Halliday as John Blakeford dictating his memoirs.

Paris When it Sizzles (1964): Audrey Hepburn and William Holden.

locations, including the mission. Old-timers are sprinkled here and there. Francis X. Bushman and Charles Ray play a director and his assistant; Betty Compson is photographed playing a scene in the studio; the director of the scene is portrayed by actor Maurice Costello; Herbert Rawlinson is a master of ceremonies in Grauman's Chinese court; Bryant Washburn is observed dining at the Beverly Hills Brown Derby; and Roy D'Arcy is an actor in a desert epic. Also on hand from Hollywood's past are Jane Novak, Harry Myers, Jack Mower, William Desmond, Frank Mayo, Pat O'Malley, Mabel Forrest, Bert Roach, Oscar Apfel and Albert Conti.

Hollywood Boulevard was released while the details of the scandal involving actress Mary Astor were fresh in the mind of the public, and not a few reviewers and people in the industry noted certain parallels, whether intended or not. *

magazine, "Modern Truth." The publisher (C. Henry Gordon) has the material sensationalized by a ghost writer, and it ultimately appears in print as "The Love Life of John Blakeford." Among the women in the actor's past is the publisher's wife (Frieda Inescort). The ex-star has a daughter (Marsha Hunt) living in Santa Barbara with her divorced mother (Mae Marsh). The daughter has fallen in love with a young Hollywood studio writer (Robert Cummings). The memoirs cause complications all around and threaten, ultimately, to involve the publisher's wife, who, it seems, has shielded from her husband her former association with the actor.

The opening credits are punctuated with assorted atmospheric shots of Hollywood in 1936. During the film we see glimpses of Sardi's, the Cinegrill, Vendome, Malibu beach and some Santa Barbara

*Mary Astor's marriage to Dr. Franklyn Thorpe ended when Thorpe secured a divorce on grounds that his wife was too dedicated to her career to make a good wife. She did not contest the divorce and agreed to let her former husband have custody of their four-year-old daughter. But as the months went by, she began to have second thoughts. The actress suddenly decided to file suit to set aside the custody agreement. She frankly admitted to her attorney that her former husband was in possession of her diaries kept from 1929 to 1934, and that they contained some startling entries. According to Miss Astor's own account, the majority of the quotes from the diaries leaked to the newspapers were forgeries, but a few pages of the authentic diary were printed by the *Los Angeles Examiner*. These quotes dealt mainly with intimate details of her extramarital romance with George S. Kaufman, the famous playwright. Then the papers printed a leak, supposedly from the diary, indicating that Mary had kept a "box score" of Hollywood's greatest lovers. Finally the custody issue was settled with divided privileges, and since the by now famous diary contained some very candid opinions and revelations about many Hollywood people, Judge Goodwin J. Knight—later Governor of California—ruled that the document be impounded in a secret place to be later removed and burned.

William Holden played his second screen writer—the first being in *Sunset Boulevard*—in *Paris When It Sizzles* (1964), a misguided comedy dealing with a hack writer living in Paris who must provide, over a weekend, a long-overdue script for a big producer (Noël Coward). He hires a stenographer (Audrey Hepburn) to take his dictation and soon falls for her. The hard-drinking screenwriter has a penchant for acting out all of his ideas in order to discover if they will work or not. The secretary soon learns to play the heroine roles to his heroes and the victim roles to his villains.

As one sequence seques into the next, Holden becomes in turn an FBI agent chased by spies, an international thief, a cowboy and a vampire. Miss Hepburn is a terrified girl in mortal danger, an aviatrix and a love goddess. In the end, the writer decides he's very definitely a hack, and the whole screenplay of the mystery-comedy to be called "The Girl Who Stole the Eiffel Tower" is junked. The basic idea developed by Geroge Axelrod had been used previously in a very amusing Julien Duvivier French film of 1955 called *Holiday for Henrietta*.

Another George Axelrod entry of 1964 was a film version of his comedy play, *Goodbye Charlie*. The one-joke premise has to do with an amorous Hollywood writer who is killed by an irate Hungarian producer (Walter Matthau) when the producer finds the writer romancing his wife. The writer, Charlie, is reincarnated as an attractive woman (Debbie Reynolds), who combines the lecherous mind and mores of her former male self with a sexy exterior and newfound femininity while announcing to the world she is the writer's widow. She decides to cash in on former affairs with Hollywood wives, and gets especially close to the producer who shot Charlie.

The Way We Were (1973) gives an insight into the likes of a prototype WASP writer (Robert Redford) with a genuine talent who was a Big Man on Campus in the 1930s. He meets and later marries an intelligent, committed Jewish political radical (Barbra Streisand) and, after writing one good novel, moves to Hollywood with his wife. She becomes a woman trapped in contempt for the way her once-talented husband collapses into a weak, mediocre person. She stands by as a boorish Hollywood director (Patrick O'Neal) bullies the writer into compromising the screen adaptation of his one good novel.

Comes the era of the Communist Menace, the Unfriendly Hollywood Ten, blacklisting and witch-hunts (late 1940s, early 1950s) and loyalties are severely strained. His wife finally walks out on him

Goodbye Charlie (1964): Sheldon Leonard and Debbie Reynolds.

The Way We Were (1973): Robert Redford and Barbra Streisand.

The Way We Were: The Marx Bros. party. Robert Redford, Barbra Streisand, Patrick O'Neal, Murray Hamilton, Bradford Dillman, Lois Chiles, Viveca Lindfors and Dan Seymour.

and returns with their daughter to New York after she learns of his cooperation as a friendly witness with the House Committee on Un-American Activities. Years later, they accidentally meet in front of the Plaza Hotel, where she's passing out Ban-the-Bomb leaflets—a radical to the end. He has become gracefully empty, a once-important novelist who now writes for television.

An extremely popular film helped considerably by the presence of its two stars, their doomed romance, the nostalgia of an Eastern college during the thirties, New York during World War II and then Hollywood, it is all blanketed with a lush, sentimental title melody. The Hollywood milieu is rendered in a hackneyed way, and the treatment of the blacklisting days, when lives and careers were ruined, seems arbitrary, abrupt and not sufficiently motivated or explained.

The longest and certainly the most expensive single movie project produced for television as of this date, *QB VII*, ran five hours and twenty minutes without commercials two nights in a row in April, 1974. Part two of the adaptation of Leon Uris' novel of retribution and horror focuses on a Hollywood writer (Ben Gazzara), who is a faithless husband and an indifferent father. He cringes at the Jewishness of his Zionist father (Joseph Wiseman) and plunges into a consuming affair with a highborn Englishwoman (Lee Remick). Later, in Israel to bury his father, he visits an Israeli memorial to Nazi victims. Tremendously moved, he creates a best-selling novel about the atrocities. The writer is depicted as a rather sour and comparatively dull character until he reaches Israel.

The Hollywood writer is rarely represented in films, or anywhere else for that matter, as a reasonably contented, mature professional who works hard at his craft, approaching each assignment with at least a fair degree of zeal and industry. He is instead usually shown as a disillusioned, once-hopeful author who has sold out and long ago given in to the lure of Hollywood and the solace of alcohol.

Part of the screenwriter's problem has always been his basic lack of control over the material he creates. Up until relatively recent years it was not unusual to have five, six or even ten or more writers working on a script—sometimes concurrently, sometimes in successive stages. Multiple collaboration tends to rob a writer of his sense of personal relation to the story. Joseph L. Mankiewicz, George Seaton and others have stated that during the 1930s and 40s, Hollywood screen writers never even met the directors of their scripts in most instances.

Also films, until the mid-1950s or thereabout, were generally considered the undistinguished opiate of the masses. For prestige and significance one created books or wrote for the theatre —literature, that is. Movies were product —ground out on an assembly line. But they paid well. Prestigious writers from the world of books and the theatre have more often than not failed to cope with the Hollywood system, including most importantly the specialized requirements of writing for the screen. Some retained an attitude of tolerant superiority to Hollywood; they neither studied nor perfected film-writing techniques. Anita Loos has said that there is a knack about dramatic writing which some very legitimate talents can't master. "It thus came about that the studio's product was actually supplied by only about ten percent of its writing staff. The most reliable were women." Adela Rogers St. Johns elaborated on this thesis to the authors of this book and cited a specific example:

Dorothy Parker and her husband Alan Campbell didn't really do very much on their scripts. Like a lot of famous writers they had been brought to Hollywood for more money than they had ever before seen, and then discovered they couldn't write a shooting script —something that the man behind the camera, the director and the actors could put on the screen. So some poor underpaid fellow would have to sweat it out to get a script. This would cause Dorothy and many like her to weep and wring their hands and say how much they hated Hollywood.

Recently writer John Gregory Dunne summed up the attitude of at least some of the current screen writers in the *Atlantic Monthly* (July, 1974). He compared writing for the screen to working as a group journalist for a magazine such as *Time*:

The professional screen writers we know are either directors or aspire to be, because only by directing your own script can you control your own material. . . .

The fact is screen writing is a drag. . . . Finish a book and there is a sense of accomplishment; finish a script and the shit starts. . . .

Why then write for films? Because the money is good. Because doing a screenplay is like doing a combination jigsaw and crossword puzzle; it's not writing, but it can be fun. . . .

Screenwriter Robert Towne has the last word: "In

190

Lady Killer (1933): Mae Clarke and James Cagney.

most situations [Hollywood] writers have about as much potency as a eunuch in a harem."

Things were far from dull for the screenwriter played by Lee Tracy in a satirical and melodramatic RKO program picture of 1937 called *Crashing Hollywood*. Tracy selects an ex-convict as a collaborator and fictionalizes a bank robbery in which the latter in reality was framed by erstwhile friends. Exhibition of the film gives the police new leads to criminals and brings gangsters to Hollywood to put an end to the exposés of underworld technique. *Crashing Hollywood* is a remake of the 1923 Robertson-Cole feature called *Lights Out*, which in turn was based on the 1922 play of the same name.

A racketeer comes to Hollywood to escape the law and is transformed into a movie star in a James

Cagney vehicle of 1933 called *Lady Killer*. Dan Quigley (Cagney) at the beginning of the film is the doorman at Warner Bros.' Strand Theatre in New York City. He is fired and hooks up with racketeers before heading west on the Santa Fe Limited. He arrives in a rainstorm, goes to the Alexandria Hotel, and later, assuming he has been spotted by the police, finds to his surprise that a director (William Davidson), looking for types and new faces, thinks he is right for a prison picture. So for "three bucks a day and a box lunch" the mobster goes to work on the prison epic and follows that up with a stint as a Sioux Indian, complete with headdress and war paint. For this he rides a mechanical horse in front of a process screen for an irascible German director (Herman Bing). Quigley continues to play bits, and his fan mail attracts attention. (He writes his own and has

Another Face (1935): Brian Donlevy, standing.

the letters postmarked from all over by a mailing bureau.) Suddenly he is a star. Complete with mustache, wig and velvet trappings, he plays a dandy in a period piece opposite his off-screen romance, a leading actress played by Margaret Lindsay. In response to a less than enthusiastic review, he forces the critic to eat a copy of the review at the Cocoanut Grove. Next the old gang from New York shows up—including Quigley's ex-girl friend (Mae Clarke). They try to use him in their plan to rob the homes of movie stars, but he resists their threats and at the grand finale is cleared of all charges.

Humorous and fast-moving, this unpretentious early Cagney film benefits enormously from the freshness of the basic situation and by Cagney's marvelous comedic playing. This was his first of four films with Hollywood and the movies as a background. *Something to Sing About* (band leader turns actor), *Boy Meets Girl* (as a madcap scenarist), and *Man of a Thousand Faces* (as Lon Chaney) were the others. To stretch a point, one might include *Starlift* (in which he plays himself) and *Love Me or Leave Me* (as Martin "The Gimp" Snyder).

In the comedy *Another Face* (1935), Brian Donlevy is an ugly gangster who has his face lifted and then yearns to be in the movies. He is discovered in Hollywood by the one remaining living person who can identify him, and his capture is framed by an enterprising studio press agent (Wallace Ford). Alan Hale was on hand playing a film producer.

Talent scouts, young hopefuls, Hollywood acting schools, drama coaches and screen tests were from time to time treated in a mostly mild, superficial manner. An early Alice Faye film, *365 Nights in*

Hollywood (1934), exposed a fictitious, phony Hollywood school of acting. The owner, a con man (Grant Mitchell), engages an ex-movie star, now has-been (John Bradford), to help lure student hopefuls. One of the students, a girl from Peoria (Alice Faye), is chosen to appear in a film to be directed by a down-and-out alcoholic director (James Dunn) as part of a maneuver by the owner-con man. The film, of course, although not planned to be by the head of the acting school, is a big hit. The final production number, "My Future Star," shows Dunn having trouble making up his mind in which mold the character played by Alice would be best suited—Lupe Velez, Mae West or Jean Harlow.

Although strictly speaking not a movie about the movies, *What's the Matter with Helen?* (1971) recreates certain aspects of Hollywood in 1934 with fidelity to both period and style. Debbie Reynolds, as a platinum blonde, comes to tinsel town with Shelley Winters (Helen) to open a dance school for budding Shirley Temples. Their showcase performance is called "The Kiddystar Revue," reminiscent of The Meglin Kiddies revues, a Hollywood staple for many years. Director Curtis Harrington handled the milieu with obvious affection and knowledge.

A Warner Bros. "B" of 1937, *Talent Scout*, had Donald Woods digging up newcomer Jeanne Madden after he has been fired from his job as studio talent scout. The discovery takes place at an amateur show in a small town. Woods brings the girl to Hollywood and manages to manipulate his ex-employers into giving her a test. The girl catapults to stardom and falls in love with her leading man (Raymond Crane).

As depicted in 20th Century-Fox's *Star Dust* (1940) Linda Darnell's experiences in getting a bid to Hollywood for a test, the resultant turndown because she is too young, and her eventual connivance to stay and register strongly in her first picture, closely paralleled her experience in real life. In the script, a once great, but now faded, film star (Roland Young) has become a talent scout for "Amalgamated Studios" and is sent by the dynamic head of production, Dane Wharton (William Gargan, doing a parody of Fox's Darryl F. Zanuck) into the sticks to round up additional talent for the studio. Aboard the train which is carrying him into the Southwest, Tom meets Bud Borden (John Payne), a gridiron star. Tom sees in him the making of a movie hero, and offers him a chance to go to Hollywood. Bud is not slow in accepting.

Tom finally lands at State College in Centerville in one of the Southwestern states. He drops into the

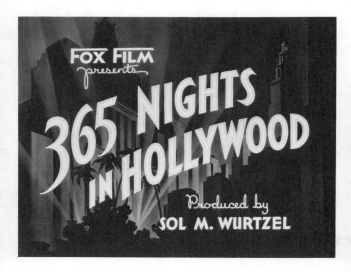

365 Nights in Hollywood (1934): James Dunn, Alice Faye
and John Bradford.

365 Nights in Hollywood: Alice Faye and James Dunn.

What's the Matter with Helen? (1971): Debbie Reynolds
and "The Kiddystar Revue."

Talent Scout (1937): Charles Halton, Jeanne Madden and a gleeful Donald Woods.

Star Dust (1940): Linda Darnell.

194

campus coffee shop and there meets vivacious, beautiful, intelligent, talented, etc. Carolyn Sayres (Linda Darnell), a student at the college. Later, after he hears her reciting lines from *Camille* and is impressed, he learns she is only sixteen, and that she is the daughter of a woman he once loved in his poverty-stricken days. He points out to Carolyn that although she has undoubted possibilities as an actress, she is too young for a career as a leading lady in Hollywood. Still determined, she sends her photographs to Dane Wharton at "Amalgamated" along with a note asking special attention for her, to which she forges Tom's name.

Carolyn goes to Hollywood, falls in love with the football player turned actor, and after many trials and errors becomes a star. Sid Grauman is shown supervising the footprinting in cement of the new star in the forecourt of his Chinese Theatre. To the initiated, the picture takes good-natured swipes at Darryl Zanuck's rapid-fire delivery. The striding and polo mallet-swinging performance of the production head is realistically imitated in one brief office sequence.

Linda Darnell had been in Hollywood less than a year when she made *Star Dust*, her third film. Previously she had been sent home to Dallas because she was too young (fourteen) when she was first brought out to Hollywood and given a test. But she was called back a year later, given a Fox contract and starred in her first screen appearance, *Hotel for Women* (1939). Fox reworked some of the ideas used in *Star Dust* for *Dancing in the Dark* (1949), which is discussed in another chapter.

In 1969 a television series, *Bracken's World*, used the Fox lot in West Los Angeles as the base of operations for the continuing behind-the-scenes story of a studio ("Century") through the private and professional conflicts of those seeking fame in the movies. All-knowing executive secretary Sylvia Caldwell (Eleanor Parker) is the only person having contact with studio boss Bracken, who is never seen (recalling Howard Hughes when he ran RKO in the late 1940s and early 1950s, and Darryl Zanuck, during his time as president of Fox when he was operating out of New York). Ambling around in contemporary clothes, but living in a studio system closer to that of twenty years earlier, are the movie producer-writer-director (Peter Haskell) with an alcoholic wife (Madlyn Rhue); the mother-hen talent-school head (Elizabeth Allen) attracted to the churlish young Brando-type method actor (Stephen Oliver); the sexpot, Marilyn Monroe-ish actress who will do anything to get a part (Karen Jensen) vying

Star Dust: William Gargan—"Is it? . . . Could it be? . . . Yes, it is!"

with the Grace Kelly-like well-bred hopeful (Laraine Stephens); and the mother-pushed starlet (Linda Harrison) in love with a stunt man who's studying for a law degree (Dennis Cole).

In the tradition of the same studio's *Valley of the Dolls* of 1967, herewith are samples from the dialogue:

Producer to wife: "Look at us. We have so much and enjoy it so little."
Wife's reply: "I remember when we had so little and enjoyed it so much."

Grace Kelly-like starlet: "But I do need the part. Can't you understand I've got to be something more than the daughter of someone with connections?"

Star Dust: The forecourt of Grauman's Chinese Theatre. Sid Grauman is the gentleman holding Linda Darnell's hand. To the left is John Payne and William Gargan. On the other side of Linda are Charlotte Greenwood and Roland Young.

Forceful and direct starlet: "You lay a script on me and I'll show you what I've got!" [Certainly an interesting play on words, if nothing else.]

Another starlet: "Just wait till I make it big, then we'll tell them all where to go!"

Hollywood sage: "He gave you too much, too soon. Stardom, Fame, Fortune. You weren't ready, Paula, you couldn't handle it."

Several years before the Universal Studio Tour, *Four Girls in Town* showed off the lot as it looked in 1956. Rita Holloway (Helene Stanton)—seen mostly from the rear with a Marilyn Monroe-inspired wiggle—is the star who refuses the leading role in "Manning National's" epic "The Story of Esther",

resulting in a talent hunt which finds four hopefuls being brought to the studio to be tested by a brilliant, but as yet undiscovered, director played by George Nader. He rehearses the girls chosen to make a test: an American (Julie Adams), an Italian (Elsa Martinelli), a French girl (Gia Scala) and an Austrian (Marianne Cook). He also looks out for them and becomes involved in their lives. Each thinks she will find something she wants in Hollywood whether or not she gets the part. The finish finds none getting the coveted role, the star having changed her mind. The director, as a result of his extraordinary job on the tests, is assigned to direct the feature.

The then-new Walt Disney Studios in Burbank were given entertaining coverage in Disney's modest but interesting *The Reluctant Dragon* (1941).

Four Girls in Town (1956): George Nader, Elsa Martinelli, John Gavin, Gia Scala, Julie Adams and Marianne Cook.

The Reluctant Dragon (1941): Robert Benchley being greeted by Walt Disney at the Disney Studio.

197

The Reluctant Dragon: Disney artist John McLeish, Frances Gifford and Robert Benchley.

The Reluctant Dragon: Multiplane camera supervisor Truman Woodworth, Robert Benchley and Frances Gifford.

198

Robert Benchley, playing himself, is urged by his screen wife (Nana Bryant), to visit the studio with the idea of persuading Disney to film Kenneth Grahame's story, "The Reluctant Dragon." Chaperoned down the lot's handsome avenues by an officious young guide spouting statistics, Benchley manages to escape and bumble with characteristic sheepishness from one department at the studio to another.

At a recording session he is intrigued to hear Clarence Nash and Florence Gill vocalizing for Donald Duck and Clara Cluck; he is startled by the Sonovox effects for Casey, Jr., a precocious locomotive that was to play a featured role in *Dumbo*. Then he sees the Multiplane camera, and guided by an extremely lovely employee, played by actress Frances Gifford, attends a story session, visits the Animation Department, the paint and chemical laboratory and gets a superficial exposition of the various steps in animation production. By the time Benchley's wanderings are over, he is asked to view a cartoon in the projection room, and learns that Disney has beaten him to his suggestion and has already made "The Reluctant Dragon."

Films about child performers in the movies are few and uneventful. Edith Fellows, Columbia's answer to Judy Garland and Deanna Durbin, figured in two—*Little Miss Roughneck* (1938) and *Girl's Town* (1942). In the former, she is unable to get a break in Hollywood because of her overly zealous stage mother (Margaret Irving) until she thinks up a publicity hoax that results in a seven-year contract. In PRC's *Girl's Town* she accompanies her beauty contest-winning sister (June Storey) to Hollywood and winds up getting the lead in a movie while her snobbish sister gets nowhere.

In *Keep Smiling* (1938), Jane Withers, Fox's second-string Shirley Temple, plays the orphaned niece of a boozing ace director (Henry Wilcoxon) who has damaged his career. With help of his former secretary and love interest (Gloria Stuart), the child manages to straighten out her uncle and crash the movies at the same time. Withers also appeared with Gene Autry in the movie-oriented *Shooting High* (1940), discussed elsewhere in the book.

As a spoiled, uncooperative child star "who is loved by millions and yet loved by no one," Patty (*The Bad Seed*) McCormack in Universal's *Kathy O* (1958) plays a ten-year-old orphan whose guardian aunt (Mary Jane Croft) treats her more as an investment than a human being. Dan Duryea is a

Kathy O (1958): Patty McCormack.

Actors and Sin (1952): Eddie Albert and Paul Guilfoyle talking to Jenny Hecht. The man with his hand over his eyes is Alan Reed.

publicity man at the insufferable brat's studio, and is handed the unwanted task of keeping her in hand while she's being interviewed by a noted magazine writer (Jan Sterling), who happens to be his former wife. The child, expecting everyone who approaches her to demand something, eventually runs away, is believed kidnapped, and is actually concealed in the publicist's house. The little actress responds with warmth to a loving home atmosphere, and as a result she mends her ways. In a slapstick suspense sequence, the child gets into the studio back lot and goes prowling through a maze of weird gargoyles and other *Hunchback of Notre Dame* leftovers. She takes the familiar horrors for granted. This leads to an almost Keystone Cops-like wind-up as the studio watchman chases her through old sets and artifical waterfalls.

A variation on Hollywood's precocious children occurred in "Woman of Sin," the second of two stories comprising Ben Hecht's *Actors and Sin* (1952). A great movie producer of the 1930s (Alan Reed) falls in love with an anonymous script titled "A Woman of Sin," erroneously mailed to the studio by an agent's secretary. The script, it turns out, was written by a skinny little nine-year-old (Hecht's daughter, Jenny) whose vivid imagination has been fed by the routine romantic films of that time. Hollywood's penchant for "producing films for child minds" reaps its logical reward: The studio head films the infantile drama—and it makes an enormous amount of money. This situation is reminiscent of *Once in a Lifetime* when "Dr." Lewis mistakenly films in 1931 a 1910 Biograph script, and it, too, is a success.

The Youngest Profession (1943): Walter Pidgeon giving his autograph to Jean Porter and Virginia Weidler.

Hecht, who wrote, directed and produced this burlesque, said that it presents "Hollywood in the late 30s, when movie making was a mad and wonderful thing—somewhat like going after whales with a bean-blower." The action revolves around an author's agent (Eddie Albert) who, in Hecht's overblown oratory, is "a ten-percenter, peddler of genius and beauty, full brother to the Headless Horseman—evasive, double-talking, irresponsible as a grasshopper, liaison officer between the Mad Hatter and the Three Little Pigs."

Virginia Weidler, another child actress, played the nation's most avid movie fan in MGM's *The Youngest Profession* (1943). As the New York fan club president who pursues Hollywood stars for their signatures (for the purpose of this picture the list was narrowed down to Greer Garson, Walter Pidgeon,

Robert Taylor and William Powell), the girl's personality has been heavily influenced and garbled by the romantic notions she has gleaned from the movies.

Probably the most interesting of the movies about child stars is Paramount's *Glamour Boy*, an unpretentious second half-of-the-bill film of 1941. The unusual interest derives from the idea of showing Jackie Cooper, ex-child star, then eighteen, playing Tiny Barlow, ex-child star, then eighteen. Has-been Barlow is a soda jerk in a Hollywood drug store. "Marathon," the same studio for which he worked as a child, has a new, young star (Darryl Hickman), but no one can find suitable story material for him. Barlow overhears a harassed producer (Walter Abel) discussing the problem and suggests a re-make of *Skippy* (Cooper played the lead in *Skippy* for

Paramount in 1931). The producer is intrigued by the idea and hires Barlow to coach the precocious new child star, who is also an intellectual giant. The coaching includes running off lengthy scenes from the original *Skippy* to show the boy how the part should be played.

In the film called *Heat* (1972), somnambulistic Joe Dallesandro plays a former child star who tries to work his way back to the top by being agreeable with a succession of older women. He pays his rent (in his own way) to a frizzy-haired, chunky, sex-starved motel landlady (Pat Ast) before moving in to a gaudy Hollywood mansion with a former semi-big time actress (Sylvia Miles) who falls in love with the stud and introduces him to her Hollywood contacts.

The characters and course of events seem to suggest a cross-pollenation and distortion of the seedier aspects of *Sunset Boulevard* and *The Day of the Locust*. The daughter of the ex-actress (Andrea Feldman) is a part-time Lesbian and masochist with a sadistic girl friend who puts out cigarettes on her breasts. She has an illegitimate baby which she carries in a tote bag. The relationship between the ex-actress and ex-child star goes nowhere, especially when the daughter decides to abandon Lesbianism temporarily to take the young stud away from her mother. But Mother finds them out and grumbles that the daughter "can't even make a good dike."

The actress then tries to unload the daughter on her ex-husband, who is now a homosexual, but he's too busy with his decorator boy friend to be bothered. Finally, the young stud leaves the aging actress. She tries to kill him, but her gun is empty (presumably symbolic). *Heat* is an Andy Warhol production, written, photographed and directed by Paul Morrissey. Morrissey has been quoted as saying that most of the lines in *Heat* were improvised and that the actors were encouraged to be natural. The result is a reflection of natural boredom, emptiness and decadence.

Nathanael West in his 1939 novel *The Day of the Locust* also dealt with the darker, seamier side of Hollywood, but with considerable insight, style and a sense of purpose. The characters who populate his story are not the glamorous stars, studio heads or directors, but the losers, the watchers and the dreamers. They are—most of them—a hapless collection of has-beens and would-bes; people who prefer dreams to fulfillment, and who cannot face reality.

For a six-month period in 1935, West, unable to find work as a screenwriter, lived in a run-down

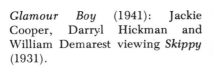

Glamour Boy (1941): Jackie Cooper, Darryl Hickman and William Demarest viewing *Skippy* (1931).

apartment hotel on North Ivar Street in Hollywood. Its residents were the people he would be writing about in *The Day of the Locust*—extras and bit players, aspiring youngsters, grotesquely ambitious stage mothers, the old and exhausted, minor racketeers, madams and prostitutes.

After all these years, the book, not a commercial success but surely a critical one, has finally been made into a motion picture (1975) produced by Jerome Hellman, directed by John Schlesinger and adapted by Waldo Salt—the team responsible for *Midnight Cowboy*. The period remains the same—1938. Salt found himself drawing on his own experiences during the 1930s, when he worked for $35.00 a week as a junior writer on the MGM lot under producer Joseph L. Mankiewicz: "Success then was a balance around the 50 percent mark between what you did and what you got. The theory was that you always had to balance the content of your work against the payment. If you got a lot of money, you couldn't do a lousy picture."

The cast, as with everything connected with a Schlesinger picture, was chosen with great care. Karen Black plays Faye Greener, a shimmering, ice-cold blonde extra player whose personality is a comic pastiche of all the attitudes and gestures she has copied from her favorite movie stars. Faye incessantly talks in platitudes, picking up her most colorful phrases from the gossip columns of the Hollywood trade papers. She also fantasizes various combinations of stock movie plots. Karen Black studied a cross-section of films made by leading film actresses of the period in order to absorb certain speech patterns and general mannerisms into her performance. Burgess Meredith is her father, an ex-vaudevillian turned door-to-door salesman; Geraldine Page portrays "Big Sister" (a character not in the novel), a faith-healing revivalist with more than a passing resemblance to evangelist Aimee Semple McPherson; real-life producer/director William Castle re-creates a 1930s cigar-chewing director complete with riding breeches, who is seen directing a historical spectacle, "The Battle of Waterloo;" Billy Barty is the pugnacious, tough-talking dwarf Abe Kusich, allegedly suggested by a well-known dwarf who sold papers on Hollywood Boulevard. Natalie Schafer plays a madam who runs a house in the Hollywood Hills. West apparently modeled this character on Lee Francis, a former actress who was Hollywood's most distinguished madam at the time. Her girls were beauty-contest winners who hadn't gotten the big break. In one

Heat (1972): Pat Ast, Sylvia Miles and Joe Dallesandro.

203

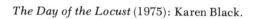

The Day of the Locust (1975): Karen Black.

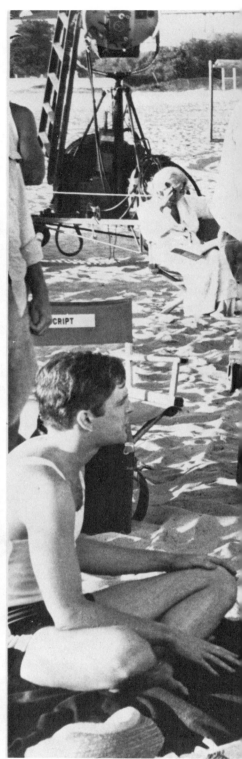

The Day of the Locust: Director John Schlesinger with his hand on the camera. Karen Black in front of him.

sequence, art director Claude Estee (Richard Dysart) takes his party guests to the brothel—not for sex but to watch what was commonly referred to as a "stag movie." A line of Estee's, delivered earlier to young sketch artist Tod Hackett (William Atherton) sums up his character: "You're a little too facile for your own good, but that can be an advantage out here."

John Schlesinger recently told us something of his approach to the film and his feelings about Hollywood:

The Day of the Locust is about people trying to cope with failed lives. It's about the enormous attraction to the promised-land quality that Hollywood has, because it's a fantasy place. And it's about the way people respond when their dreams and hopes aren't realized.

The book was difficult to adapt because it's not really a story, and in order to adapt it for film, we've had to try to give it some dramatic shape and form. We had to develop the characters as real people, but at the same time I did not want to lose that nightmarish quality.

I was not at all interested in making a picture about power and success in Hollywood—the tycoons, the stars. I am fascinated more with losers. What drew me to West's book was its study of delusion; people's dreams unfulfilled. The picture's not a putdown of Hollywood. I'm fascinated by Hollywood. It is much more all-embracing than about disappointed people in tinsel town; much more an allegory about people whose fantasies do not come true and who therefore become violent. And the holocaust at the film's conclusion is not literal; it takes place largely in the mind of Tod Hackett, who in a sense is the spokesman for Nathanel West.

As for Hollywood—there is no point in making it out to be anything other than extremely hard. The facts of life in the film business are tough. To say they are not would be a delusion, and delusion is the substance of this film.

Producer Jerome Hellman responded to the book in similar ways:

Many of the films of the thirties, by their denial of the harsh realities of life at that time, encouraged their audience to an attempt to duplicate, in their own lives, something that was unreal and therefore unattainable. As a result I believe that many people became more and more dissatisfied with the reality of their own experience and perhaps less well equipped to do something about it in creative, personal and legitimate ways. In this sense I feel the input was deadly, retarding growth and cultural maturity.

In this exceptionally well-made film, the evocation of period is impeccable, but not forced and self-conscious as so often is the case. Although some material was shot at actual locations in and around Hollywood, many sets were built on the Paramount lot. Meticulous research and an eye for just the right details resulted in a marvelous manufactured composite of every tacky Hollywood apartment court and bungalow complex of the 1930s—here called The San Bernardino Arms (The "San Berdoo" for short), where some of the principal characters live. Production designer Richard MacDonald found Hollywood movies of the late thirties no help at all in his research. "Studios then never shot on location in Hollywood."

The huge sign in the hills overlooking Hollywood which spells out the word Hollywood in letters four stories high was partially simulated for an early sequence in the picture. The real sign—put up in 1923 to advertise parcels of land in an unsuccessful development called "Hollywoodland"—was not used because it couldn't be approached from the required angle. In the film, Faye Greener and Tod Hackett take a tourist trip to the site, but pay no attention to the guide who bellows out a story based on the true account of a disappointed would-be film actress called Peg Entwistle, who in 1932 climbed to the top of the letter H and threw herself off in a successful suicide attempt.

Faye invites Tod, along with Earle Shoop (Bo Hopkins), a cowboy bit player, to a showing in Glendale of Eddie Cantor's film, *Ali Baba Goes to Town*, in which she is glimpsed fleetingly. Actual footage from *Ali Baba* is seen with newly filmed shots of Karen Black intercut.

The Hollywood studio atmosphere of the late 1930s is reproduced with great style for several sequences, the biggest and most effective being the filming-within-a-film of "The Battle of Waterloo." Tod, the sketch artist, is on the set during the massive battle sequence. As the camera begins to turn, Tod discovers that "Danger" signs have been removed from the still-uncompleted set. He watches horrified as hundreds of extras crash through the scaffolding of the studio hill. Later, in the studio barber shop, the head of the studio, coolly played by Paul Stewart, conducts a casual investigation while having his hair cut. There is routine talk of insurance and a general coverup of responsibility. Perhaps the most trenchant comment is that of an injured extra as he is being carried from the set: "A broken leg is worth at least five hundred bucks."

The climax of *The Day of the Locust* takes place outside Grauman's Chinese Theatre. A huge crowd has assembled to watch celebrities arrive for the gala film premiere of Cecil B. DeMille's 1938 production of *The Buccaneer*. Dick Powell, Jr., plays his father.

206

A child actor (Jackie Haley) confronts Homer, the shy, awkward bookkeeper from Iowa (Donald Sutherland), and teases and torments him, as he has done often before. After the boy throws a rock at Homer's head, the ineffectual bookkeeper finally expresses the fury he has suppressed all his life. He chases the child into a parking lot and kills him. People in the crowd witness the murder. They drag Homer onto Hollywood Boulevard and tear him limb from limb.

Tod tries in vain to reach Homer in an effort to save him from the frenzied mob. Tod is knocked to the ground, his leg badly broken. Finally, pinned against the hood of a car he watches helplessly as Homer is killed and the crowd, now bent on destruction, explodes in mass fury. In terrible pain and overwhelmed by the savagery and violence around him, Tod begins to hallucinate. In a sequence intended to be more surreal than literal, Tod visualizes an apocalypse as cars are overturned, stores are looted, and the facade of the movie palace collapses in flames.

In his book *The Four Seasons of Success* (Doubleday, 1972), Budd Schulberg discusses his friend "Pep" West and *The Day of the Locust* novel. This small extract is interesting and appropriate:

Reacting to the mass hysteria of Pep's climax, I remembered as a young teen-ager driving to just such a World Premiere at Grauman's Chinese Theatre as Pep described. . . . Suddenly a fat girl who looked about sixteen broke from the crowd, ducked under the rope and jumped onto our running board. "Who are you? Who are you?" she screamed into my face. "I'm nobody," I said. "Nobody." Clinging to the running board, in a paroxysm of self-abasement, she turned her head to the crowd and shouted, "He's nobody! Nobody! Just like us!" Then the loyal police moved in and dragged her roughly back into the crowd waiting to devour her.

The Day of the Locust: Real-life producer-director William Castle directing "The Battle of Waterloo" film-within-the-film.

The Day of the Locust: Dick Powell, Jr., playing his father, arriving at the premiere.

CHAPTER EIGHT

CALLAWAY (AND OTHERS) WENT THATAWAY

The public's response to MGM's *Callaway Went Thataway* in 1951 was considerably less than it deserved. The film satirized television's exploitation of movie Westerns, and the producers discovered what others had found before—that poking fun at the celluloid West was not, with few exceptions, particularly profitable. It is ironic that the American West as portrayed by Hollywood is largely an invention, and that it had managed for the most part to resist satire and burlesque until the arrival of such comedies as *Red Garters, Cat Ballou, Support Your Local Sheriff* and *Blazing Saddles*. Mythology is difficult to debunk, especially when it is as warmly and universally regarded as the Western lore of motion pictures.

Of the films dealing with life in the picture business the least successful, certainly, have been those about the making of Westerns, although they are not without interest for the film buff. Probably the earliest of these is a two-reeler titled *The Moving Picture Cowboy*, made by the Selig Polyscope Company in 1914 and starring Tom Mix, who also wrote the story and produced the picture. The public's concept of the West at this time was influenced mostly by dime novels, and Hollywood chose to perpetuate that concept. Tom Mix, who had started his film career in 1910, had yet to reach great popularity, and it was to be only a short while before William S. Hart would become a major attraction. By 1914 the only actor who had been extremely popular as a movie cowboy was Broncho Billy Anderson, and *The Moving Picture Cowboy* may possibly have been a spoof on his heroic antics.

This little picture was presented in two parts. Its slight plot is about Luke Barns (Mix), a cocky young fellow who works in film Westerns. He writes to his rancher uncle explaining that the arduous duties of his career have made a vacation necessary. He

211

Tom Mix in *The Moving Picture Cowboy* (1914).

Tom Mix in the early days of his film career.

212

arrives at the ranch wearing elaborate Western regalia, to the amusement of the real cowboys, and proceeds to swagger about the place boasting of his stunts in making pictures. He claims to be an expert rider and roper, and tells of saving his leading lady from Indians while on location. Luke vividly describes his adventures, and his listeners see in their mind's eye how he does all these things, like hoisting himself from a galloping horse onto a train, bulldogging a runaway steer, and being chased on horseback by bandits, who panic when they catch up with him.

The second part of *The Moving Picture Cowboy* tells the truth about Luke Barns. All of the scenes in the first part are reproduced, except that the climax of each scene is entirely different, with the boastful Luke involved in comical mishaps at the conclusion of each attempted stunt. *The Moving Picture Cowboy* proves, if nothing else, that the film people were given to ribbing their own kind even as far back as 1914.

Tom Mix made other short pictures for Selig with a movie-business angle, all of them written, produced and sometimes directed by himself. In *Sagebrush Tom* (1915) he played a cowboy who idolizes an actress and tries to woo her, unsuccessfully, when her company is on location at the ranch where he is employed. In 1916 Mix made two such pictures—*A Mix-Up in Movies* and *Shooting Up the Movies*. In the former he was a cowboy who takes the opportunity to rob a bank when he spots a movie company doing the same thing as part of a picture but changes his ways at the persuasion of a sympathetic actress (Babe Chrisman). In *Shooting Up the Movies*, Mix was an outlaw who stumbles into a film location and rescues the heroine (Victoria Forde), not realizing that her predicament is part of a movie set-up. They fall in love, and by the fade-out Tom has switched to the right side of the law and become a deputy sheriff. Similarly, years later in Universal's *The Crimson Canyon* (1928), a cowhand (Ted Wells) rescues a young lady (Lotus Thompson) from a runaway wagon only to discover that he has interrupted the filming of a motion picture sequence.

Apparently the first Western feature to stress the theme of movie-making was *The Texas Streak*, produced by Carl Laemmle for Universal in 1926, and starring the popular Hoot Gibson. Gibson, who had come to Hollywood following his success as a trick rider in rodeos and circuses, differed from most other Western stars in that he emphasized humor and tried to get away from the deadpan William S.

Hart image. Authenticity was of no concern to Gibson, who enjoyed stunting with racing cars and motorcycles even more than galloping horses. In *The Texas Streak* he is a happy-go-lucky drifter employed as an extra by a film company on location in Arizona. After working on a Western, he and his two buddies (Jack Curtis and Slim Summerville) lose their railroad tickets and find themselves stranded. Gibson takes a job as a guard with a surveying company and gets involved in their conflict with ranchers over water rights. He falls in love with the daughter (Amy Hollis) of the chief rancher, and after a number of adventures, manages to settle the differences of the opposing parties. His heroics also bring him to the attention of the motion picture company for which he recently worked, and they announce that they intend to feature him as a star in their Westerns.

Leonard Maltin in a recent issue of *Film Fan Monthly* describes RKO's *Scarlet River* (1933) as "a delightful surprise amid the Tom Keene 'B' Westerns of the early 1930s. This one opens with Keene and [Betty] Furness as sole survivors of a wagon train, when suddenly it's revealed that they're actors on location filming a Western movie. The real plot gets going when the Tom Baxter (Keene) company hires [Dorothy] Wilson's ranch for its next movie site, interfering with foreman [Creighton] Chaney's* plans to steal the unsuspecting lady blind. Numerous highlights dot this fast-moving outing: A scene in the RKO commissary with Joel McCrea, Myrna Loy, Julie Haydon and Bruce Cabot as themselves . . . Edgar Kennedy as the movie director . . . [Yakima] Canutt pre-dating his famous *Stagecoach* stunt almost exactly, dropping from a horse team to the ground, letting the wagon run over him, then grabbing the back of the cart."

By 1936 New England-born Charles Starrett had been in pictures for six years, and he persuaded Columbia to let him take a crack at the Western market. Among the first of his efforts in this new line was *The Cowboy Star*, which presented him as a cowboy star tired of his limited opportunities and income, and bored with make-believe adventures and romances. He leaves Hollywood incognito and heads for the real West to live the life of a genuine cowboy. But he is recognized by a young fan (Wally Albright) and his attractive sister (Iris Meredith). He pledges them to keep his secret, but he becomes involved in some real drama, which takes the form of the kind of adventures he usually performs in his

---

* Later known as Lon Chaney, Jr.

The Texas Streak (1926): Slim Summerville, Jack Curtis and Hoot Gibson.

Scarlet River (1933): Billy Butts, Tom Keene and Yakima Canutt.

movies. His exploits receive wide attention and he returns to Hollywood—with the girl and to a much better contract. In reality Charles Starrett did well by his Columbia contract, retiring in 1953 after making a great many Westerns for them.

Republic's *The Big Show* in 1937 was the first Western to show the customers something about the tricks of stunt men in Westerns. It was also Gene Autry's best film to that time. By the end of 1937 he had dislodged Buck Jones as Hollywood's most popular cowboy star. In *The Big Show*, which gets its name from being set at the Texas Centennial in Dallas, Autry appears in a dual role—as a petulant cowboy star named Tom Ford and as his stunt man double. When the unreliable Ford refuses to make his appearance at the Dallas show, his press agents persuade the double to go on in his place. He is, of course, a big hit. Not only is he more affable than Ford but he also sings, and when he foils the crooks who are trying to steal the profits from the show, his employers at "Mammoth Studios" realize that this is the man they should be starring in their pictures. By the end of *The Big Show* it is ex-star Ford who is being used to double for the ex-double. This ploy probably created some confusion in the minds of young movie-goers of 1937 and caused the film's

The Cowboy Star (1936): Charles Starrett and Iris Meredith.

The Cowboy Star: Wally Albright, Iris Meredith, Charles Starrett, Si Jenks and fans.

Gene Autry watching his double (also Autry) in *The Big Show* (1937).

editors to be particularly careful, since Autry was incapable of most of the spectacular stunt work, and Yakima Canutt had to double for him in both of his guises in this picture.

This backstage Western was given better than usual production values by Republic, clearly in an attempt to promote Autry, and it contains some interesting sequences showing the filming of running shots and stunt set-ups. There is a tightly edited montage, near the beginning of the film, featuring stock action shots from earlier Republic and Mascot films of transfers, collapsing wagons, Indian chases, falls from horses, wagons and horses toppling over cliffs, and Yakima Canutt's famous leap from one pair of horses pulling a coach to another pair, followed by his fall between the lead horses and his hanging on to the coach tongue and dropping to the ground with horses' hooves and coach wheels missing him on both sides.

In 1940 20th Century-Fox borrowed Gene Autry to appear in *Shooting High*, his first film away from Republic and, as it turned out, a film he might well have avoided. In view of his popularity, it is surprising that Fox would require him to take second billing to Jane Withers in a sixty-five minute feature that was no better than a run-of-the-mill "B" Western.

Here Autry appears as a fellow named Will Carson in the small town of Carson's Corners, the grandson of the town's heroic first marshal. Since the days of the marshal the town has been divided in a feud between the Carsons and the Pritchards, but young Will is in love with a daughter of the opposition (Marjorie Weaver), to the delight of her mischievous young sister, Jane (Withers). A motion picture company arrives in town to film the story of Wild Bill Carson, to be played by Robert Lowery, and Will is hired as his stunt double (and, ironically, Autry is doubled in the stunts). Jane concocts a scheme to scare Lowery out of town, telling him the

Pritchards may lynch him for playing Carson. When he leaves town, Will is given the role of his grandfather.

In the course of making the film-within-the-film, he foils the attempts of a trio of bank robbers, who appear to be actors robbing a bank according to the script, and he captures them in the conventional end-of-film chase. A real hero, worthy of his grandfather's name, Will politely declines the offer of the film company to go to Hollywood and become a star. He prefers to stay in Carson's Corners and settle down to a quiet life with his girl.

The trite *Shooting High* received poor notices and Autry wisely thereafter stuck to his tried-and-true packaging for Republic until he joined the Army Air Corps in 1943. His only other film to touch upon the picture business was *Down Mexico Way* in 1941. This showed nothing about film-making, but its villains were a group who posed as film producers, raising money from people in small towns with the notion of making pictures in their communities and then taking off with the funds. After one such bilking

Autry pursues them into Mexico and puts an end to their endeavors.

Gene Autry, a man with the Midas touch, parlayed a genial personality and a small singing voice into a multimillion-dollar empire, and overtook in popularity all the Western stars considered to be much more authentic and vigorous than himself—men such as Buck Jones, Tim McCoy, Ken Maynard and George O'Brien. Perhaps it was a sign of changing times, but the relatively soft, expensively tailored Autry, with no background as a cowboy and no great ability in action sequences, nonetheless trounced the opposition at the box office.

In 1937, the year of Autry's ascent, the husky George O'Brien appeared in *Hollywood Cowboy*. O'Brien, who became a boxing champion during his years with the Navy, got his start in pictures in 1924 in John Ford's *The Iron Horse*, and after playing a variety of roles, gradually settled for being a movie Westerner. In 1936 he signed a contract with RKO, which resulted in twenty Westerns over the next four

The Big Show: Champion, Gene Autry and Kay Hughes.

217

years. The third of them was *Hollywood Cowboy*, with O'Brien as an actor who takes a vacation in the West under an assumed name in company with a dyspeptic writer buddy named G. Gadsby Holmes (Joe Caits). Posing as an ordinary cowboy, he woos and wins a ranch heiress (Cecilia Parker) and steps in to stop the depredations of racketeers from Chicago. The crooks run a protective association and cut in on livestock shipments until the cowboy from Hollywood foils their plans. Slower paced and a little more mature than most "B" Westerns of its time, *Hollywood Cowboy* had something to say about the new West, with airplanes being used to stampede cattle and labor unrest being exploited by racketeers, but the Saturday matinee audiences doubtlessly preferred the rugged, smiling George O'Brien in more conventional stuff.

It Happened in Hollywood was the third of three pictures in which Richard Dix starred in 1937. Although never attaining super-stardom, Dix nonetheless was consistently on a firm level of popularity and appeared in almost a hundred films between 1921 and 1947. Most of his pictures hovered

Shooting High (1940): Jane Withers, Champion and Gene Autry.

Shooting High: Gene Autry, and to the left, Jane Withers and Marjorie Weaver.

218

Hollywood Cowboy (1937): George O'Brien and Maude Eburne.

between the "A" and "B" status. *It Happened in Hollywood* is typical, running sixty-seven minutes and probably returning its investment for Columbia in short order. Here Dix is co-starred with Fay Wray, as an actor and actress whose love for each other is disrupted by twists of career. Dix, a famous Western star named Tim Bart, finds his fortunes sliding away with the coming of sound in Hollywood, while she, Gloria Gay, goes on to greater success. Unable to cope with dialogue and adamantly unwilling to accept small roles as a villain, feeling this would offend his juvenile fans, he is let go by his studio. Years later, he and Gloria are brought together again when they both come to the aid of a crippled boy (Billy Burrud—now television's travel-adventure host and producer Bill Burrud), a faithful fan of the actor. Bart shortly after becomes involved at the scene of a bank robbery and guns down three robbers. As a result of the publicity he is re-hired by his old studio and given another chance at stardom. Sentimental and improbable, *It Happened in Hollywood* gives little insight into the plight of washed-up stars, but does contain one remarkable

It Happened in Hollywood (1937): Richard Dix and Fay Wray.

sequence. At a Hollywood party the likes of Clark Gable, James Cagney, Charlie Chaplin, W. C. Fields, Mae West, Bing Crosby, Fred Astaire and Ginger Rogers all appear as played by their doubles, with Arthur McLaglen pretending to be his brother Victor.

By 1938 Buck Jones was past his peak as a king of movie cowboys. A star by 1920, he was now forty-seven and like several other veterans he was somewhat dismayed by the rise in popularity of the singing cowboys. *Hollywood Roundup* was an attempt by Columbia to give Jones something a little more interesting than his usual traditional Western. Here he played a movie stunt man assigned to double for a soft and temperamental cowboy star, Grant Drexel (Grant Withers), who takes a disliking to Jones when he realizes that his leading lady, Carol Stevens (Helen Twelvetrees), is growing fond of him. Drexel tries to get rid of Jones by embarrassing him and managing to have him fired. Unwittingly mixed up in a bank robbery, Jones is jailed, but Carol's young brother Dickie (Dickie Jones) helps him escape and Jones takes off after the bandits and captures them. Drexel then steps up to claim that he himself captured the villains, but Dickie saves Jones and ruins Drexel by revealing snapshots he had taken of the actual capture. Drexel is disgraced and the stunt man is elevated to stardom.

Buck Jones was clearly not very comfortable in this offbeat item in his catalogue, but *Hollywood Roundup* is of interest because of its peek behind the scenes in the making of Westerns and the manner in which cowboy stunts are faked by trick camera work. However, the producers of "B" Westerns found that attempts to deviate from the norm seldom pleased, and in this case the revelation of movie trickery may have alienated the Buck Jones admirers.

In 1941 20th Century-Fox paired young George Montgomery with Mary Beth Hughes in *The Cowboy and the Blonde.* This limp little yarn served its term as the bottom half of Fox programs and quickly returned to the studio vaults. It tells of Lank Garret (Montgomery), who is signed to a movie contract by "Consolidated Pictures" because of his success as a rodeo star but fails to pass his screen test. He and Crystal Wayne (Hughes) strike up a romance and the studio decides to keep him on salary because of his calming influence on the temperamental actress. But once he discovers the reason for his pay checks, the proud cowboy heads back to the ranch, where he is joined in short order by the tamed

Crystal, who then turns her back on Hollywood in favor of rural bliss.

The theme of picture-making did not turn up again in a Western until 1945, when Republic used it as a twist in Roy Rogers' *Bells of Rosarita.* Rogers supplanted Autry as that studio's chief draw and,

like Autry, he used his own name on the screen, dressed elaborately and set his stories in the contemporary West. In this picture he plays himself and the story begins with his having just finished a location film on a ranch owned by Dale Evans. She is the daughter of a recently deceased ex-circus man, whose crooked partner (Grant Withers) has stolen the mortgage papers and is about to cheat Dale of her inheritance. A group of orphans, wards of Dale, persuade Rogers to stay on and save the situation just as he would do in a movie. Realizing this can't be done alone, Rogers calls the Republic Studios in

It Happened in Hollywood: Billy Burrud and Richard Dix.

North Hollywood and asks a group of fellow actors to ride to the rescue. The entire roster of Republic cowboy stars soon arrives on the scene—"Wild" Bill Elliott, Allan Lane, Donald "Red" Barry, Robert Livingston and Sunset Carson, plus Bob Nolan and the Sons of the Pioneers. The villains are, inevitably, put in their place, and Rogers and the stars appear at Dale's circus in order to raise the money to pay off notes against her property. Perhaps *Bells of Rosarita* should have been called *Altruism Rides the Range.*

There was nothing altruistic about the way Herbert Yates ran his Republic Studios. When Gene Autry left the studio for wartime service, Yates immediately moved Roy Rogers into first position, and when Autry returned three years later, he considered it best to go with another studio, Columbia. In case he should lose Rogers, Yates kept a lookout for possible replacements. One of them was Monte Hale, a young singing cowboy from Texas. His pictures were precisely the same format as the Autry and Rogers products, packing in half a dozen songs in a running time of sixty to sixty-five

minutes. *Out California Way* (1946) has him as a cowboy trying to break into the movies. Monte comes to the attention of a casting director and gets the opportunity that sends him on the way to success at "Global Studios" (allowing for plenty of shots of Republic), but a jealous, fading cowboy star (John Dehner) does his best to ruin Hale's chances. His best, of course, is not good enough. Herbert Yates' best was something else and, to make sure that Monte Hale came to the attention of Western fans in *Out California Way,* one of Republic's first Westerns to be shot in color, Yates required guest appearances by Roy Rogers, Dale Evans, Allan Lane, Donald "Red" Barry, Foy Willing and the Riders of the Purple Sage, the St. Luke's Choristers, and syndicated columnist Jimmy Starr. For all that, Monte Hale was not destined to become a star. Roy Rogers stayed with Republic, but by the early fifties television had put an end to the whole "B" Western industry.

The best of the minor Westerns with movie themes is *Grand Canyon,* a Robert Lippert production, well

222

Hollywood Round-Up (1938): Dickie Jones, Buck Jones and Lester Dorr.

The Cowboy and the Blonde (1941): Mary Beth Hughes and George Montgomery.

224

Bells of Rosarita (1945): Allan Lane, Roy Rogers, Dale Evans, Donald Barry, Robert Livingstone and Sunset Carson.

Callaway Went Thataway (1951): Dorothy McGuire, Howard Keel, Fred MacMurray, and Clark Gable.

Callaway Went Thataway: Dorothy McGuire and Howard Keel, with Mickey Little and B.G. Norman.

226

Callaway Went Thataway: Charlita, Howard Keel and Jesse White.

photographed by Ernest W. Miller (sepia-toned prints) in 1949 and starring Richard Arlen. Arlen was Hollywood's journeyman-hero par excellence, appearing in dozens of adventure yarns as a pilot, racing driver, highway engineer, boat skipper, oil rigger, forest ranger and sundry soldiers of fortune. In *Grand Canyon* he is Mike Adams, an operator of a team of mules, who leases them and himself to a film company on location for a Western. *Grand Canyon* is not without humor. The director, Mitch Bennett (Reed Hadley), has to persuade the head of the studio that a film about the Grand Canyon should be shot there and not at the studio. Ironically, weather problems forced the real company to leave the Grand Canyon after a few days, and the bulk of the film was made in Hollywood. The screenplay of *Grand Canyon* is by Carl K. Hittleman, who also produced it, and the frequent mention of Lippert Productions suggests it was the price Hittleman paid for gibing at the boss. Once again the leading man is an unpleasant, temperamental fellow (James Millican) and once again he needs to be replaced. He

breaks a leg tackling a mule, and mule skinner Mike is persuaded by the director to take his place. He falls in love with the leading lady (Mary Beth Hughes) and is outraged when he discovers that his tender moments with her have been shot by the wily director for inclusion in the film. Mike storms off, but the director, realizing that the actress really loves him, affects a reconciliation by staging yet another scene, one which requires her being rescued by Mike, after which he surrenders to his fate—as a husband and presumably a movie actor.

The only major item in the films about Westerns, as of the writing of this book, is MGM's *Callaway Went Thataway* (1951), which is actually more of a spoof on the television industry than on picture-makers. Produced, written and directed by Norman Panama and Melvin Frank, it deals with the resurgence in popularity of a wayward and almost forgotten Western star named Smoky Callaway when his old pictures are run on television. The fractious, womanizing, hard-drinking Callaway (Howard Keel) is considered no loss to Hollywood,

Slim Carter (1957): Tim Hovey and Jock Mahoney.

Callaway becomes a nuisance and demands some of the proceeds from his old films, but Stretch saves the situation by assigning all the Callaway income to a trust fund for needy youngsters, thereby bringing honor to the name of Callaway—something in keeping with his supposed image. At this, Callaway agrees to return to his life as a boozing beachcomber in Mexico.

Callaway Went Thataway satirized television's exploitation of old movies and the merchandising gimmicks of tie-in products such as clothes, guns and games. Howard Keel regards this as one of his best films but admits that it was only moderately successful at the box office. "Television Westerns were too popular—the public wouldn't accept satirizing them."

While *Callaway Went Thataway* was in production it was generally thought in Hollywood that certain aspects of the film were remotely suggested by William "Hopalong Cassidy" Boyd, who had astutely acquired the rights to his old

but when his televised films create a public demand for more, the network executives instruct hucksters Mike Frye (Fred MacMurray) and Deborah Patterson (Dorothy McGuire) to find Callaway and bring him back into the business. An agent (Jesse White) tracks him down in Mexico, but Callaway is too unpleasant and alcoholically bleary to present to the public. In the meantime a Colorado cowboy, Stretch Barnes (also Keel), writes to the network and complains that his similarity to Callaway is causing him embarrassment, and he encloses a snapshot of himself to prove his point. Seeing the snapshot, the frantic Mike and Deborah, who have money at stake in Callaway, rush to Colorado and persuade Stretch to come to Hollywood and pose as the famous cowboy. The gauche cowboy knows nothing about the movie business. Mike and Deborah try hard to educate him, but he greets Clark Gable in the Mocambo as "Sam," and almost fells Elizabeth Taylor with a hearty slap on the back. The real

228

Westerns and earned a fortune leasing them to television. Boyd's manager, Bob Stabler, demanded a screening of the picture before it was released, but afterwards agreed that there was no reason for Boyd to be offended and that he found the movie to be "good fun." MGM nonetheless felt constrained to preface the film with a title card: "This picture was made in the spirit of fun and was meant in no way to detract from the wholesome influence, civic-mindedness and the many charitable contributions of Western idols of our American youth, or to be a portrayal of any one of them."

In 1957 Universal came up with a mild spoof called *Slim Carter*, starring ex-stunt man Jock Mahoney as an egotistical Western singer elevated to movie stardom through the efforts of a studio publicist, Clover Dale (Julie Adams), who also loves him but has reservations about his probable worth as a husband. The studio builds him up as a genuine Westerner and publishes a ghost-written book of Indian lore under his name, which he has to read in

order to find out about Indians. He also has to learn to ride and rope, and a top stunt man (Ben Johnson) is assigned as his double. One of the title cards for this picture is a bit of an inside joke—pointing out that Mahoney's singing and stunts were actually performed by Mahoney. Slim Carter is not liked at the studio because of his glib, selfish nature, but a big—and improbable—change comes over him when an orphaned boy, Leo (Tim Hovey), is brought to Hollywood by the studio as a contest winner to spend a month as the house guest of Slim Carter. Everybody at the studio is impressed by the nice young lad and they do nothing to detract from his belief in Carter as the personification of all that is noble about a true Western hero. By the end of the month Carter is such a splendid fellow Clover agrees to marry him and the orphanage consents to their adopting Leo.

Since then, the only Hollywood movies even to touch upon the making of Westerns have been *Blazing Saddles* (1974), directed and partly written

The finale of *Blazing Saddles* (1974), with the entire cast exploding from the main gate of Warners.

229

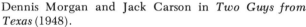
Dennis Morgan and Jack Carson in *Two Guys from Texas* (1948).

by Mel Brooks, and *Hearts of the West* (1975). A broad and raw burlesque of Westerns, sufficiently vulgar to require a restricted rating, *Blazing Saddles* has nothing to do with film-making until the last reel when Brooks pulls back his cameras on a brawling crowd in a street and continues pulling back until it becomes obvious it is a set on the backlot at the Warner Bros. studio in Burbank. The brawlers drift and spill over to the set of a musical film, continuing through the cafeteria, onto the street and out the main gate to Olive Avenue, where the villain (Harvey Korman) jumps into a taxi and tells the driver, "Drive me off of this picture." He is driven to Grauman's Chinese Theatre, where he buys a ticket to see—*Blazing Saddles*.

Hearts of the West, not yet released at the time of this writing, seems to have a lot going for it. Rob Thompson's script is a comedy with a moral, and the story is filled with enthusiastic idealism. It is set in the early 1930s and deals with a young man (Jeff Bridges) from the Midwest who wants to become a Western novel writer in the Zane Grey-Max Brand tradition. His adventures in Hollywood, which lead him to become a Gower Gulch "B" movie extra, are somewhat reminiscent of the *Merton of the Movies* lineage. Director Howard Zieff worked closely with Thompson for several months on the script and then invited him to stay on during filming at MGM and at locations in and around Los Angeles.

Two Guys from Texas (1948), one of several pictures in which Warners co-starred Dennis Morgan and Jack Carson, had nothing to do with Hollywood, but it does contain the only song so far written to satirize film Westerns, "I Wanna Be a Cowboy in the Movies."* Morgan and Carson, a pair of third-rate vaudevillians stranded in Texas, take a job on a dude ranch and at one point entertain the guests with this song by Sammy Cahn and Jule Styne:

I wanna be a cowboy in the movies,
I wanna chase those rustlers 'cross the screen,

*Copyright 1948, M. Widmark & Sons. Copyright renewed. All rights reserved. Used by permission of Warner Bros. Music.

230

I'd like to sit astride a critter,
A pluckin' on a beat up guitter,
And be a hero like Tex Ritter in a scene.

I wanna be a cowboy in the movies,
I wanna yell Iy Yippee Oh Kiy Yay,
It's swell to win a maiden's praise,
Because you've cleansed the Santa Fe's,
And the villain's afeared 'cause you've raised a beard,
That's the envy of Gabby Hayes.

I wanna be a cowboy in the good old movies,
California, I'm on my way.
I'll ride the trail for RKO,
I'll rope for Paramount,
I'll get more mail for MGM than they can ever count,
Republic and Columbia will star me in the lead,
And Monogram will call me to stop a small stampede,
All the independents will offer me a piece,
A Technicolor feature, United Artists release.
Are you list'nin' Goldwyn, Selznick and the others?
Is there anyone I've forgotten?
I thank you Warner Brothers!
I wanna be a cowboy in the good old movies,
California, I'm on my way!

Hearts of the West (1975): Jeff Bridges and Andy Griffith.

CHAPTER NINE

THE STUDIO MURDER MYSTERIES

Charlie Chan, Philo Vance, Nick Charles, Mr. Moto, The Lone Wolf, Ellery Queen, Sam Spade, Philip Marlowe and the rest of the detectives, private and otherwise, did not become involved on the screen in murder mysteries taking place inside Hollywood studios; nevertheless there have been quite a few instances of behind-the-screen who-dunits.

The Third Eye, a fifteen-chapter serial of 1920, seems to be the first American film of any length to place an apparent murder on a shooting stage. The story tells of a pretty motion picture star (Eileen Percy) becoming the victim of a group of criminals, the head of which (Warner Oland) is in love with her. She refuses to aid his schemes. Then a murder is committed in the studio. Later, it is found that a moving picture camera has recorded the event, leaving the hand that cranked the camera a mystery. Circumstantial evidence points to the guilt of the young woman. The chief argument of the prosecution is the reel of film which supposedly shows the girl in the act of committing the crime. The gang, to serve their own ends, seeks to fasten the crime upon the girl. A struggle then begins between the star, aided by her sweetheart (Jack Mower), and the leader of the gang for possession of the film.

The reviews at the time were laudatory, referring to the serial as one of the "swiftest moving of the season" with "thrilling situations . . . suspense in every foot of film . . . elaborate backgrounds . . . convincing performances . . ." and, to quote *Photoplay*, it is a serial that "has everything—absolutely everything." The chapter titles are typically lurid: "The Pendulum of Death," "In Destruction's Path," "Daggers of Death," "The Race for Life," "The House of Terrors," "At Bay"—and, of course, "Triumph of Justice."

The device of a motion picture camera recording a murder or an attempted murder and the film later being used as evidence had previously been used for a picture produced in Italy in 1914 called, appropriately, *The Film Detective*. The story has Jack Daingerfield (Gustavo Serena) accepting a commission from a film company to make a movie about lion-hunting in Africa. While there he is shot in the back by two men, a rival in love and an old creditor.

233

In a Lonely Place: Frank Lovejoy, Jeff Donnell, Humphrey Bogart and Gloria Grahame.

The Studio Murder Mystery (1929): Warner Oland, Fredric March and Doris Hill.

The cameraman captures this (and the African veldt in the background) on film. When the group returns to England the villains are exposed by the indisputable filmic evidence.

The potential of the studio murder case was dormant during the 1920s until the end of the era. In England, Anthony Asquith's first credited feature (he wrote the story and assisted director A. V. Bramble) was *Shooting Stars* (1928), and although not a murder mystery, it did curiously combine a dramatic triangle, a murder on the set and a look at life among the film people of Britain. The plot: A film actor (Brian Aherne) threatens to divorce his film star wife (Annette Benson) when he discovers that she is having an affair with a slapstick comedian (Donald Calthrop). She realizes that the scandal will ruin her career, so she decides to kill her husband. Her scheme involves inserting a live bullet in a prop gun to be used in one of her husband's scenes, but the plot miscarries and the lover is killed instead. The husband goes on to become a famous director, whereas his former wife is forgotten and some time later applies for work as an extra. She eventually works on one of his films, but he does not notice her.

Before leaving the set, she goes to the preoccupied director: "Do you want me any more?" she asks. Without looking, he replies, "No, thank you." Making a long exit, the ex-star crosses the empty studio stage and goes out through a door in the far, dark distance.

The story takes second place to the insight the film gives into silent movie-making at the end of the twenties in England. In the picture the two stages shown in the large "Zenith Films" studio building operate simultaneously. The lower one is occupied by a unit shooting a romantic cowboy thriller against very flimsy sets; the upper one used by another unit is making a crude slapstick farce. Both films have their attendant small orchestras on the sidelines to work up mood. The films being shot are obviously "quickies," with no one involved taking more than a routine, workmanlike interest.

The style of the production was heavily influenced by the then-fashionable German school (and, to a degree, the Russian school). There is much subjective camera, satiric cutting, moving camera, expressionistic touches and the like. One extremely unusual bit: an establishing shot reveals the interior

234

of a large cathedral set on the shooting stage. After a few seconds, the camera begins dollying in —revealing to the audience that a great portion of the cathedral has been painted on glass in the foreground, and only parts of the set are full scale. This is the only instance, presumably, in which a matte painting deliberately gives itself away in a theatrical film. Seen recently, the effect is quite striking.

The first dialogue film in the genre is Paramount's *The Studio Murder Mystery* (1929), released during the height of the vogue for Philo Vance and other fictional detectives. The story, adapted from a *Photoplay* magazine serial, was typical of the whodunit patterns and formulas of the time, with only the locale being a novelty. The mandatory inclusions were a murder, many varied suspects (each with more than enough motivation), false leads, sundry detective work, a red herring or two, accumulated evidence, twists, a final gathering of the suspects for the reconstruction of what really happened, and then the unmasking of the murderer.

In this instance we have Rupert Borka (Warner Oland), a film director who had been a ventriloquist, suspecting Richard Hardell (Fredric March), a philandering young actor, of having had relations with his wife. Hardell's own wife (Florence Eldridge) has promised that he will meet with an "accident" the next time he is unfaithful. Besides incurring the enmity of these two, Hardell is not exactly a favorite of young Ted MacDonald (Gardner James), whose sister, Helen (Doris Hill), is the studio watchman's daughter, and who has been beguiled by Hardell with false promises of an early divorce. It isn't surprising when the romantically busy actor is found murdered on a deserted studio set the morning after he had been seen with some of the suspects. The evidence points to the watchman's daughter, who is jailed and sentenced, but she is saved at the last minute by a studio gag writer (Neil Hamilton) in love with Helen, who stumbles on a clue while talking to himself on the telephone. As it turns out, Borka's talents as a ventriloquist allowed him to perfect an alibi. Tedious and stilted, with far too much emphasis on strained humor, *The Studio Murder Mystery* has all the faults of the very early microphone-dominated talkies.

Paramount waited seven years before doing a similar film. A modest "B," *The Preview Murder Mystery*, running a scant sixty-two minutes, manages through the efforts of its director, Robert Florey, to present an interesting picture with considerable atmosphere and style.

The Studio Murder Mystery: Warner Oland.

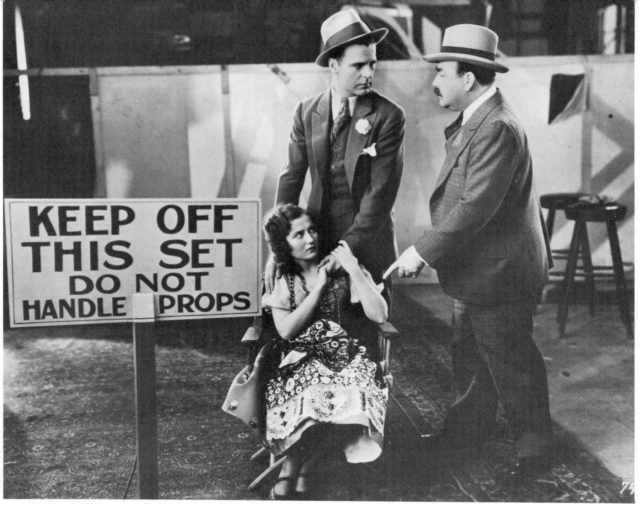

The Studio Murder Mystery: Doris Hill, Neil Hamilton and Eugene Pallette.

The Preview Murder Mystery (1936): Rod La Rocque, Gail Patrick and Ian Keith.

A terrorized star (Rod La Rocque) fears that he will never live to see his latest film previewed. At a theatre, in which all the attendant color and excitement of a preview night of the times are illustrated, the carefully guarded star is found in his seat, murdered. Almost concurrently—but in the studio—the film's director (Ian Keith) is also slain. The police come to investigate, but studio publicity director Moran (Reginald Denny), aided by his secretary, Peggy (Frances Drake), gets on the job to protect the producer's (George Barbier) interests. The action roams all over the studio—from the front office to the film vault. Finally, Moran gets to the bottom of the mystery. He traps Edwin Strange (Conway Tearle), an old star who is supposed to be dead, and who believes that the murdered director and actor ruined his career.

The studio scenes were particularly good, and other than the preview, the action is all on the lot, with the police holding everyone within the gates—convinced the murderer is among them. A premature angle for 1935 involved a television camera being used for studio surveillance.

Ian Keith's eclectic director sported riding pants in the manner of DeMille, a whistle on a string around his neck à la Rouben Mamoulian, a leather-bound stick in imitation of Josef von Sternberg, and a filter glass on a cord as used by King Vidor.

Florey wanted to use faded star John Gilbert in the picture, but he turned it down because of not enough money. Gilbert died before the picture was completed.

The Death Kiss (1933), a cheap blend of mystery and ineffective humor, starts promisingly, but quickly disintegrates. An expensive automobile is standing in front of a fashionable apartment-hotel entrance. A woman in evening clothes explains to four companions that the man she is about to kiss will thus be identified as their victim. Then a man in formal attire walks to the entrance. To his astonishment the woman kisses him. As he resumes walking, guns go off and he drops. At this point, there is a cutback to a long shot, and it is revealed that the action is taking place in a studio with director, cameras, lights, etc. It promptly develops that the actor playing the supposed gun victim in the gangster movie has really been murdered. The leading lady, played by Adrienne Ames, is involved as the suspected murderess, and the balance of the story concerns the efforts of a young screen-writer (David Manners) to apprehend the real criminal. In what amounts to a minor supporting role, Bela Lugosi,

The Preview Murder Mystery: Reginald Denny and Frances Drake.

237

The Preview Murder Mystery: The extra and bit part players line up to take their turn at the phone—probably to call Central Casting or their agents. Note Hank Mann on stool and Chester Conklin in top hat.

receiving featured billing, has a few scenes in a role which turns out to be a red herring.

In Edward Small's *Super Sleuth* (1937) Jack Oakie portrays a popular screen hero of detective and mystery stories. He is so expert at solving film crimes that he takes it upon himself to graduate into real-life sleuthing in competition with the Police Department, and is soon the central figure in a murderous blackmail scheme. His investigating methods used to track down a "Poison Pen Killer" are based on the routines his script writers think up for his screen character.

The antics of the egotistical star when he discovers that the criminal plot is aimed against himself comprise considerable opportunities for Oakie's style of comedy. Ann Sothern plays the studio publicity head, whose job is to trail Oakie and get him back to picture making. Eduardo Ciannelli is the menace. Most of the scenes in this better-than-average programmer take place inside the studio, with a location unit of camera cars and sound trucks also prominent in the action.

In an RKO "B" of 1938, *Fugitives for a Night*, a producer (Russell Hicks) is murdered at the opening of an elaborate Hollywood nightclub. A young publicity man (Frank Albertson) is suspected, but he flees the scene of the crime with his girl (Eleanor Lynn), and by morning the fugitives return to accuse the real murderer. Although strictly a formula murder mystery, there were some interesting Hollywood and film industry touches. Frank Albertson played a publicity man in an earlier film, a low-budget trifle called *Hollywood Hoodlum* (1934), which was also known as *Hollywood Mystery*.

In 1941 RKO began a series of mystery films "suggested" by a character created by Michael Arlen. *The Gay Falcon* featured George Sanders as a debonair "modern Robin Hood of crime." The role was almost an exact duplicate of The Saint, also played by George Sanders and made into a series by RKO from 1938 to 1942. After three Falcon entries, Sanders decided to bow out and passed the baton to his real brother, Tom Conway, in *The Falcon's Brother* (1942). Conway carried on for nine subsequent films, including *The Falcon in Hollywood* (1944)—oddly enough the only detective series entry to deal with a studio murder mystery. (*Boston Blackie Goes Hollywood*, 1942, could just have easily been called "Boston Blackie in Peoria" for all it had to do with Hollywood and/or the movies.)

Visiting Hollywood, the Falcon stumbles on the corpse of the leading man of a picture which is

The Preview Murder Mystery:
Frances Drake and Reginald
Denny.

encountering so many obstacles that the producer
(John Abbott) insists that efforts are being made to
sabotage his first film effort. There are more murders
and attempted murders with lots of behind-the-
scenes Hollywood suspects, ranging from an aspiring
actress (Barbara Hale), the obligatory temperamental director (Konstantin Shayne), to a
producer who speaks only in Shakespearean verse.
Clues crop up in plaster models and miniatures, on a
reel of film, in an exotic jewel from an idol's eye, and
in time-honored stage superstitions. It turns out that
it is the Shakespeare-quoting producer who wants to
keep the picture from being completed so that he can
pocket the money put into the project by a group of
backers.

In 1950, Humphrey Bogart's independent production company, Santana, released through
Columbia an offbeat and downbeat treatment of the
after-hours world of Hollywood, called *In a Lonely
Place*. Studios, sets, cameras, stars, premieres, etc.,
are those of a psychopathic screenwriter (Bogart), a
struggling actress (Gloria Grahame), a loyal agent
(Art Smith), a broken-down actor (Robert Warwick), a hat-check girl (Martha Stewart) and a
detective and his wife (Frank Lovejoy and Jess
Donnell).

The film begins with Dixon Steele (Bogart) un-
dertaking the scripting of a trashy novel that he can't
face reading. He induces a hat-check girl who has

The Death Kiss (1933): Adrienne Ames and David Manners.

Fugitives for a Night (1938): Frank Albertson, Russell Hicks, Adrienne Ames and Bradley Page.

The Falcon in Hollywood (1944): Tom Conway, Konstantin Shayne, Emory Parnell, Frank Jenks and John Abbott.

read the book to come to his apartment and tell him the story. Later she is found murdered and Steele is suspected, but is released after Laurel Gray, a neighbor (Gloria Grahame), testifies that she was watching from her balcony as the writer sent the girl home in a cab.

Laurel gives Steele renewed confidence, and he begins to work on the script in earnest. She helps him by typing the manuscript, preparing meals, and handling otherwise distracting details. But Steele is given to occasional nasty outbursts in which he beats up friends, acquaintances and perfect strangers when provoked. Laurel begins to wonder about him—and to fear him. Only a phone call from the police who have caught up with the real murderer (the hat-check girl's boy friend) keeps the writer from strangling her during an aberrated moment. But they both know that it is all over, and Bogart walks out of her life.

This moody film was rather slow and somber, but it did catch much of Hollywood's ambience and loneliness. Bogart and Gloria Grahame were excellent in difficult characterizations. Bogart altered between dry cynicism, tender affection, and uncontrollable rage. Graham was pouting, brooding, wary, and sensual.

In a Lonely Place was not a critical or commercial landmark, but *Sunset Boulevard*, released a few weeks later, was so impressive that it ushered in a deluge of films about movie people. Over the next few years, directly as a result of *Sunset Boulevard*, every studio got into the act with their "Hollywood story": there was *The Bad and the Beautiful* and *Singin' in the Rain* from MGM, *The Star* from Fox, *Valentino* from Columbia, the remake of *A Star Is Born* from Warners, *The Big Knife* from United Artists and *Hollywood Story* from Universal.

Hollywood Story (1951) is interesting for several reasons, not the least of which is its subject matter, which bears a superficial resemblance to the still officially unsolved murder of director William Desmond Taylor in 1922. Unfortunately, the idea for the film was far superior to its execution. All kinds of potential in the contrasting of Hollywood in the silent days with the Hollywood of 1951 was thrown away and merely given a once-over-lightly treatment. Arbitrarily introducing old-time favorites Francis X. Bushman, William Farnum, Betty Blythe and Helen Gibson in one scene was pointless and awkward, as contrasted with a scene in *Sunset Boulevard* featuring silent stars which enriched the story development.

When the film was previewed at the Academy

In a Lonely Place (1950): Humphrey Bogart.

In a Lonely Place: Robert Warwick, Alice Talton, Art Smith, Gloria Grahame and Humphrey Bogart.

Award Theatre, press agents invited veterans of the silent screen and saluted them in publicity handouts as "the Hollywood greats who reigned before the days of Oscar. . . . Headliners whose glamour gave the film community its worldwide fame." To a newsman at the screening, sixty-year-old Elmo Lincoln, the original Tarzan in films, offered a bitter reaction: "Every time they want to exploit something like *Hollywood Story,* they call on us. We're not getting any money out of this. . . . All of us who worked in *Hollywood Story* got $15.56 a day, the minimum extra rate for one day's work. The principals like Helen Gibson and Francis X. Bushman, who had dialogue, got $55.00 for their day's work. They paid us for that one day and they've gotten $15,000 worth of publicity out of it. If I had the opportunity, I'd stand right there on that stage tonight and say: 'Why don't we get work?'. . . . The motion picture industry is the most unappreciative, selfish business in America today."

The intriguing plot of *Hollywood Story* begins with the arrival in Hollywood of the character played by Richard Conte, who is going to produce an independent picture. Space has been rented for

him at a studio which hasn't been used much since the silent days (actually the Chaplin Studio on La Brea Avenue near Sunset Boulevard). A casual inspection of the premises brings him to the site of the murder in 1929 of famed director Franklin Ferrara. Against all sorts of advice and pressure, he drops his original picture idea and starts preparing a film revolving around the crime committed twenty-two years previously. But he needs the solution of the unsolved crime before he can begin production. Word of his project begins to hit the Hollywood gossip vine. Sally Rousseau (Julia Adams), the daughter of silent screen star Amanda Rousseau (also Julia Adams), who was involved with the director, tries to stop the renewed investigation. Vincent St. Clair (Henry Hull). Farrara's writer—missing for eighteen years–is discovered by the producer living in a shack on Zuma Beach, north of Malibu, and is engaged to write the script after the producer screens several of Ferrara's and St. Clair's old films. (One so-called Ferrara film being run off in the studio projection room is the 1925 Lon Chaney *Phantom of the Opera!*) Roland Paul (Paul Cavanagh), an ex-silent screen star reduced to playing bits, is discovered to

244

Hollywood Story (1951): On the set with Richard Conte, Francis X. Bushman, Helen Gibson, William Farnum and Betty Blythe.

be the secret husband of deceased Amanda Rousseau and Sally's father—a prime suspect.

The producer's sleuthing takes him to the *Los Angeles Times* building, the Hollywood Hills, The Motion Picture Country Home and Mission San Juan Capistrano. He breakfasts poolside at the Hollywood Roosevelt Hotel, lunches at La Rue's, dines at Jack's at the Beach, drops in at Universal Studios to see Roland Paul do a scene with Joel McCrea, and passes the Christmas parade on Hollywood Boulevard.

Fred Clark, playing Conte's backer, is revealed to be Ferrara's onetime business manager and the victim of an attempted frame-up on the night of the murder. Meanwhile, Ferrara's long-vanished secretary turns up and is murdered. Finally, the one crucial missing piece falls into place: writer Vincent St. Clair is discovered to be Ferrara's brother, who was extraordinarily jealous of his success. In reality, the director wrote as well as directed all of his pictures. The business manager years ago found out that St. Clair actually could not write, so St. Clair, after murdering his brother, left clues to place the guilt on the business manager.

The actual case that "inspired" this picture would

have been difficult to depict because of the legal complications, but it might have been a gem. Flash-back to 1922: William Desmond Taylor, a hand-some, cultivated gentleman of forty-five, was one of the top Famous Players-Lasky directors (*Sacred and Profane Love, Morals, The Witching Hour,* etc.). He lived in a bungalow court on South Alvarado Street in what was then regarded as the fashionable Westlake Park area of Los Angeles. Early in the evening on the night of February 1 he was visited by screen star Mabel Normand. At 7:45 P.M. he was observed walking her to her chauffeur-driven automobile. Taylor left his front door open. Miss Normand was driven off in her car and he went back into his cottage. At approximately 8:15 P.M. Douglas MacLean, the actor, and two other residents of the court heard a sound that they decided later must have been a shot. A few minutes passed and Mrs. MacLean happened to open her front door and saw a man leave the Taylor house—or, she said later, possibly a woman dressed like a man. Later in the evening actress Edna Purviance saw lights on in Taylor's house—she lived in the court, too—and went across to his cottage for a

Hollywood Story: Richard Conte, Fred Clark, Jim Backus and Henry Hull.

Hollywood Story: Richard Conte, hands in pockets, looks over a sound stage at Universal.

Hollywood Story: Richard Conte and a scene shot at the well known seafood restaurant.

visit. She rang the doorbell, but there was no answer. It was Taylor's servant (!) who discovered the body at 7:30 the next morning. Taylor had been shot in the back in his living room. Close by were framed and inscribed photographs of Mabel Normand and actress Mary Miles Minter. There were also amorous notes and monogrammed handkerchiefs from Miss Minter and letters from Miss Normand. Indeed, there were dozens of love letters from many different women and also lingerie and sheer nightgowns.

Later it was discovered that Taylor had for years been engaged in an elaborate masquerade. He was not at all the man everyone thought him to be—in fact there was evidence of a double life and a mysterious brother (who may have been his missing secretary-valet) who had forged checks with Taylor's signature. Before his death, Taylor had gone to the Federal narcotics agents of his own volition to tell them what he knew about the dope traffic in Hollywood. Taylor didn't use drugs, but it is presumed that Mabel Normand was an addict, and

it was possibly his bitterness about her addiction that led him to the agents. Perhaps the narcotic ring was behind his death. Apparently robbery was not the motive, but it was learned that the dead man's home had been ransacked a day or two after the murder.

Mary Miles Minter's mother also was involved. It was suggested by some that she was romantically interested in Taylor. Everybody in Hollywood had known that she had been trying to end the romance between her daughter and the apparently indefatigable director.

In a short time both Mabel Normand and Mary Miles Minter were through with pictures. Mabel died in 1930. As time went on, Mary Miles Minter began to be regarded as something of an eccentric. She is still alive. As far as the District Attorney's office is concerned, the file on the murder of William Desmond Taylor is formally closed, but the case has never been officially solved.

The file on *The Phantom of the Opera* is very definitely still open. There have been two official

248

William Desmond Taylor.

The Phantom of Hollywood (1974):
Skye Aubrey and Jack Cassidy.

remakes of the 1925 Lon Chaney classic and several other unofficial productions heavily indebted to the basic idea and situations. In early 1974 The Phantom was transplanted to MGM for a movie made for television, *The Phantom of Hollywood*. As with *Hollywood Story*, the idea had marvelous promise, but the script was weak and implausible. Someone decided to take advantage of the destruction of the back lot at the MGM studios in Culver City, following the decision to sell the lot for a real estate project. Why not photograph some of the key standing sets and the razing of the area and then integrate this material with the basic story line from the original *Phantom*?

In this version a subterranean room on the back lot becomes The Phantom's home, and for years rumors crop up about his presence in a medieval executioner's costume among the old sets. Later, he kills any who would desecrate the lot, including teen-age vandals, engineers and workmen. Peter Lawford plays the cold studio chief of "World Wide Studios" whose primary mission, apparently, is to dispose of studio assets. "We need the cash flow," he explains. "The day of the Hollywood back lot is over." His daughter is portrayed by Skye Aubrey, the daughter of James Aubrey, who was MGM's president at the time so many of that studio's assets were liquidated.

The Phantom does his usual terrorizing, including capturing the studio head's daughter and holding her in his underground lair. The spectacular finale has The Phantom, armed with longbow and arrows, desperately trying to fight off the bulldozers from the battlements of a back lot fortress. He falls and dies in the debris of the crushed set.

Detective work reveals that The Phantom was a onetime classic actor and matinee idol (Jack Cassidy) who, at the peak of his fame, was horribly disfigured by an explosion. At the time, he was playing D'Artagnan in a film version of Dumas' tale being shot on the lot. He became a recluse, and with the aid of his brother, the curator of the studio photograph vault, made his home among "the ghosts of a thousand movies."

The opening is intriguing: The camera probes some of the old exterior sets as they were just prior to being levelled, then there are cuts to the scenes in the pictures in which they were used. A rundown, tacky railway station gives way to a scene from *Waterloo Bridge*, with Robert Taylor and Vivien Leigh making their way through the crowds in the station set. In another area the camera roams down a dusty, cobblestoned street to a Parisian square where a

Madhouse (1974): Vincent Price and fan.

guillotine rests in the sun. Then that same street swarms with life as the aristocrats and Ronald Colman are being taken to have their heads chopped off in *A Tale of Two Cities*. There are similar effects created with the *Tea and Sympathy* school exterior, the *Young Tom Edison* station house and a street used in *Pride and Prejudice*. Later, in a screening room, studio head Lawford is viewing a retrospective compilation showing clips from several of "World Wide's" classic films put together by an old-time film editor played by Jackie Coogan. The brief scenes are from MGM's 1925 *Ben-Hur*, *Grand Hotel*, *Dinner at Eight*, the 1935 *Mutiny on the Bounty*, *San Francisco*, and *The Philadelphia Story*.

A number of clips from old AIP movies are put to good use in *Madhouse* (1974), an entertaining and well-made Vincent Price horror item produced in England with some interesting twists. Price plays a dignified movie star who has risen to fame and fortune in a number of films featuring Dr. Death, a monstrous killer given to disguises and sadistic slayings. In a pre-title sequence, his fiancée (Julie Crosthwaite) is exposed as a former porno queen and then mysteriously decapitated. A nervous breakdown prevents the actor from knowing whether or not he committed the Dr. Death-like crime.

Some years later, he journeys to London to star in a television series as Dr. Death. A number of murders, all copied from old Dr. Death movies, ensue. Peter Cushing plays the writer of the series, an

251

Madhouse. Vincent Price and Julie Crosthwaite.

apparently sympathetic friend who proves to be a traitor. The old AIP clips featuring Boris Karloff and Basil Rathbone double for Dr. Death movies.

In this survey of movie murders, two peripheral titles worth mentioning are *The Whole Truth* and *The Last of Sheila*. Romulus Films' slick and sophisticated *The Whole Truth* (1958) presents Stewart Granger as an American film producer making a film in the south of France with a lovely but temperamental actress (Gianna Maria Canale) with whom he once had a brief affair. She is determined to rekindle the old flame, but he has reconciled with his wife (Donna Reed) and wants nothing further romantically to do with the actress. When Granger is told that she has been murdered, he embarks on a frantic series of lies and maneuvers to keep the police and his wife from knowing of his connection with her, only to find that the supposed victim is very much alive. But then the delayed killing does take place, and Granger realizes that he has set himself up to look like a murderer.

An intriguing twist to the proceedings is that the audience knows of Granger's innocence and the guilt of George Sanders. The latter plays the suave husband of the murdered actress. Consumed with hate because of her philanderings, he kills her and cunningly devises the evidence to incriminate Granger. Granger is forced into escaping in a police

car in order to reach his wife before Sanders has a chance to dispose of her as well, since Sanders has learned she holds the clue to his guilt—a cigarette lighter left behind at the time of the murder. Granger arrives in time and Sanders is killed by the police as he tries to make a getaway.

Listening to the imperious Granger and Sanders fence verbally with one another is reason enough to make a point of seeing this better-than-average production. Jack Clayton produced and John Guillermin directed in a slick manner.

The "Sheila" in *The Last of Sheila* (1973) is the name of a luxury yacht named after the late wife of a Hollywood producer (James Coburn) killed by a hit-and-run driver shortly after leaving a raucous Bel Air party. A year later, Coburn asks six of the party guests for a week's Riviera cruise aboard the "Sheila." They include a glamorous Hollywood star (Raquel Welch), her business-agent husband (Ian McShane), a fading director (James Mason), a struggling scriptwriter (Richard Benjamin), his wealthy wife (Joan Hackett) and an aggressive talent agent (Dyan Cannon).

On board, Coburn initiates a week-long game in which each guest is given a card indicating a secret to be discovered by the others. Though the printed secrets do not apply to the person holding them, they do, it is revealed, apply to one of the fellow guests.

252

The Whole Truth (1958): Donna Reed, Stewart Granger and Gianna Maria Canale.

The Last of Sheilah (1973): James Mason, Raquel Welch, James Coburn, · Joan Hackett, Ian McShane, Dyan Cannon and Richard Benjamin.

The Whole Truth: George Sanders and Stewart Granger.

Since one of the cards reads "I am a hit-and-run driver," the mystery concerns the person responsible for Sheila's demise.

Flashbacks, betrayals, premature confessions and more murders flesh out this interesting and unusual but not entirely successful combination of *Sleuth*, *And Then There Were None* and searing melodramas about film people. The script, direction, and performances are cold, precise and cerebral. The final explanation of what actually took place, how, by whom, and for what reason is quite ingenious and almost plausible. Perhaps the film's failure is the result of its being too bizarre and peopled with unsympathetic types—the faults of so many movies about the film business.

CHAPTER TEN

STAR SPANGLED RHYTHMS

In the first three years of the sound era Hollywood swamped the theatres with musicals. The path from New York to Hollywood was beaten by hordes of singers, dancers, musicians and songwriters, eager to get in on the new bonanza. But the movie musicals, prior to the Busby Berkeley breakthrough in late 1932, were much of a muchness, and, for the most part, were filmed with little cinematic concept. Among them were several extravaganzas in which the studios displayed their talent rosters: MGM's *Hollywood Revue of 1929*, Warners' *The Show of Shows*, *Paramount on Parade* and Universal's *The King of Jazz*. These were all revues devoid of plot lines, in which stars and featured players sang, danced and appeared in skits.

The first musical to utilize a Hollywood setting fully in its story was *Married in Hollywood*, made by Fox in 1929 and starring J. Harold Murray and Norma Terris, neither of whom ever became popular players. Harlan Thompson wrote the story and the lyrics, adapting them from a stage musical for which the distinguished Oskar Straus had supplied the music, some of which was retained for the picture. The story begins in Vienna with a Prince (Murray) falling in love with a pretty American singer (Terris). Their love appears hopeless, with the prince forced to stay in his own social class, so the saddened girl returns to America. On the boat she sings for her fellow passengers, one of whom happens to be a film producer who offers her a contract. Stardom swiftly follows, and she gets a chance to devise a screenplay of her own. She decides to tell the story of her love affair in Vienna, and invents a dramatic ending in which the girl kills the aristocrat the Prince plans to marry. However, the Prince himself happily spoils her ending by turning up in Hollywood, telling her a revolution has made him an exile and that they are now free to marry.

In 1930 Fox boasted they were making a musical which would show intimate scenes of the real Hollywood. This was *Let's Go Places*, with Lola Lane and Joseph Wagstaff, but it turned out to be a conventional backstage musical placed in a movie setting, with its musical numbers shown being filmed. In this "mistaken identity" farce a young singer (Wagstaff) goes to Hollywood intent on

255

Music is Magic: The gentlemen in the check jackets are Frank Mitchell and Jack Durant, and the girl in the abbreviated striped number is Alice Faye.

Married in Hollywood (1929): Norma Terris and J. Harold Murray.

Show Girl in Hollywood (1930): Jack Mulhall and Alice White.

making good in the movies and is mistaken for a more important man of similar name, which gives him the opportunity he needs. By the time the error is discovered, the young man is already a success.

First National's *Show Girl in Hollywood* (1930) was described as being "13% color." It was the dull and heavy-handed sequel to the 1928 *Show Girl*, by J. P. McEvoy, which starred Alice White as a struggling entertainer named Dixie Dugan (who then moved to the comic strips). In the sequel, directed by Mervyn LeRoy, Dixie is spotted in a nightclub by a movie director (John Miljan) and given a chance in Hollywood. She becomes a leading player but acts in such a conceited and temperamental fashion—demanding changes in the story and a different director—that the studio fires her. However, once humility takes over, Dixie gets back on the track. The most memorable sequence in this picture is the performance by Blanche Sweet, as a fading movie star, singing a song by Bud Green and Sam H. Stept titled "There's a Tear for Every Smile in Hollywood:"

There's a tear for every smile in Hollywood,
Every mile's a weary mile in Hollywood,
A million dreams are born with each day,
A million dreams keep fading away,

Three years went by before the next musical with a filmland setting—MGM's *Broadway to Hollywood*. In 1929 the studio had shot material for a lavish musical to be called *The March of Time*, but shelved it because of generally poor results. Director Willard Mack and writer Edgar Allan Woolf labored for a long time to find a way of presenting some of the material and finally came up with a story about a theatrical family called the Hacketts, following them through three generations from vaudeville to the movies. In the Hollywood segment the grandparents (Frank Morgan and Alice Brady) watch over the career of young Ted (Eddie Quillan), who becomes a hit in Hollywood but lets success go to his head. Ted becomes irresponsible and cocky, and it takes a good deal of talk from his grandfather to point out that expensive schedules and the fortunes of many other people rely on the behavior of the star.

Ted sees the light. As he does his stuff for the cameras, his grandfather collapses on the set and dies in the arms of his wife, sinking contentedly as he watches Ted carry on the family tradition. Very little of the material shot for *The March of Time* appeared in the final print of *Broadway to Hollywood*, but a number of stars were used as guests, including Jimmy Durante, Fay Templeton and Nelson Eddy in his first film appearance.

The Broadway-to-Hollywood plot device has been a staple in movie musicals. One of the early uses of

257

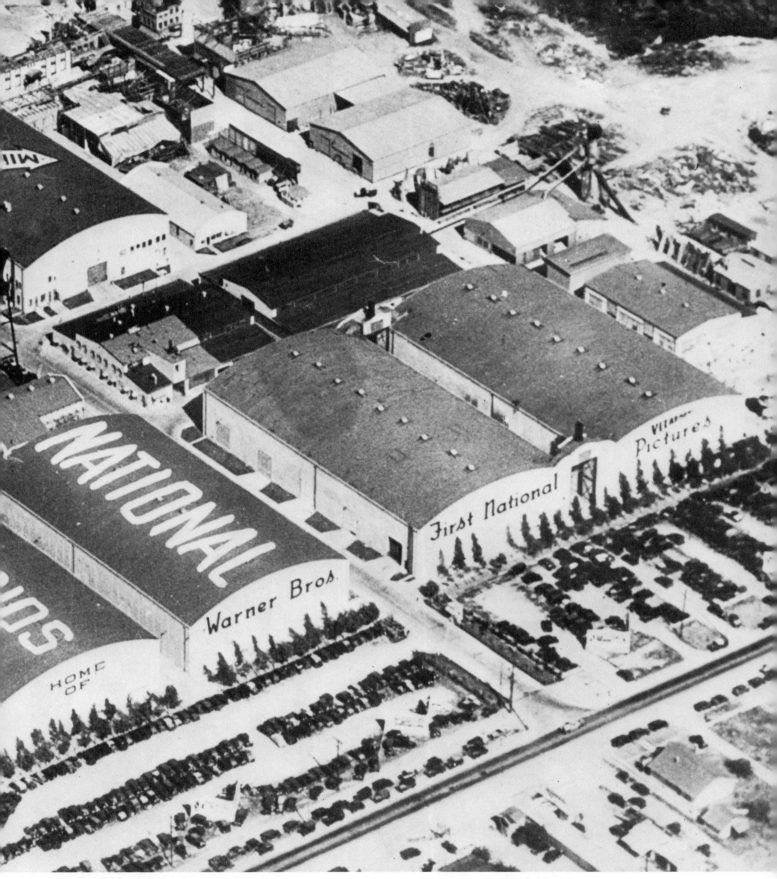

The Warner Bros. — First National Studio in Burbank,
as it appeared at the time of making *Show Girl in
Hollywood*.

this theme was MGM's *Excess Baggage* in 1928. In this non-musical William Haines and Josephine Dunn appear as a pair of vaudevillians whose marriage goes on the rocks when she finds success in Hollywood and he doesn't—until the end of the picture, when all their problems happily resolve. A similar situation was dealt with the following year in Fox's *Big Time* (also not a musical) with Lee Tracy and Mae Clarke as a vaudeville team who split up. She becomes a movie star and he drifts downhill, ending up as an extra in movies—until the day he is assigned to one of her pictures, which brings about a reconciliation. *Big Time* is of note because of the appearance of director John Ford as himself.

In 1933 another movie musical employed the migration from New York to Hollywood theme —*Sitting Pretty*, directed by Harry Joe Brown for Paramount. The songs were written by lyricist Mack Gordon and composer Harry Revel, and both of them appeared in the picture. The story concerns a pair of songwriters, a breezy one played by Jack Oakie and a more serious one, played by Jack Haley in his movie debut. A music publisher (Mack Gordon) encourages them to try Hollywood, where

scores of musicals are being made, and a pianist (Harry Revel) seconds the opinion. But the two are short on cash and have to hitchhike their way across the country, in the course of which they meet a pleasant lunch-wagon proprietress (Ginger Rogers), who happens to be able to sing and dance. She falls for Haley and helps the pair get to Hollywood. Oakie gets involved with a flamboyant actress (Thelma Todd), but she drops him when he loses his job. Once he gets over being swellheaded he finds success easier to manage.

Sitting Pretty was the best of the Hollywood-oriented musicals up to this time. Of the Gordon-Revel songs "Did You Ever See a Dream Walking?" became a standard, and the Busby Berkeley influence was obvious, with the director aping some of his overhead shooting of ensemble numbers. Gregory Ratoff contributed an amusing lampoon as an agent, and Ginger Rogers' performance resulted in her being selected to play opposite Fred Astaire for the first time in *Flying Down to Rio*.

MGM's *Hollywood Party* in 1934 was described by one reviewer as being a "long short." Its string of songs, dances and comic bits are held together by a

Show Girl in Hollywood: Supervisor Robert Lord and director Mervyn LeRoy confer with their star, Alice White.

Broadway to Hollywood (1933): Frank Morgan, Alice Brady and Eddie Quillan.

Excess Baggage (1928): William Haines and Josephine Dunn.

Sitting Pretty (1933): Jack Haley and Jack Oakie.

Sitting Pretty: Ginger Rogers and Jack Haley.

yarn about Jimmy Durante, a jungle picture star playing "Schnarzan," trying to get the better of his rival (George Givot). Both of them want to persuade big game hunter Baron Munchausen (Jack Pearl) to let them use the animals he has just brought back from Africa in their next pictures. Durante stages an elaborate party to impress the Baron, and Givot turns up disguised as a Greek ambassador to try and wreck the festivities. Among the guests are Mickey Mouse, Laurel and Hardy, Polly Moran, Lupe Velez and Charles Butterworth, who has the film's only memorable line: Commenting on the party he says, "This place is littered with movie celebrities—and that makes some litter." Even in 1934 *Hollywood Party* was regarded as poor.

Let's Fall in Love (1934) was Ann Sothern's first major film. As Harriette Lake she had appeared in several bit parts, but in grooming her for stardom Columbia invented a new name and gave her the role of a girl who becomes a movie star. The story has her as a Brooklyn-born circus girl who catches the eye of a Hollywood director (Edmund Lowe). He passes her off as a European singer-actress when his star (Tala Birell) becomes difficult and has to be replaced. The ruse is successful until the director's jealous fiancée (Miriam Jordon) exposes the girl, but the spiteful ploy backfires because the public takes to her in spite of the phony publicity. This pleasant little musical was written by the estimable Herbert Fields and gave Harold Arlen his first crack at Hollywood. The lyrics to the three Arlen pieces were written by Ted Koehler, and the title song became a standard. And once again Gregory Ratoff roared across the screen as a harried movie producer. He and Adolphe Menjou should have received special Academy Awards for their innumerable performances as producers.

Music Is Magic, directed by George Marshall, was among the last films made by Fox in 1935 before their merger with the Twentieth Century Company. It was also the last Hollywood film in which Bebe Daniels appeared, before she left for England. In this she played the part of a slipping movie star and although it was the principal part in the film, Fox gave top billing to the upcoming Alice Faye, thereby suggesting that the fiction was rather close to fact.

The thin plot deals with the star's attempts to hang on to her position, even passing off her daughter as her younger sister. While making a picture to be called "Music Is Magic," Bebe refuses to sing one of the songs and chorus girl Alice is asked to do it. She does it so well that everyone thinks that she is the one who should be playing the lead. When the daughter

Sitting Pretty: Jack Oakie, Jack Haley and Gregory Ratoff.

263

Hollywood Party (1934): Jimmy Durante as Schnarzan and Charlotte Greenwood as his mate.

The sequence was re-shot with Lupe Velez, and that version remained in the film.

Hollywood Party: Johnny Weissmuller in a sequence cut from the film.

Let's Fall in Love: Edmund Lowe, as a director.

(Rosina Lawrence) is slightly injured in an accident, Bebe's maternal instincts surface and she admits to parenthood, which also brings her to her senses about her career. She accepts the role of a mother in another picture and tells the studio that Alice should play the lead in the musical.

Music Is Magic did nothing for the career of Bebe Daniels except possibly make her realize, like the lady in the picture, that it was necessary to make a change in her life. However, for Alice Faye it was a definite step in the right direction. This modest programmer soon led to popularity in 20th Century-Fox musicals.

Musicals with Hollywood settings were not in evidence again until 1937, and then came a flood of them. The least of the lot is *Start Cheering*, a Columbia effort starring Jimmy Durante as a thick-headed agent who has to try to persuade Charles Starrett (taking time off from his career as a cowboy star) to return to Hollywood, after having given up fame in favor of a college education. Starrett finds school life fretful, what with the adulation of the girls, the hatred of the boys and the conniving of his agents to get him kicked out of college. The only song to last beyond the run of the film was Durante's own "When I Strut-away in My Cutaway."

Eddie Cantor's *Ali Baba Goes to Town* (1937) is not set in Hollywood, but it has the comedian as a movie fan on his way to the film capital to get the autographs of his favorite stars. Eddie is first seen making his frugal way on a freight train and being thrown off by a pair of truculent tramps. He staggers through the desert and comes across a movie company on location making an Arabian Nights epic (as in *Souls for Sale*). The director is played by Alan Dinehart. Eddie is pressed into service as an extra and finds the work so taxing he takes pills to fall asleep. The bulk of this picture is built around Eddie's dream, in which he is transported back to the days of Old Bagdad. Fortuitously, he becomes a minister to the Sultan (Roland Young) and solves Arabia's problems by employing the policies of President Franklin Roosevelt's New Deal. He wakes from the dream when he falls from a magic carpet ride, and the picture ends with him in Hollywood ogling the stars. This was Cantor's first and only film for 20th Century-Fox, but it failed to bring him the kind of success he achieved from his earlier Samuel Goldwyn vehicles and the popularity he enjoyed in radio. The songs by Mack Gordon and Harry Revel, including a love song for young Tony Martin, were pleasant but not memorable, although Cantor

269

Let's Fall in Love (1934): Ann Sothern and Edmund Lowe.

Let's Fall in Love: Edmund Lowe, Tala Birrell and Gregory Ratoff.

Slightly French (1949): Don Ameche and Dorothy Lamour in the re-make of *Let's Fall in Love*.

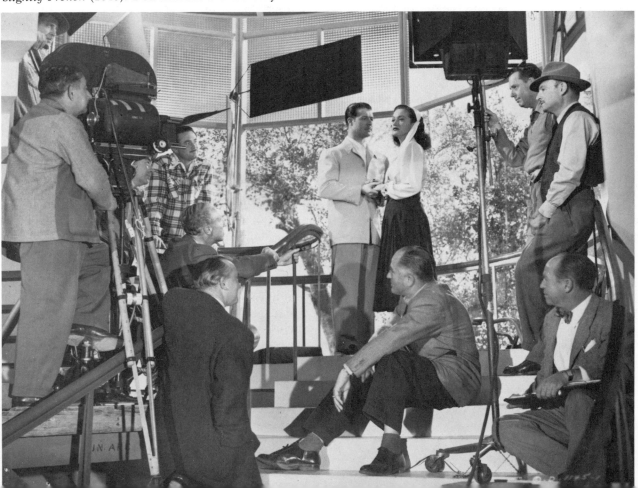

Music is Magic (1935): Bebe Daniels doing the celebrity arrival routine.

Start Cheering (1937): Jimmy Durante, Charles Starrett and Walter Connolly.

Ali Baba Goes to Town: Alan Dinehart, Eddie Cantor and Sidney Fields.

admirers will recall his characteristic eyeball-rolling, hand-clapping rendition of "Swing Is Here to Stay."

Samuel Goldwyn's only sound film about Hollywood was *The Goldwyn Follies* (1937), an expensive but overblown and largely hollow picture. Its only distinction is that it contains the last three songs written by George Gershwin, who died before the picture was completed. The screenplay is by the estimable Ben Hecht, but it is nonetheless trite and ridiculous, telling the tale of a prominent producer (Adolphe Menjou) who hires a nice, uncomplicated girl (Andrea Leeds) to advise him how to make pictures. The producer, out of touch with "real life," finds his recent films failing with the public. He happens to meet the character played by Miss Leeds, newly arrived in Hollywood from a good, simple life in the country, and she points out that his films lack the common touch. So impressed is he with this revelation that he hires her and titles her "Miss Humanity," which results in his product once again receiving public approval. Not unnaturally, he falls

Ali Baba Goes to Town (1937): Eddie Cantor and Alan Dinehart.

272

The Goldwyn Follies (1937): Adolphe Menjou, Vera Zorina, Charlie McCarthy and Edgar Bergen.

The Goldwyn Follies: Kenny Baker and Andrea Leeds on the piano bench, and around the piano: Helen Jepson, Phil Baker, The Ritz Bros., Ella Logan, Bobby Clark, Vera Zorina, McCarthy and Bergen, and Adolphe Menjou.

Something to Sing About (1936): Gene Lockhart, William Frawley and James Cagney.

in love with her, but she loves a handsome young fellow (Kenny Baker), a tenor who works at a hamburger stand. Also not unnaturally, she gets him his break in the movies. Then the producer throws a party for his cast to announce his engagement to "Miss Humanity," until he realizes that she and the tenor are meant for each other, and magnanimously gives them his blessing and his backing.

Goldwyn hoped to make his *Follies* prestigious by hiring ballet star Vera Zorina and choreographer George Balanchine, along with opera star Helen Jepson and the *corps de ballet* of the Metropolitan Opera. After Gershwin's death, Vernon Duke was hired to compose the music for the ballet sequences, and to contrast the cultural aspects with more plebeian tastes, Goldwyn brought in comics Phil Baker, Bobby Clark and the Ritz Brothers. The two-million-dollar budget, a hefty one for 1937, is apparent in production values, but the total effect is plushly tedious. The behind-the-scenes look at Hollywood is even more false than usual, particularly in the relationship between the producer and his "Miss Humanity." A presumably top-line producer would not have needed to be told his pictures were failing because the dialogue was stilted and his players grotesquely hammy.

However, *The Goldwyn Follies* is not a film to completely dismiss—it has Kenny Baker singing "Love Walked In" and "Our Love Is Here to Stay," and Ella Logan singing "I Was Doing All Right."

In 1936 James Cagney broke away from Warner Bros. after years of bickering with them about money and he signed with modest little Grand National for two pictures, the second of which was a musical spoof on Hollywood, *Something to Sing About*. In this, Cagney appears as a New York band leader who accepts an offer from Hollywood to star in a movie, somewhat against his better judgment. At the studio he resents the attempts to improve his appearance and manner with elocution lessons and make-up, and resorts to fisticuffs both on and off camera. Convinced he is a flop as a screen personality, Cagney marries his girl friend Rita (Evelyn Daw), and they take off for a quiet life in the South Pacific. But his movie becomes a great success and the studio urges him to return to Hollywood and sign a seven-year contract. After signing it, he discovers it requires him to pretend he is not married. Eventually his wife tires of the sham and returns to New York, convinced that he is now romantically involved with the studio's foreign-born siren (Mona Barrie), an affair which actually exists only as a publicity stunt. Growing more and more sick of a life style he neither wants nor admires, Cagney returns to New York, his wife and his band.

Something to Sing About was a change of pace for

275

Cagney and gave him an opportunity to take a few jabs at the film industry. Like the character in the picture, Cagney had been heard to make deprecating remarks at the way studios were run and about the men who ran them. At one point he claimed he might give up his film career and become a doctor. However, it was not until 1961 that he threw in the towel, after which no amount of persuading could interest him in returning to the picture business. *Something to Sing About* is amusing to Cagney fans because it allows him to sing and dance, long before *Yankee Doodle Dandy* proved he was a master hoofer with a unique style. But he actually started his career as a song-and-dance man on Broadway in 1920.

Warners' *Hollywood Hotel* (1938) was far from their most exciting musical of the thirties, even though it was directed by Busby Berkeley and starred Dick Powell. By 1937 Warners' cycle of lavish production number musicals had almost spent itself, and the studio was no longer willing to indulge Berkeley in his expensive surrealistic choreography. In this picture the emphasis is on comedy and music, with seven new songs by Richard Whiting and Johnny Mercer, and specialties from the orchestras of Benny Goodman and Raymond Paige. The title refers both to the real hotel on Hollywood Boulevard at Highland Avenue and the popular radio program "Hollywood Hotel" which featured Powell and columnist Louella Parsons in a potpourri of gossip stories, interviews, songs and excerpts from current movies sung and acted by the stars. The musical director of the program at one time was Raymond Paige, the announcer Ken Niles, and among the singers contracted to the program was Frances Langford. They all appear in the film, broadcasting from The Orchid Room, which was really a mythical setting and not the sumptuous cavern created by Warners. The Hollywood Hotel, pulled down in 1956, was a modest and somewhat passé place to stay in 1937, and although its exterior appears in the film, the interior sequences are pure invention, making it appear like a Waldorf-Astoria.

Dick Powell in *Hollywood Hotel* is Ronny Bowers, a saxophone player from Benny Goodman's band, who wins a talent contest which takes him to "All-Star Pictures." His first job is to escort Mona Marshall, a conceited, temperamental star, to the premiere of her newest picture at the Carthay Circle Theatre. (In almost all movies about Hollywood, premieres are staged either at the Carthay or Grauman's Chinese Theatre). However, the girl he

The Hollywood Hotel in 1910.

Hollywood Hotel (1938): Rosemary Lane, Dick Powell, Ted Healy, Ronald Reagan, Allyn Joslyn, Hugh Herbert and Lola Lane.

Hollywood Hotel: Lola Lane, as a temperamental star, giving Louella Parsons an interview. Glenda Farrell at far left. Curt Bois with cigarette holder.

279

Hollywood Hotel: On the set — Glenda Farrell, Lola Lane and director Busby Berkeley talking to Louella Parsons. Cameraman Charles Rosher by lamp.

takes is actually Mona's look-alike stand-in, Virginia. With Mona played by Lola Lane and Virginia by her younger sister Rosemary, Ronny has reason to be confused. When Mona finds out she has been misrepresented in public, she throws a temper tantrum at the studio and causes Ronny to be fired. He takes a job working in a drive-in restaurant, loved and encouraged by Virginia, and one night when he is singing on the job he is heard by a director (William B. Davidson), who offers him a job. To his disappointment, Ronny finds he has to dub the singing of the pompous, hammy actor (Alan Mowbray), who is Mona's co-star in a Civil War romance. The idiotic actor is so thrilled by the compliments about his dubbed singing that he accepts Louella Parsons' invitation to vocalize on her radio program. It later dawns on him that he can't sing and that he must feign a throat infection to excuse him from appearing. But Virginia and her friends abduct the actor and clear the way for Ronny to appear on the broadcast with Mona—to inevitable acclaim.

Hollywood Hotel is trivia, but it also is a useful reminder of a long-gone landmark and a radio program which helped make Hollywood a major network broadcast center. Louella Parsons, who enjoyed a considerable reputation with her widely syndicated columns, appears in the picture, but some of her footage was cut in the final released version. Even her influence in the industry could not hide the fact that she looked stiff and faintly ridiculous. Of great musical interest is the work of Benny Goodman in this film. He and his band were at the peak of their popularity at this time, and their sequences were shot during the summer of 1937, when they were engaged at the Palomar Ballroom in Los Angeles. Gene Krupa, Harry James and Ziggy Elman were still members of the Goodman band, and for one number Goodman and Krupa are joined by pianist Teddy Wilson and vibraphonist Lionel Hampton (The Goodman Quartet).

This was the eleventh film to associate Dick Powell with Busby Berkeley, and it was the last. The two had both shot to prominence with *42nd Street* in

Hollywood Hotel: Alan Mowbray, Lola Lane and Louella Parsons.

1933, and Powell had been the singing star, often in tandem with Ruby Keeler, in most of Berkeley's famous movies. But times were changing. Berkeley claimed he wanted to be a serious director and Powell was eager to escape the narrow image of juvenile crooner. By 1939 both Powell and Berkeley were free of their ironclad Warner contracts, and a movie era came to an end.

Hollywood Hotel was the film for which Dick Whiting and Johnny Mercer wrote "Hooray for Hollywood," the best song ever written about the industry and its veritable anthem. Always played as a salute to Hollywood, the lyrics nevertheless contain some sharp jabs at the lunacy of the place, referring to it as "screwy, bally-hooey Hollywood, where any office boy or young mechanic can be a panic, with just a good-looking pan. And any barmaid can be a star-maid if she dances with or without a fan." The puckish Mercer also worked in the snide line, "Hooray for Hollywood, where you're terrific if you're even good."* He wasn't alone in his ribbing on this picture. Scenarists Jerry Wald, Maurice Leo

and Richard Macauley got in some pointed comments on egocentric actors and conniving publicists, and in one scene where Powell pulls up outside "Miracle Pictures," the sign reads, "If it's a good picture, it's a Miracle."

Louella Parsons was paid $40,000 for her work in *Hollywood Hotel* and wrote a tongue-in-cheek review of it, referring to herself as "pretty and slender," and modestly claimed, "As an actress we are a good columnist, and even not so bad on the radio." For all her seeming joviality, Parsons intimidated Hollywood with her power. By the time she appeared in this picture she had already been writing about the community for twenty-three years, fifteen of them for the journals of William Randolph Hearst.

Guided all the way by the newspaper czar, Hearst, Marion Davies' film career spanned the twenty years from 1917 to 1937. Acting in movies was practically a sideline to Davies, who as Hearst's celebrated

* Copyright 1938, Harms, Inc.

281

mistress played host to the cream of Hollywood society at Hearst's great estate at San Simeon. Among her last pictures was *Going Hollywood* in 1933, in which she played a young (she was then thirty-six) schoolteacher who moons over the voice and the likeness of a singing movie star, played by Bing Crosby. Crosby by this time had enjoyed popularity on the radio and recordings, and his movie career was just entering its ascendancy. In this pleasant musical, Davies goes to Hollywood to be near her idol and runs afoul of his co-star and girl friend, Fifi D'Orsay, a fiery, temperamental type. She finds him in the course of making a picture directed by Ned Sparks, and she so impresses Crosby that D'Orsay whisks him away to Mexico. Davies follows and manages to persuade Crosby to return to Hollywood minus D'Orsay and, once the film is back in production, Davies herself takes over D'Orsay's role and becomes a sensation. This incredible accomplishment also includes winning Crosby.

Aside from being the film in which Crosby introduced the song "Temptation," *Going Hollywood* is interesting more for what went on behind the camera than in front of it. In his autobiography, *Call Me Lucky* (Simon and Schuster, 1953), Bing Crosby recalls that the making of the picture was an easygoing, luxurious experience backed by Hearst, who particularly wanted Davies to star in a musical. Hearst persuaded MGM to borrow Crosby from Paramount at two thousand dollars a week, and as Crosby admits, "It was the most leisurely motion picture I ever had anything to do with. It took six months to complete." Davies' dressing room was a large bungalow, complete with kitchen and office, and she never arrived on the set until late morning. Part of her entourage was a five-piece orchestra, which played on and off all through the day because she loved music and felt that it created a nice atmosphere. Director Raoul Walsh amused himself by practicing golf, and about all that was accomplished before lunch was a conference on the scenes to be shot that day. Davies conducted the luncheons in her bungalow, and Crosby remembers them as being epicurean intervals in which the conversation ranged around everything but the picture. It would be midafternoon before they got back on the set, by which time Davies' make-up needed adjusting, followed by refreshments. Scenes might be filmed starting at five, but Hearst, who could be economyminded, objected to the company's working past six because of the heavy expense of overtime.

Bing Crosby has every reason to look back fondly at *Going Hollywood;* it helped to put him in the top

283

Hollywood Hotel: Benny Goodman and his Orchestra.

Hollywood Hotel: Dick Powell, Rosemary Lane, Louella Parsons and Allyn Joslyn.

Going Hollywood (1933): On the set, song writers Nacio Herb Brown and Arthur Freed with Bing Crosby and Marion Davies.

ten at the box office and gave him a chance to work with an actress he describes as one of the most charming and generous he has ever known. He refers to his half-year working with Marion Davies as "an example of the way the big movie queens of a bygone era—stars like Barbara La Marr and Clara Bow and Pola Negri—sailed into action. In its day it spelled glamour. I got in on the twilight of this colorful era. It was quite an experience."

The studios missed no tricks in gibing at each other's publicity schemes. David O. Selznick's long search for an actress to play Scarlett O'Hara in *Gone With the Wind* resulted in two musicals built on a similar theme, 20th Century-Fox's *Second Fiddle* in 1939 and Paramount's *Kiss the Boys Goodbye* two years later. The Fox picture was a vehicle for Tyrone Power and Sonja Henie, reuniting them after *Thin Ice*, with Rudy Vallee and Mary Healy in support. The thin story line, allowing for four Irving Berlin songs and several skating sessions, tells of the search by "Consolidated Pictures" for a girl to play Violet Jansen in their production of the best-selling novel, "Girl of the North." The search has been going on for months and the newspapers are tired of the studio's attempts to get publicity. The head of the publicity department (a character suggested by Fox's own head publicist Harry Brand) is played by Alan Dinehart. Brash young publicist Power is sent on yet another mission, this time to Bergen, Minnesota, to interview a schoolteacher (Henie) whose photo has been sent to the studio by her boy friend (Lyle Talbot). Henie doesn't know about this and even when Power explains it to her, she doesn't think she has a chance. He doesn't think so either but he persuades her that a trip to California will at least be a holiday.

Henie turns out to be the 436th girl to be tested for the part—and she wins. She is pleasantly dumbfounded: "I'm not an actress." Replies rival Mary Healy, "Don't worry. The movies can cover up the worst acting," which brings a retort from haughty Edna May Oliver, who has accompanied niece Henie to Hollywood: "I don't know. I've seen some of *your* pictures." Healy is miffed because Power has concocted a publicity romance for Henie with her fiancé, Vallee, a popular singer who has just made his first picture for Consolidated. The above ex-

Going Hollywood: Bing Crosby and Marion Davies.

Going Hollywood: Patsy Kelly, Marion Davies and Fifi D'Orsay.

Going Hollywood: Marion Davies and the gargantuan finale, "Our Big Love Scene."

Second Fiddle (1939): That's Rudy Vallee at the top of the set.

Second Fiddle: Mary Healy, Rudy Vallee, Tyrone Power and Lillian Porter.

Second Fiddle: Sonja Henie and Tyrone Power.

change of dialogue takes place in Earl Carroll's nightclub in Hollywood. The conservative Vallee objects to having to submit himself to a publicity romance, and Power assures him, "Phony romances are nothing new—they're done time and time again." It must have amused Tyrone Power to deliver these lines, because he and Sonja Henie had faked such an affair at the request of Fox when she first appeared in Hollywood in 1936.

Second Fiddle is a limp satire. With a more incisive script, it could have worked more humor from its basically good idea, but as it is every turn is predictable. Power writes Vallee's love letters to Henie, which causes her to fall in love with him (shades of *Cyrano de Bergerac*) because she doesn't know the romance is contrived. When she finds out, she leaves Hollywood in anger and returns to her home town. Shortly after, "Girl of the North" has its glittering premiere at the Carthay Circle Theatre, and both she and the picture are acclaimed triumphs, but this doesn't seem to impress her and Power is sent to get her back. By this time he realizes that he is in love with her himself, and in the nick of time manages to prevent her marriage to her patient boy friend. The latter ends the picture in disgust, as he watches Power kiss Henie: "And I had to go and send her picture to Hollywood." Had he been merely a movie-goer watching this film, he might have added, "Is *this* all they could get out of it?"

Kiss the Boys Goodbye was an acid play by Clare Boothe which satirized Selznick's search for Scarlett and did it so mercilessly that Selznick made it known that he would protest a film version. To avoid any possible battles between Paramount and the Selznick interests, the studio instructed scenarists Harry Tugend and Dwight Taylor to alter the location to New York and make it a story about a Broadway director's problems in finding a Southern star to play in his musical set in the Old South. The film is amusing and provides Mary Martin with ample opportunity to spoof ambitious Southern ladies and to sing the pleasant songs of director Victor Schertzinger and lyricist Frank Loesser, but what might have been a devastating dig at Hollywood was completely vitiated by Paramount's caution.

That's Right, You're Wrong, produced by RKO in 1939, was the first of several pictures featuring band leader Kay Kyser, whose popularity had grown with his radio show, "Kay Kyser's Kollege of Musical Knowledge." The program was a quiz show with music, and the film's title derives from Kyser's enthusiastic response to contestant's answers, "That's right—you're wrong!" Kyser's vocalists, Ginny Sims,

Kiss the Boys Goodbye (1941): Mary Martin.

Harry Babbitt, Sully Mason and Ish Kabibble appear with him in this picture, as do a number of Hollywood's syndicated columnists—a ploy that obviously paid off because the film grossed a million dollars in one year on a cost of $300,000. It was financed jointly by Kyser, director David Butler (who also had a hand in the screenplay) and RKO. Lucille Ball was brought in to supply glamour, and once more Adolphe Menjou was called upon to play a producer. The story had Kyser being brought to Hollywood to make a movie because of his radio show and finally being paid off by the studio without making the film because they find him impossible as an actor—an ironic reversal of fact. Kyser never bothered to act and his little movie musicals turned in handsome profits.

The Second World War brought a boom to Hollywood and saw the production of a kind of film never likely to be made again—the all-star musical comedy in a studio setting, with hordes of famous performers "doing their bit" to entertain both the home front and servicemen based all over the world. Thus solid showmanship was tinged with a patriotic motivation. Perhaps the best of these was the first one, Paramount's *Star Spangled Rhythm* in 1942. Seemingly everybody who was anybody at Paramount was pressed into service. Written by Harry Tugend and directed by George Marshall, the film was well served by the songs of Harold Arlen and Johnny Mercer, of which "That Old Black Magic" and "Hit the Road to Dreamland" remain popular. The former was sung by Johnny Johnston and danced by Vera Zorina, and the latter by Dick Powell and Mary Martin as a "film-within-a-film" sequence directed by Preston Sturges.

Star Spangled Rhythm has an amusing plot device. An old studio gateman (Victor Moore) has allowed his son (Eddie Bracken) to believe that he is head of production at Paramount. The son, now in the Navy, turns up with a gang of his buddies in the hope of touring the lot. A studio switchboard girl (Betty Hutton), who has been corresponding with Bracken, takes pity on the old man and devises a mad scheme to make him appear the man he claims to be, which causes consternation for the actual head of production (Walter Abel). The sailors are royally greeted around the studio and they urge Moore to bring the stars to San Pedro to stage a gigantic show for the naval base. Somehow this amazing proposal gets put into effect. The master of ceremonies is Bob Hope, of course. Among the many acts are Paulette Goddard, Dorothy Lamour and Veronica Lake

singing "A Sweater, a Sarong and a Peekaboo Bang," reprised by Walter Catlett, Sterling Holloway and Arthur Treacher; "Old Glory," sung by Bing Crosby; Betty Hutton stating the case for the whole company with "I'm Doing It For Defense"; and Betty Rhodes, Marjorie Reynolds and Donna Drake performing a production number set in an airplane factory, "On the Swing Shift," which is shown being filmed.

The Paramount picture remains an interesting item, especially as a reminder of what certain actors were doing at that time, and how they kidded themselves. Alan Ladd, who had rocketed to popularity shortly before in *This Gun For Hire*, appears here in a vignette: He strolls into a dingy poolroom and his victim recoils at the sight of him. Ladd reaches into his trenchcoat and pulls out a weapon—a tiny bow and arrow. Ray Milland and Fred MacMurray lampoon their drawing room comedy style with a skit about men playing cards in the manner of women, and Bob Hope does a jealous husband skit with William Bendix. *Star Spangled Rhythm* now reeks of nostalgia, particularly for any veteran Paramount employee.

Warners' *Thank Your Lucky Stars*, made in 1943, stands up better than most all-star wartime entertainments because it is strung together with a fairly amusing plot line and presents some of that studio's major players in a few memorable moments, set to words and music by Frank Loesser and Arthur Schwartz. The highlights are Bette Davis chanting "They're Either Too Young or Too Old"; Errol Flynn mocking heroics as a Cockney sailor in "That's What You Jolly Well Get"; Ann Sheridan singing the facts of life to a group of girls in "Love Isn't Born, It's Made"; and Jack Carson and Alan Hale doing a vaudeville song-and-dance, "I'm Going North." It also has John Garfield singing a dramatic version of "Blues in the Night," and an unshaven Humphrey Bogart being browbeaten by a flabbergasted S. Z. Sakall.

The core of *Thank Your Lucky Stars* is a gala benefit stage show being produced by Sakall and Edward Everett Horton, and as such it is more a backstage show than a look behind the scenes in Hollywood. The story is about a singer (Dennis Morgan) and a songwriter (Joan Leslie) who hope to break into the picture business and are befriended by a tourist guide named Joe Simpson (Eddie Cantor), who has had to give up his own hopes of being an entertainer because he looks exactly like Eddie Cantor. Cantor himself is approached by the

290

That's Right, You're Wrong (1939): Adolphe Menjou, Kay Kyser and Lucille Ball.

Star Spangled Rhythm (1942): Victor Moore and Betty Hutton.

Star Spangled Rhythm: William Haade, Gil Lamb, Betty Hutton, James Millican, Eddie Bracken and Victor Moore.

Bette Davis in *Thank Your Lucky Stars* (1943).

distraught producers because they want to use his contracted singer, Dinah Shore, on their show, but not Cantor, who is shown in this film as an egocentric bore. However, they have to agree to use Cantor in order to get Shore, and as they feared, he tries to take over the direction of the show. Morgan and Leslie strike upon the idea of abducting Cantor and substituting the mild, obliging Joe, thereby getting into the production themselves and allowing the producers to go about their business un-Cantored.

Thank Your Lucky Stars is so packed with star turns that Eddie Cantor's considerable participation in the film tends to go unremembered. He performed well both as himself and as Joe Simpson. He sang "We're Staying Home Tonight," a song about the need for conserving energy and materials in wartime, and subjected himself to various comic indignities as the abductee. Producer Mark Hellinger and director David Butler appear briefly in the picture as they stop and chat with Simpson, and Spike Jones and his City Slickers accompany Dennis Morgan as he sings "I'm Riding for a Fall," in a supposed area of Hollywood called Gower Gulch, where extras and job-seekers band together. No such place exists, and certainly not with the camaraderie here shown. In actuality, Gower Gulch was the name given the area around Sunset Boulevard and Gower Street, which was a kind of gathering place for actors and others connected with inexpensive (Poverty Row) Westerns.

Except for "Ice Cold Katy," a woefully outdated "colored" production number with Hattie McDaniel and Willie Best, *Thank Your Lucky Stars* is a genial movie which stands the test of time and gives a nostalgic glow to the Warner studios of a long-ago, peak period. The film kids Hollywood in an agreeable way, and it remains a pleasure to watch such great amateurs as Bette Davis, John Garfield, Errol Flynn, Olivia de Havilland and Ida Lupino tackling musical routines.

Universal's 1944 contribution to the all-star movies made to salute Hollywood and parade a multiplicity of talents in one package was *Follow the Boys*. More than the other pictures in this league, it pointed out the efforts being made by Hollywood's entertainers in their extensive travels to the war fronts. Running more than two hours, *Follow the Boys* contains some twenty musical sequences and flash appearances by a huge number of famous actors, singers and dance bands. The connective tissue is a story about Tony West (George Raft), who rises from vaudeville to Hollywood stardom in partnership with lovely Gloria Vance (Zorina). With the outbreak of war he tries to enlist in the services but is rejected because of age. West is despondent, but it occurs to him to form a Hollywood Victory Committee and organize entertainment for the forces at home and abroad. His plan is an instant success and it becomes part of the USO.

The Victory Committee seems to include every player under contract to Universal, from stars like Maria Montez and Robert Paige to character types like Nigel Bruce and Samuel S. Hinds. In the parade of performances staged for the fighting men around the world are Arthur Rubinstein, the Delta Rhythm Boys, Dinah Shore, the Andrews Sisters, and Jeanette MacDonald singing "Beyond the Blue Horizon," which she originally sang in *Monte Carlo* (1930). Within his characterization George Raft danced to the tune of "Sweet Georgia Brown" in the back of a truck on a distant front. "I'll Walk Alone," written by Jule Styne and Sammy Cahn, turned out to be one of the most enduring songs of the second World War. For film buffs the highlight of *Follow the Boys* is a magic act performed by Orson Welles with Marlene Dietrich as his assistant. Welles, who had long been an amateur magician, here saws Marlene in half as a pair of puzzled soldiers stand by. This picture also provides a record of one of W. C. Fields' most celebrated accomplishments—his amazing dexterity at the pool table, using hideously bent cues. By this time in his life Fields had been doing this bit of eccentric pool playing for forty years and here, at sixty-five, he had lost none of his hilarious skill.

Follow the Boys saluted Hollywood's war efforts without calling too much attention to the fact, but Warners' *Hollywood Canteen* (1944) seems particularly smug in dealing with the film industry's entertaining of service men. United Artists had made *Stage Door Canteen* the year before and peopled it with a great many theatrical celebrities as hosts to the services in New York. As written and directed by Delmer Daves, the Hollywood equivalent appears to be almost the exclusive enterprise of one studio—Warner Bros.

The president and vice-president of the Hollywood Canteen are Bette Davis and John Garfield, who mingle with the guests and tell them something about the history of the canteen. The sliver of a story line concerns a pair of soldiers, a shy one played by Robert Hutton and a brash one played by Dane Clark, who visit the canteen just prior to their being sent overseas. Hutton turns out to be the millionth serviceman to enter the canteen and as such is

Follow the Boys (1944): George Raft and Vera Zorina.

heralded and pampered. He is a doting fan of Joan Leslie and, to his simple-minded astonishment, he finds that the canteen has arranged a date for him with her. Dane is likewise amazed to find himself actually dancing with Joan Crawford. Both Leslie and Crawford are presented in this picture as forms of deities. Some of the other stars, like Paul Henreid, Barbara Stanwyck, Peter Lorre, Eleanor Parker and Ida Lupino appear only a little less awkward as they wait on tables and engage the troops in conversation. Luckier are Dennis Morgan, Eddie Cantor, Jack Carson and Jane Wyman who relieve the tension by getting up and singing.

Hollywood Canteen is, like the others of this kind, important for its rare moments, such as Joseph Szigeti joining Jack Benny in a violin duet, and a fine performance of Cole Porter's "Don't Fence Me In," sung by Roy Rogers astride a dancing Trigger. Other musical sequences strung through the long two hours are provided by the Sons of the Pioneers, the Golden Gate Quartet, Kitty Carlisle, the Andrews Sisters, and the bands of Jimmy Dorsey and Carmen

Follow the Boys: Orson Welles involving Marlene Dietrich in his magic act.

296

Cavallaro. Except for the coy adventures of Hutton and Dane, *Hollywood Canteen* is fairly pleasing entertainment and at best serves as a reminder that once there was such a canteen in Hollywood and that it did provide admirable services for the services.

Columbia's ephemeral *Jam Session* (1944) starts out in the Mertons and Marys of the Movies tradition. The story deals with the trials and tribulations of Ann Miller as a small-town contest winner of a trip to Hollywood and introductory letter to a major studio producer. She becomes romantically involved with a screenwriter (Jess Barker), and by the usual plot manipulations gets the dancing lead in her boy friend's picture. Every few minutes the story stops for specialties by the orchestras of Louis Armstrong, Charlie Barnet, Glen Gray, Alvino Rey, Jan Garber, Teddy Powell, etc., and the vocalizing of the Pied Pipers and Nan Wynn.

Anchors Aweigh is one of the mightiest of Metro's wartime musicals, running two hours and twenty minutes, with a half-dozen songs by Jule Styne and Sammy Cahn, and three major dance sequences by Gene Kelly. It touches upon Hollywood's hospitality to servicemen, but that is not the theme of the story, which is about a pair of sailors (Kelly and Frank Sinatra) who decide to spend a few days in Hollywood—mainly to look for girls. Kelly plays the breezy one and Sinatra the shy type. They get their chance to tour MGM when Kelly makes the acquaintance of Susan Abbott (Kathryn Grayson), who makes her living as a movie extra while studying singing with José Iturbi. The Iturbi angle also affords "serious" music interludes, including a concert at the Hollywood Bowl, with Iturbi conducting a group of young concert pianists.

The Hollywood Canteen is featured in *Anchors Aweigh,* and it is there that Sinatra meets a girl from Brooklyn (Pamela Britton) and falls in love with her. The flippant Kelly at first treats Susan with little interest, but then gradually comes to realize she is the girl for him. At the MGM studios he shows her how he would romance her if he had been a cavalier of long ago as he dances across a huge set with a style combining the Latin grace of Rudolph Valentino and the athletic prowess of Douglas Fairbanks, Sr. The dance takes Kelly around the courtyard of a Spanish castle—scaling the walls, leaping from parapet to parapet and swinging to the balcony of his beloved. Kelly's "Mexican Hat Dance" with a little girl is charming, but his elaborate routine with Jerry Mouse (of "Tom and Jerry"), combining live action with animation, is a major sequence in the history of movie musicals.

Hollywood Canteen (1944): Bette Davis, Robert Hutton and Joan Leslie.

Hollywood Canteen: Joseph Szigeti, Jack Benny and Bette Davis.

297

The director (Eddie Kane), at far left, preparing to test Ann Miller in *Jam Session* (1944). George Eldredge on the right.

Anchors Aweigh: Gene Kelly, Jose Iturbi, Frank Sinatra, and Pamela Britton.

Anchors Aweigh: Gene Kelly and girls on the MGM lot.

Anchors Aweigh: Kathryn Grayson, with director George Sidney seated in front of her.

Duffy's Tavern (1945): Charles Quigley, Walter Abel and Eddie Bracken.

In 1945 Paramount did another all-star musical, *Duffy's Tavern*, built around the long-running radio comedy starring Ed Gardner as the manager of a restaurant "where the elite meet to eat." The picture met with little enthusiasm despite the appearances of a wealth of stars doing skits, blackouts and musical numbers, but it does contain one excellent sketch in a movie studio setting. In this Eddie Bracken appears as a double for a handsome cowboy actor (Charles Quigley). The director (Walter Abel) treats the actor with deference and the double with the indifference usually shown inanimate objects. Every time the actor is about to do anything involving action, risk, pain or indignity the director stops the filming and poor Bracken is pushed in to receive the "treatment."

Paramount's *Variety Girl* in 1947 bears some similarity in style to the wartime all-star musicals in the way it trundles out all the stars for songs and skits and little vignettes of them at work. But, instead of visiting servicemen, the device here is a pair of young girls trying to break into the movies. The picture is dedicated to the Variety Clubs of America, which was founded by a group of theatre men in Pittsburgh in 1929 to provide for a foundling who had been abandoned in a local movie house. The child was christened Catherine Variety Sheridan and subsequently adopted. This picture purports to be about that girl but changes her name to Catherine Brown (Mary Hatcher) and tells of her arrival in

Hollywood, where she rooms with a girl who calls herself Amber La Vonne (Olga San Juan). The two girls visit all the usual Hollywood spots before descending upon the Paramount studios in their quest for work. Their luck is bad until Catherine's identity is known, and then as the Variety Girl she is given the opportunity she wants.

George Marshall, who directed the picture, is seen directing Amber's screen test. Cecil B. DeMille is glimpsed during the filming of *Unconquered*, and director Mitchell Leisen and writer Frank Butler are seen in the Vine Street Brown Derby sizing up Amber as a typical movie hopeful. Amber's screen test is humorously done as she plays opposite a Cagney-like William Bendix and receives the grapefruit treatment à la Mae Clarke in *Public Enemy*. One of the film's most interesting sequences involves the voice-dubbing of a George Pal-Puppetoon short, a frantic and complicated bit of business. Bob Hope and Bing Crosby are, of course, present in *Variety Girl* and sing a comic duet called "Harmony," about two men who apparently lack it.

Much of the picture centers around the annual Variety Club Banquet at the Cocoanut Grove in Los Angeles, which, for the purposes of this picture is an entirely Paramount affair. Aside from the appearances of stars like Gary Cooper, Alan Ladd, Dorothy Lamour, Veronica Lake, Barbara Stanwyck and Burt Lancaster, the mammoth variety show offers music by Spike Jones and his City Slickers, and the Original Dixieland Jazz Band. *Variety Girl* is among the best movies of this kind, with genuine warmth and humor, providing a generous inside view of Paramount and the many people who were once so indelibly identified with it.

Most of the great American songwriters have written for Hollywood and a few of them have had movies made about their lives—*Rhapsody in Blue* (George Gershwin), *Till the Clouds Roll By* (Jerome Kern), *Night and Day* (Cole Porter), *Deep in My Heart* (Sigmund Romberg), *Three Little Words* (Bert Kalmar and Harry Ruby) and *Words and Music* (Rodgers and Hart). An oddity of these films is the scant attention paid to their Hollywood activities. An exception is *The Best Things in Life Are Free*, directed by the veteran Michael Curtiz for 20th Century-Fox in 1956. This account of the careers of Buddy De Sylva (Gordon MacRae), Lew Brown (Ernest Borgnine) and Ray Henderson (Dan Dailey) presents a dozen of their best songs, and accurately places the trio as successful Broadway songwriters of the late 1920s. But it fictionalizes the manner in which their partnership came into being.

Here it seems song plugger Henderson stumbles across Brown and De Sylva as they are preparing a stage musical, with De Sylva talking a truculent Brown into admitting a new partner. Actually the three became a team in 1925 when they were contracted by George White to provide songs for his *Scandals* as successors to George Gershwin, who had backed away from the assignment. Thereafter, they provided songs for several editions of the *Scandals*, and for other producers wrote the scores for *Good News*, *Hold Everything*, *Follow Through*, and *Flying High*. If anything, they were even more successful than this film suggests.

Of interest to film buffs is the scene in which the songwriters get a call from Al Jolson in Hollywood, begging for a song needed immediately for his film *The Singing Fool*. Explaining that it must be a serenade to a little boy sitting on his knee, Jolson more or less dictates the line of the lyrics. De Sylva, Brown and Henderson consider the idea so corny that they sit down to deliberately write the most maudlin ballad they can compose, believing it will never be accepted. To their surprise, "Sonny Boy" becomes a smash hit. The film exaggerates the glee with which the writers tackle their "joke," but the account is a true one. Less true is the reluctance of Henderson and Brown to join De Sylva in his enthusiasm for writing songs for the movies. The team was hired to score one of the early Hollywood musicals, *Sunny Side Up*, for which they wrote the memorable title song, "I'm a Dreamer" and "If I Had a Talking Picture of You." This last song is shown as it is being filmed at Fox as a lavish production number, making for an interesting sequence. The premiere of *Sunny Side Up* at Grauman's Chinese Theatre is also re-created.

According to *The Best Things in Life are Free*, Buddy De Sylva became estranged from his partners because of his ambition to be a producer, which is true. But in the film he gives up the ambition and resumes working with them, which is false. After *Sunny Side Up* Henderson and Brown returned to New York and De Sylva stayed in Hollywood to follow a long and successful career producing films and as an executive in charge of production. The picture contains one very pertinent comment, as a dazed De Sylva complains to his studio boss, correctly identified as Winfield Sheehan (Larry Keating) at a big party, "All we do at these things is talk business. Couldn't we have a little fun?" To which Sheehan unhesitatingly replies. "In Hollywood that's what parties are for—to talk business."

Variety Girl (1947): Dorothy Lamour, John Lund, William Holden, Veronica Lake, Alan Ladd, Macdonald Carey and Diana Lynn obliging the fans.

Variety Girl: Olga San Juan trying to make an impression on director Mitchell Leisen and writer Frank Butler in the Vine St. Brown Derby.

Variety Girl: Olga San Juan and the grapefruit-in-the-face bit screen test with William Bendix.

The Best Things in Life are Free (1956): Gordon MacRae, Ernest Borgnine and Dan Dailey.

You're My Everything, made by 20th Century-Fox in 1949, was a hark-back to the early musicals with a "Broadway to Hollywood" concept, and dealt with the late Twenties and the Thirties in the film business. This is a picture fairly reeking with Fox expertise, using a backlog of famous songs from previous Fox (and other) musicals, and employing such past masters as Alfred Newman as music director, Walter Lang as director and Nick Castle as choreographer. The original story by George Jessel is about a vaudeville entertainer (Dan Dailey) who marries a wealthy girl (Anne Baxter) and takes her to Hollywood when he gets the call. But Dailey can't make the grade in silent pictures, and it's his wife who becomes a star. With the coming of sound their situation reverses—he shoots to popularity and her career subsides. When the cycle of musical pictures phases out, Dailey's career plummets and the couple decides to retire altogether. However, they have a talented daughter (Shari Robinson) and her parents split when they disagree on whether or not she should be in the movies. Baxter is against it, but when Shari is a smash hit she changes her mind and the couple resumes the happy marriage.

Dan Dailey was in fine fettle during this period in his career, and here he cavorts in some splendid song-and-dance routines like "The Varsity Drag" and "California, Here I Come." Anne Baxter also revealed ability as a dancer, and in one sequence she

302

Variety Girl: The entire cast on stage — a grand melange.

303

You're My Everything (1949): Anne Baxter, Alan Mowbray and Dan Dailey.

You're My Everything: Dan Dailey and Shari Robinson reprising an old Shirley Temple specialty — "On The Good Ship Lollypop."

You're My Everything: Anne Baxter as a composite "It Girl," "Dancing Daughter," "Modern Maiden" and "Baby Vamp."

304

does a Charleston on a tabletop in the fashion of Joan Crawford in *Our Dancing Daughters*, although the star Baxter is gently lampooning in her characterization as a silent picture luminary, who is clearly Clara Bow. *You're My Everything* includes some amusing bits about the making of silent movies, with Buster Keaton doing a cameo, and Shari Robinson and blackfaced Dailey performing the famous Shirley Temple routine "On the Good Ship Lollypop."

Also in 1949 at Fox, a picture supposedly based on the 1931 Broadway musical *The Band Wagon* was filmed as *Dancing in the Dark*. Since the Broadway show was a revue without a story, the only material retained was four songs from the original score by Arthur Schwartz and Howard Dietz. Much of the production is set inside the actual Fox studio, including a reproduction of Darryl F. Zanuck's office and a portrayal of a dapper, forceful, obviously Zanuck-inspired producer by Adolphe Menjou. The central character is a faded, impoverished movie star, Emory Slade (William Powell), whose plight brings no pity from the film community because in his days of affluence he behaved in an arrogant and selfish manner. However, Slade becomes useful to the studio when they realize that he is the only person likely to persuade Broadway star Rosalie Brooks (Randy Stuart) to overcome her dislike of Hollywood and appear in their filming of "The Band Wagon." Instead, the cavalier and frequently drunk Slade takes it upon himself to promote an unknown hopeful (Betsy Drake), and after a variety of misadventures manages to get her the job. In this scheme he is greatly aided by a studio press agent (Mark Stevens), who falls in love with the girl.

Dancing in the Dark is one of the better entries in this genre and quite trenchant in its comments on various Hollywood types, with a witty and knowing performance by Powell. Sid Grauman appears in a sequence shot at his Chinese Theatre and Mike Romanoff is seen presiding over his once-popular restaurant. Although not a remake of Fox's 1940 *Stardust*, there were certain parallels.

Warners, ever an economy-minded studio whose stars always complained they were treated like clock-in workers, made a considerable number of movies about movies. Perhaps they were less costly than the creations of other environments. *It's a Great Feeling*, in 1949, was among the last of this kind, and a few years later it would have been impossible to make because so many of the Warner stars had been "let go." Warners tightened their belts with the coming of television, sold their pre-1949 product to the enemy (thereby creating their own stiffest

Dancing in the Dark (1949): Adolphe Menjou, Mark Stevens, William Powell and Don Beddoe.

Dancing in the Dark: William Powell and Mark Stevens.

305

It's a Great Feeling (1949): Music Director Ray Heindorf, Doris Day, Jack Carson and Dennis Morgan.

It's a Great Feeling: Doris Day doing her "Mademoiselle Fifi" number on the set built for *Adventures of Don Juan*.

competition), and terminated the contracts of many famous faces long identified as Warner players. *It's a Great Feeling* is not a great picture, but it does afford a good look at the studio near the end of the halcyon period, including an opening aerial shot of the huge lot and many scenes played in its streets, dressing rooms and offices. Dennis Morgan and Jack Carson appear as themselves and carry the story—a very slight and incredible one concocted by Jack Rose and Melville Shavelson from a plot by I. A. L. Diamond.

It's a Great Feeling has Carson as a star so poorly thought of on the Warners lot that no one wants to work with him. He finds he has to direct his next picture himself when King Vidor, Raoul Walsh, Michael Curtiz and David Butler are shown adamantly refusing to direct any film with the hammy, cocky and thick-headed Carson. However, it was Butler who directed *this* picture and it is interesting to see Vidor, Walsh and Curtiz no matter how fleetingly. But with Jack Carson set to direct his own movie, his friend Morgan backs away from the project and no actress will agree to play in it. Jane Wyman faints at the suggestion. Carson, apparently broke and desperate for work, hires studio waitress—and movie hopeful—Judy Adams (Doris Day) to pose as his pregnant wife and win the sympathy of Morgan, causing him to sign the contract. Afterwards, Morgan asks Carson what he promised Judy to pull the trick and learns, "A part in the picture—the usual malarkey." But Judy is not a girl to be put off, and the two actors are shamed into giving her the part. When she says that success will make her "the happiest girl in Hollywood," Carson dryly remarks, "Nobody's happy in Hollywood."

The Carson movie, to be called "Mademoiselle Fifi," never gets made because Judy tires of all the malarkey involved in Carson's attempts at picture-making. When he makes a test of her, he operates the camera himself because he can't wait for the cameraman (a union impossibility), and mixes up the tracks in the dubbing session so that Morgan sings with Judy's voice and vice versa. At the recording session Ray Heindorf, then music director at the studio, takes pity on Carson and agrees to record the songs. Morgan asks Carson, "How can she sing a song she's never seen before?" and gets this explanation from the harried director: "I don't ask questions about *your* pictures." Finally, with every Carson ploy a failure, disgusted-with-Hollywood Judy takes a train back to her little home town of Gerky's Corners, Wisconsin, and marries her old boy friend, Jeffrey Bushdinkel, who looks exactly like Errol Flynn—and is.

The plot of *It's a Great Feeling* does not bear analysis, but the nonsense is pleasant, and much helped by half a dozen Jule Styne-Sammy Cahn songs. Gary Cooper, Ronald Reagan, Danny Kaye, Eleanor Parker and Patricia Neal appear briefly with a line or two, but some of the other stars had better bits: Joan Crawford, overhearing Carson and Morgan speaking in what she thinks is a disrespectful way about a lady, slaps their faces and berates them. They ask why and she blithely replies, "Oh, I do that in all my pictures"; Doris Day, as waitress Judy, bumps into Sydney Greenstreet and explains she's running to Jack Carson's dressing room. He chortles, "That's a switch, they're usually running *from* it"; Edward G. Robinson, doing his tough-guy routine to impress Judy, explains to a studio guard afterwards that he has to keep up his image. But the best line is that of a publicity boss, who has to invent a background for the French star Carson is importing for his picture, Yvonne Amour (Doris Day in a black wig and appearing at a welcoming party held on the sound stage containing the massive staircase built for Errol Flynn's recently-completed *Adventures of Don Juan*). Knowing nothing about her, he immediately dreams up an exotic birthplace, with father a colonel in the Foreign Legion and mother a White Russian exile. Then returning to his aides, the publicity wizard says, "So much for the facts. The rest you can make up."

In 1951 Warners produced *Starlift*, a guest-star-studded package along the lines of the wartime efforts, but rather devoid of the former spirit. It saluted the industry's entertainment of servicemen at Travis Air Force Base in Northern California, but by the time the picture came out, the enterprise had collapsed for lack of funds from Hollywood. *Time* rapped Warners for making it look as if it was the only studio involved, and pointed out that some of the stars in *Starlift* had never actually made the journey to Travis.

The thin plot is about an airman who falls in love with a movie actress, an item that is picked up and publicized by Louella Parsons, bringing attention to the need of Korea-bound soldiers and airmen for entertainment at Travis. Soon such Warner stars as Doris Day, Ruth Roman, Gordon MacRae, Virginia Mayo, Jane Wyman and Randolph Scott transport themselves to Travis to perform in a variety of songs and skits. Gary Cooper, looking understandably ill-at-ease, joins Phil Harris and Frank Lovejoy in croaking his way through a song called "Look Out, Stranger, I'm a Texas Ranger."

The one memorable moment in the ill-timed *Star-*

Starlift (1951): James Cagney, Dick Wesson, Ron Hagerthy, Doris Day and Ruth Roman.

lift is a fleeting one in which James Cagney, to please an airman admirer, does a little imitation of himself and explains some of his famous gestures. If *Starlift* has any distinction, it is only that it was the last of Hollywood's studio all-star musical packages.

In 1952 Columbia produced a movie musical set in its studio—*Rainbow 'Round My Shoulder*, starring Frankie Laine and Billy Daniels as themselves, and Charlotte Austin as a Pasadena socialite with movie aspirations who takes a job as a messenger girl at Columbia. Through a misunderstanding, she gets to audition a song for Frankie Laine's new picture and so impresses the director (Arthur Franz) that he gives her the lead. But Charlotte's stuffy family are dead set against her being involved in the entertainment business, and since she is underage, they manage to sever her contract. At this, Frankie Laine, Billy Daniels and lots of other Columbia talents decide to appear at a charity benefit sponsored by Charlotte's family and turn it into such a success that the family backs down and consents to Charlotte's becoming a star. *Rainbow 'Round My Shoulder* merits little attention except for the opportunities it gives to view the Columbia lot, now just another Hollywood memory. In 1972 Columbia evacuated their premises on Gower Street and moved to Burbank to share the Warner Bros. lot, now known as the Burbank Studios.

Good Times (1967) is a movie about a movie that is

Rainbow 'Round My Shoulder (1952): Arthur Franz, Charlotte Austin and Frankie Laine.

Good Times (1967): Sonny and Cher Bono.

never made, incorporating fantasy episodes of a few that might have been. The plot line holding the episodes together concerns the efforts of a powerful film tycoon (George Sanders) to cash in on the fame of Sonny and Cher with a hoary rags-to-riches potboiler movie. Sonny, who seeks a measure of creative control and is almost as anxious to avoid selling out as Cher, has ten days to come up with something better. The major fantasy episodes deal with "The Saga of Irving Ringo" (Sheriff of Broken Elbow, Nebraska), "Johnny Pizzicato—Private Eye" and "Jungle Morry—King of the Jungle." The latter, a spoof on the old MGM Tarzan films with Johnny Weissmuller and Maureen O'Sullivan, features Zora, Morry's mate (Cher), his faithful companion Pizza the chimp and "Boy," who is a small, bald-headed man. They call "Jungle Delight" for dinner in their tree house with the elephant-operated lift, and try to stop the safari led by no-good George Sanders from stealing ivory from the legendary elephants' graveyard, but when Morry calls the animals to help, they ignore him.

The as-yet unchallenged high-water mark in musicals with a Hollywood setting is *Singin' in the Rain*, produced by Arthur Freed for MGM in 1952 and directed by Gene Kelly and Stanley Donen. Many regard this as the best of all Hollywood musicals, and it certainly is the most enjoyable spoof on the industry at the transition from the silent to the sound era. This delightful picture lovingly pokes fun at the ridiculousness of certain kinds of film people and the problems that plagued the business when it made The Big Change. It is in fact a perfect musical comedy, its songs and dances easily flowing in and out of its situations.

Singin' in the Rain is also a fairly accurate account of this period in movie history. Says Gene Kelly: "All of us involved in making the picture went around the studio talking to the veterans of the various departments to get their recollections. We gathered far more material than we were able to use, but what we did use was based on actual happenings. We spent a lot of time with the sound people talking about the problems of recording in those days, when they had to hide microphones all over the set to pick up the actors. This used to drive the directors crazy. From what I understand, it was Lionel Barrymore who brought about the idea of the mike boom. He refused to work with the stationary and hidden mikes, and told a sound man, 'Put it on a fishpole and let it follow the actor.' We also collected a lot of old equipment and trappings, and to show you how far we went with our authenticity, the costume I

Singin' in the Rain (1952): On the set with Gene Kelly, Donald O'Connor, Louis B. Mayer and Arthur Freed.

Singin' in the Rain: Donald O'Connor, Madge Blake, Gene Kelly and Jean Hagen.

Singin' in the Rain: Donald O'Connor, Gene Kelly, Douglas Fowley and Bill Lewin.

309

Singin' in the Rain: Filming "The Dueling Cavalier," with Gene Kelly and Jean Hagen in costume, Donald O'Connor at the piano and Douglas Fowley in the director's chair.

wear in 'The Dueling Cavalier' sequence is the one worn by Rudolph Valentino in *Monsieur Beaucaire*."

The film came into being through Arthur Freed's wish to make a musical that would use the best of the songs he had written with Nacio Herb Brown. Since 1939, Freed had been Metro's foremost producer of musicals, and his success in this field had somewhat eclipsed his distinction as a lyricist and the fact that he and Brown had been responsible for supplying the songs for the earliest movie musicals. Freed contacted writers Adolph Green and Betty Comden, whom he had used before on *Good News*, *The Barkleys of Broadway* and *On the Town*, and asked them to come up with a concept, telling them only that the film would be titled *Singin' in the Rain*. First there were discussions about remaking an early MGM picture—Jean Harlow's *Bombshell* (1933) being a particularly strong possibility after many of the older films were screened. This plan was abandoned in favor of an original. Comden and Green, along with actress Judy Holliday, had for some years written, produced and performed an act called "The Revuers," and among their material were skits about the early days of sound movies. Green played the actor confused by microphone placements and Holliday did the actress with the high, whining nasal voice, which she later used to

great advantage in *Born Yesterday*. Adolph Green is well known among his friends as a film buff with seemingly limitless knowledge. As Comden and Green recall:

Many of these songs had been written by Freed and Brown for the earliest musical pictures made, between 1929 and 1931, during the painful transition from silence to sound, and it occurred to us that, rather than try to use them in a sophisticated, contemporary story, or a gay-nineties extravaganza, they would bloom at their happiest in something that took place in the very period in which they had been written. . . . Our thoughts kept coming back to the dramatic upheavals of that period, when great careers were wrecked because the public's image of a favorite would be instantly destroyed by a voice that did not match the fabled face. We remembered particularly the downfall of John Gilbert, the reigning king of the silent screen in 1928, whose career was finished off by one talking picture, in which, with his director's encouragement, he improvised his own love scene, consisting of the phrase "I love you" repeated many times with growing intensity, exactly as he had done it the year before in front of the silent camera. The audience roared with laughter. We decided our leading character should be just such a star. The trick of course, was to make the stuff of tragedy like this fit into a lighthearted satirical comedy that featured . . . Freed-Brown songs along the way. . . .

Freed supplied Kelly, Donen, Comden and Green with his backlog of songs and allowed them complete

310

Singin' in the Rain: Millard Mitchell, Debbie Reynolds, Gene Kelly and Donald O'Connor.

Singin' in the Rain: Donald O'Connor, Bobby Watson and Gene Kelly.

Singin' in the Rain: Kathleen Freeman, Jean Hagen, Gene Kelly, Douglas Fowley and the microphone hidden in the bushes.

311

312

freedom of choice. Freed's only stipulation was that he didn't want to have to write anything new, but when it came to a knockabout song-and-dance solo for Donald O'Connor, it was found that none of the old material was quite suitable. Freed and Brown thereupon wrote "Make 'em Laugh," which is reminiscent of Cole Porter's "Be a Clown" from Freed's production of *The Pirate*. When Comden and Green pointed out that they needed a song for the spoof on diction coaches and elocution lessons Freed told them to write their own lyrics and have Roger Edens supply the melody. The late Edens, who was Freed's right-hand man, could turn his talents to any kind of musical activity. The other songs, and their sources, used in *Singin' in the Rain* are these:

"Broadway Melody," "The Wedding of the Painted Doll," and "You Were Meant for Me," from *The Broadway Melody* (1929).

"Singin' in the Rain," from *Hollywood Revue of 1929*.

"Should I?" from *Lord Byron of Broadway* (1929).

"Fit as a Fiddle," from the stage revue *George White's Music Hall Varieties* (1932).

"Beautiful Girl" and "Temptation," from *Going Hollywood* (1933).

"All I Do Is Dream of You," from *Sadie McKee* (1934).

"I've Got a Feelin' You're Foolin'," "You Are My Lucky Star," and "Broadway Rhythm," from *The Broadway Melody of 1936*.

"Would You" from *San Francisco* (1936).

"Good Morning," from the film version of *Babes in Arms* (1939).

All these songs were written by Freed and Brown, with the exception of "Fit as a Fiddle," which Freed wrote with Al Hoffman and Al Goodhart.

Singin' in the Rain begins with a premiere at Grauman's Chinese Theatre, where there are crowds of fans and the customary hoopla. A jovial, rotund lady commentator (Madge Blake), obviously a take-off on Louella Parsons, broadcasts: "What a night, ladies and gentlemen—what a night! Every star in Hollywood's heaven is here to make Monumental Pictures' premiere of 'The Royal Rascal' the outstanding event of 1927 . . ." Then the stars arrive—Don Lockwood (Kelly) and Lina Lamont (Jean Hagen)—and the commentator invites Don to say a few words to his audience. He says more than a few, giving a capsule account of his rise to fame, with his claims totally at variance with the illustrated facts. He and Lina have co-starred in several pictures and the fan magazines assume them to be romantically attached, an assumption shared by Lina, who is neither very bright nor very talented. The shrewd Don deftly sidesteps the issue. When he later meets movie hopeful Kathy Selden

Singin' in the Rain: Carl Milletaire, Jean Hagen and Gene Kelly.

Singin' in the Rain: Donald O'Connor, Debbie Reynolds and Gene Kelly.

(Debbie Reynolds), he falls in love with her and after a few misunderstandings the feeling is mutual.

At a party at the home of Monumental's boss, B. F. Simpson (Millard Mitchell), a demonstration of a talking picture is presented. On the screen flashes a crudely made piece of film in which a nervous, pinched-faced gentleman (Julius Tannen) over-articulates: "Notice—it is a picture of me—and I am talking! Note how my lips and the sound issuing from them are synchronized together in perfect unison . . ." After the demonstration the guests make inane remarks about its novelty and Simpson doubts whether the method will ever be used. "Warner Brothers are making a whole talking picture with this gadget—*The Jazz Singer*. They'll lose their shirts . . ." Much of the humor in *Singin' in the Rain* arises from Simpson having to eat his words and the attempts by his studio to crack the sound barrier.

During the course of production on the new Lock-wood-Lamont movie, "The Dueling Cavalier," the great success of *The Jazz Singer* forces Simpson to halt production and re-shoot with sound, which is disastrous, because Lina's voice is thin and ugly and she cannot read lines. Diction coach Phoebe Dinsmore (Kathleen Freeman) tries hard to give her elocution lessons, but the results make the poor actress appear even more ludicrous. Her director, Roscoe Dexter (Douglas Fowley), is driven almost insane trying to cope with the new manner of filming and the problems of dealing with Lina. At the premiere of "The Dueling Cavalier," the audience is convulsed with laughter at the errors in sound synchronization, Lina's vocal quality, the hideously loud pick-up of extraneous noises and Lockwood's repetitive "I love you" dialogue. With suggestions coming from Kathy and Lockwood's pal Cosmo (Donald O'Connor) Simpson decides to turn the picture into a musical, "The Dancing Cavalier," with Kathy dubbing the songs and dialogue for

Lina. (Lina is referred to as "a triple threat: can't sing, can't dance, can't act.")

At the premiere of the new version, the dim-witted Lina can't ignore the pleas of the audience to encore some of her songs in person, and Kathy is quickly brought in to stand behind a curtain and sing while Lina mouths the words. This gives Lockwood the chance to reveal Kathy as the entertainer she deserves to be—and the opportunity to become his co-star as well as his wife. He pulls up the curtain and the audience sees the real singer.

Singin' in the Rain runs a smooth, delightful 103 minutes. So concisely written was the Comden-Green script that little needed to be deleted after filming and editing, but for reasons of timing it was decided to drop Kelly's reprise of "All I Do Is Dream of You" and to cut some of the choruses of "You Are My Lucky Star." A little swordplay footage from MGM's *The Three Musketeers* with Kelly was spliced into "The Dueling Cavalier" sequence.

The longest number in the picture, the elaborate "Broadway Ballet," depicting the rise to fame of a song-and-dance man, was filmed after the rest of the picture, by which time Donald O'Connor had to meet a television commitment and could not be involved. Kelly decided to use Cyd Charisse for the ballet portions because they were beyond Debbie Reynolds' ability. And Kelly dubbed Reynolds' tap dancing for the "Good Morning" number. Some of Debbie Reynolds' singing and dialogue dubbing for Jean Hagen's character was later in actuality dubbed by singer Betty Royce and Jean Hagen, thereby compounding the dubbing.

Says Kelly, "Almost everything in *Singin' in the Rain* springs from the truth. It's a conglomeration of bits of movie lore. Douglas Fowley's director is a little bit of Busby Berkeley, and Millard Mitchell's producer has a touch of Arthur Freed in him, and Jean Hagen's marvelous Lina was an amalgam of every poor woman who couldn't make it with the coming of sound."

Star Without Life, a minor French film made four years before *Singin' in the Rain*, dealt in a heavy, melodramatic way with a similar situation during the advent of talking pictures. A star (Mila Parely) is threatened with obscurity because of her voice quality. Her lover (Marcel Herrand), gets a hotel maid (Edith Piaf) to do her singing in a film. When the secret is discovered, the actress commits suicide.

CHAPTER ELEVEN

BIG KNIVES

Those movies which have dealt with the manipulation of power in Hollywood and with the ruthlessness of ambition are the *films noir* of this genre. None of them is flattering, although they range from fascinating (*The Bad and the Beautiful*) to spurious (*The Oscar*) according to quality of concept and production. Typical of this dark group is *The Big Knife*, produced and directed by Robert Aldrich in 1955 as an independent production, with a screenplay by James Poe based on Clifford Odets' Broadway play of 1949. The play, superficially a conflict between a movie star and a movie mogul, but more importantly the conflict between affluence and ideals, ran for a modest one hundred and eight performances with John Garfield and J. Edward Bromberg in the leads.

Clifford Odets had spent some time in Hollywood, writing the scripts for such films as *The General Died at Dawn* (1936), *Golden Boy* (1939), and *Humoresque* (1947). He apparently worked up a considerable dislike for the place. *The Big Knife* is his railing against Hollywood's vulgarity and materialism, its temptations for the flesh and the soul, and its population of pampered stars and powerful bosses. Quite Faustian in tone, dealing with a star who has sold himself to success and now wants to extricate himself, Odets' play was trounced

by the critics as being unbalanced and much too vitriolic to make sense. The film, shot in fifteen days on a budget of less than half a million dollars and mostly on one set, is a literal transcription of the play, and the same criticism applies.

According to Odets, it is veritably impossible for a sensitive artist to come to terms with the powerful businessmen of the film industry. Certainly there is evidence to support this view, but there is also plenty of other evidence that good actors and writers have settled down to success and an affluent life in Hollywood without debasing themselves. Odets claims that *The Big Knife* is an indictment of ruthlessness and evil, but most critics feel that he ruined his case by overstating his points. Some have said that the play's bitterness is far too personal, and in writing a play about the burdens of wealth and success Odets could hardly hope to touch a vast audience. The average ticket buyer probably wondered, "What's all the fuss about a guy who's unhappy because he's making millions, living high, and loved by his attractive wife and the public?"

The central character of *The Big Knife* is Charlie Castle (Jack Palance), who is considered by his studio to be such a valuable property that they want to renew his contract for another seven years. Castle doesn't want the contract, or even to continue with

317

The Bad and the Beautiful: Kirk Douglas and Barry Sullivan ransacking the MGM back lot.

The Big Knife (1955): Ida Lupino and Jack Palance.

his screen career. He is a tortured man: "Look at me! Can you face it? Look at this dripping fat of the land. Could you ever know that all my life I yearned for a world and people to call out the best in me? How can life be so empty? But it can't be! It can't! It's proven—statistics and graphs prove it—we are the world's happiest, earth's best . . ." And so on—and on.

Impinging upon Castle are his long-suffering, loving wife, Marian (Ida Lupino), his kindly but spiritually broken agent, Nat Danziger (Everett Sloane), an arrogant columnist, Patty Benedict (Ilka Chase), who considers it her right to walk into his home and demand all the facts about his existence, a sad-sack starlet, Dixie Evans (Shelley Winters), and, most of all, Stanley Hoff (Rod Steiger), the head of "Hoff-Federated Pictures." With Hoff at all times is his efficient lieutenant, Smiley Coy (Wendell Corey).

Charlie hates what he has become—a bored, superficial player of meaningless parts—but there is no escape for him because Hoff won't let him go. The situation is more complex than it seems. Hoff has a blackmail hold on Castle, who years previously killed a child in a drunken driving accident, which was hushed up and paid off by the studio. When Castle makes known his refusal to sign the contract, Hoff and Coy arrive to bring pressure to bear. Coy reminds him, "Just keep in mind that the day you first scheme . . . you marry the scheme and the scheme's children." After much discussion the cool, quiet, humorless Hoff loses his temper and screams at Castle, "Who are you? Snotty aristocracy because the female admissions wanna sleep with you? Who are you? You, with your dirty, unmanicured fingernails? What are you without Hoff-Federated behind you? I built that studio with my brains and hands—I ripped it out of the world!"

Adding to Castle's grief is a writer (Wesley Addy), who is in love with Marian and trying to persuade her to leave Castle. The writer has known him for many years and points out to Castle that he is not the man he used to be—an idealist interested in classical literature and in performing Shakespeare and other fine dramatists on the stage. "No, you're not! You've sold out! You'll be here for another fourteen years. Stop torturing yourself, Charlie—don't resist! Your wild, native idealism is a fatal flaw in the context of your life out here. Half-idealism is the peritonitis of the soul—America is full of it! Give up and really march to Hoff's bugle call. Forget what you used to be! That's the only way you'll find a reasonable happiness and pass it on to your wife. No half-man ever made a woman happy!"

318

The Big Knife: Rod Steiger, Jack Palance, Wendell Corey and Everett Sloane.

The Big Knife: Ida Lupino, Paul Langton, Ilka Chase and Jack Palance.

The Big Knife: Everett Sloane and Jack Palance.

Trapped by Hoff and surrounded by confusion, weakness, and cruelty, Castle decides on death. He quietly excuses himself and proceeds upstairs, where, unseen by the audience, he cuts his wrists and immerses himself in a hot bath, thereby scoring a victory over the vicious Hoff. *The Big Knife* ends with his distraught wife crying the word "Help!" over and over.

The film is well staged and well acted, but its appeal is minimal because of the oppressive dramatics. What defeats the picture more than anything else is the casting of Jack Palance as Charlie Castle. This fine, intense actor is simply unbelievable as a major-league movie star—the kind a studio would go to great lengths to retain, such as a Gable, a Cooper or a Cagney. On the other hand, the performance of Rod Steiger as Hoff was so painfully acute that it angered most of Hollywood's tycoons—particularly Harry Cohn, the tough, crude head of Columbia, and MGM's Louis B. Mayer, who allegedly cried when he saw the film, feeling that Odets had singled him out for vilification. It was generally thought in Hollywood that the weeping, pleading side of the Hoff characterization was based on Mayer and the furious, raging aspect on Cohn.

The Big Knife was not a commercial success. It was widely viewed and discussed in Hollywood but even within the community it was considered a conspicuously black account. Producer-director Robert Aldrich maintains that the film is honest, but feels he failed in communicating the essential predicament—a man trapped by affluence and a sense of compromised integrity. Says Aldrich: "It is a portrait of a man—an actor—who is not strong enough to live with himself and resolve his doubts. He is a confused idealist. I think the point of the story, as Odets expressed it, is that 'half-idealism is the peritonitis of the soul.' But the mass audience couldn't identify with this man. To them it was an alien situation, and I don't know that this dilemma could have been resolved anyhow. Had we been able to use John Garfield in the lead, we might have partially overcome the public's not being able to identify with Charlie Castle, but my father spelled out what most people thought when he said, 'If a guy has to take or not take $5,000 per week, what the hell is the problem?' Our problem was that that was not the real point of the story. It was a question of internal integrity such as anyone might have. I thought Jack Palance had—and has—the kind of intensity and burning integrity the part required. To say that it never occurred to me the public wouldn't accept him as a movie star is hindsight."

Rod Steiger played another movie tycoon in *The Movie Maker*, a Universal picture produced for television in 1967. This time his characterization was less vicious but not much happier. His Mike Kirsch starts out as the owner of a nickelodeon who goes to Hollywood with the ambition of being a producer. He gets himself a job in the publicity department of "Globe Pictures" and seizes upon the opportunity of turning a lackluster picture into a hit by drastically editing it—changing its melodramatics into comedy (as in *Stand-In*). Kirsch does so well that it starts him off on the way to becoming the head of the studio. Concerned only with success, the compulsive, intense and seemingly humorless Kirsch has less and less to do with his family and retreats into the small world of his office, where he finally loses touch with public taste. The studio begins to sink and the financial backers appoint Kirsch's faithful young lieutenant (Robert Culp) as the new head of the studio. Alienated from his wife (Anna Lee) and his daughter (Sally Kellerman), the deposed Kirsch sits in a projection room and, with tears in his eyes, watches again the film he edited years before.

Rod Serling collaborated on the script of this picture, and once again the public could hardly be blamed for inferring that this was yet another knock at poor Louis B. Mayer, who by now had been dead ten years. Certainly they could not be blamed for thinking that gaining command of a film studio was tantamount to courting misery.

Other than in *The Bad and the Beautiful* the producer is the one Hollywood figure rarely explored to any degree except as a cliché supporting character played by the likes of suave, sophisticated Adolphe Menjou, sturdy, father-like Charles Bickford, absurd, foreign-accented Gregory Ratoff or crude, ruthless Rod Steiger.* His exact functions misunderstood or not understood at all by most people (including those in the business), the producer will finally emerge as the leading character in the forthcoming production of F. Scott Fitzgerald's unfinished Hollywood novel, *The Last Tycoon*. Fitzgerald's protagonist, Monroe Stahr, is based to a degree on an idealized Irving Thalberg, for whom Fitzgerald had worked at MGM in the 1930s, and there is a considerable amount of Fitzgerald himself—romanticized and otherwise—imbued in the complex man. Perhaps there is also a touch of Budd Schulberg's father, who was the West Coast head of

* Richard Basehart played the leading role of a producer in the 1956 British-made *The Intimate Stranger*—called *Finger of Guilt* in the U.S.—a modest but unusual production with the British film industry as a backdrop.

The Movie Maker (1967): Sally Kellerman and Rod Steiger.

production at Paramount for several years. Young Schulberg spent considerable time with Fitzgerald in his last few years, and the older novelist encouraged Schulberg to tell him Hollywood stories. Schulberg had grown up in the film capital and gladly regaled Fitzgerald with anecdote after anecdote—many of which later turned up as part of the fabric of *The Last Tycoon*. Even the book's narrator, a second-generation daughter of a producer, turned out to be a composite of Budd Schulberg and Fitzgerald's own daughter.

In the novel, Stahr is attracted to Kathleen by her resemblance to his dead wife, as Fitzgerald had been drawn to Sheilah Graham, the Hollywood columnist, an attractive woman who somewhat resembled his wife, Zelda. Sheilah Graham has said that all during their close relationship she could never tell Fitzgerald enough about Hollywood and, again, many of her recollections were woven into the text.

Fitzgerald failed as a Hollywood writer. His incapacity to function under Hollywood conditions drove him, finally, back to his serious fiction. In *The Last Tycoon*, he succeeded in identifying his own predicament with that of his hero, a brilliant producer, an old-fashioned American individualist, with ideals of artistic excellence. He has always been in the habit of doing everything for himself in his own way but is eventually to be destroyed by the crass, uncreative elements which are depicted as converting moving pictures into a big, mechanical industry that has no regard for persons or for quality.

Since *The Last Tycoon*'s posthumous publication in 1941, several announcements of forthcoming productions have been made periodically, with no follow-through, but apparently the Sam Spiegel–Elia Kazan version is to be a reality.

The Bad and the Beautiful (1952) is among the dozen most interesting films ever made about Hollywood, giving a wide impression of the workings of a studio and the power play behind the scenes. Its variety of characters includes producers, directors, writers and actors and, even allowing for the fact that its story is pure fiction, the film does convey a sense of industry and purpose. The principal character is a chillingly charming and compulsive producer called Jonathan Shields, who walks over everyone and uses everyone on his ruthless path to success. The character is a recognizable one to

The Bad and the Beautiful (1952): Dick Powell, Lana Turner, Barry Sullivan and Walter Pidgeon.

anyone in the picture business, and as played by Kirk Douglas, an actor with an authentic success drive, Shields is a compelling and engrossing figure.

The film has a *Citizen Kane*-like structure and comes closer than any other to explaining the mysteries of movie megalomania. Its credentials largely explain its quality—production by John Houseman (who was an associate of Orson Welles and had worked on the scripting of *Citizen Kane*), direction by Vincente Minnelli, a literate screenplay by Charles Schnee (based on two short stories by George Bradshaw, "Memorial to a Bad Man" and "Of Good and Evil"), photography by Robert Surtees, skillful art direction by Cedric Gibbons and Edward Carfagno, and a superb musical score by David Raksin.

At the start of the picture a veteran producer and associate of Jonathan Shields, Harry Pebbel (Walter Pidgeon), calls three very successful people to his office—actress Georgia Lorrison (Lana Turner), director Fred Amiel (Barry Sullivan) and writer James Lee Bartlow (Dick Powell). All three owe their success in films to Shields, but none of them is interested in Pebbel's plea to come to the aid of Shields

now that he needs help in re-establishing his collapsed career. In a series of flashbacks we learn why.

The talented Shields is not a popular man and his film pioneer father was even less popular. After the funeral of his father, Shields is seen handing out money to the mourners, all of whom are extras he hired for the occasion. He admits that his father was a despicable man ("He wasn't a heel—he was *the* heel"), and yet he loved him, and vindicating the collapse of his father's business seems to be a compelling force in his own drive to scale the Hollywood peaks.

He and fledgling Amiel go to work for experienced, level-headed executive producer Pebbel, and together they make a series of small pictures, including "B" horror items. It doesn't take them long to form their own studio. Amiel is an artistic and clever man, but it is Shields' astute drive and judgment as a producer that turns Amiel into a topflight director. Their association is friendly and fruitful until the day Shields agrees to another director taking over a film on which Amiel has already spent much time and effort, adapting and developing. Since it is a big

The Bad and the Beautiful: Gilbert Roland, Kirk Douglas, Paul Stewart, Vanessa Brown, Barry Sullivan and Peggy King.

picture he particularly wanted to direct, Amiel walks out on Shields, declaring their partnership ended. His leaving appears to make little impression on Shields, who cold-bloodedly believes in assigning the right director at the right time to the right picture, regardless of friendship or ethics. Amiel goes on to great success, independent of Shields.

Georgia Lorrison is a beautiful but depressed and alcoholic actress who spends her time in her dingy apartment, idolizing her late actor-father. The father was a John Barrymore type, and the recording of him declaiming Shakespeare was made by Louis Calhern. The role of Georgia vaguely suggests Barrymore's daughter, Diana. Knowing her to be an actress of potential star caliber, Shields visits her and taunts her into returning to her profession. He angers her by disparaging her father, describing him as a fine artist but a personal failure, and telling her that she is emulating his weaknesses, but not his style. His rough tactics work, and Georgia is soon putty in his hands—and a box-office champion for Shields' studio. She falls in love with him and assumes the love is returned. But he fails to appear at a party after the premiere of her first starring film, and when she afterwards rushes to his home to share with him her triumph, she finds him with a lovely young actress (Elaine Stewart). The deeply hurt and disillusioned Georgia leaves Shields and his studio, not to return to the bottle, however, but now strong enough to continue her ascent as a star.

The Bad and the Beautiful: Kirk Douglas.

The Bad and the Beautiful: Lana Turner and Kirk Douglas.

James Lee Bartlow is an affable college professor of medieval history who writes a best-selling novel, which Shields buys and plans to turn into a film. Bartlow is not particularly interested in moving to Hollywood, but Shields marks him as a man with a talent for screen writing, and Bartlow's young, social-climbing Southern belle of a wife, Rosemary (Gloria Grahame), persuades him to go. Bartlow is under contract to Shields and living in California in short order. He, too, is molded by Shields into becoming a Hollywood success, but at the price of losing his wife. Shields sees Rosemary as a time-wasting, interrupting force in Bartlow's productive life, and to get her out of his way while he and Bartlow go off to a cabin near Lake Arrowhead to work on the script, he arranges an affair for her with a dashing, hedonistic Latin actor, Victor "Gaucho" Ribera (Gilbert Roland). The film briefly shows Bartlow writing at Arrowhead while Shields edits his script. (Shades of the producer of *The Bad and the Beautiful*, John Houseman, going off with writer Herman Mankiewicz to a California guest ranch for three months in order to work without distractions on the screenplay of *Citizen Kane* for Orson Welles in 1940.)

Tragedy strikes when Rosemary and "Gaucho" are killed in a plane crash. In consoling Bartlow, Shields trips on his own words and it becomes obvious to Bartlow that Shields knew the couple was going away. The writer smashes a fist in Shields' face and another association ends.

The only partner who stays with Shields is his head of production, Pebbel, ever economy-minded and realistic, and something of a surrogate father. He advises and tries to contain the eager, ambitious Shields, but his counsel is seldom heeded. He finds himself standing by as Shields begins to make decisions that invite disaster. Shields argues with the quietly arrogant German, von Ellstein (Ivan Triesault), whose concept of direction differs widely from that of Shields. With much riding on the success of a huge costume epic, Shields takes over the direction himself after von Ellstein walks off the set. Months later, sitting in a projection room, Shields admits his mistake. The film has no dramatic pacing or style, and is a lavishly mounted but turgid bore. "I butchered it. Shelve the picture." The studio is forced to close.

Shields retreats to Europe. Time passes and Harry Pebbel calls Fred Amiel, Georgia Lorrison and James Lee Bartlow into his office to tell them Shields wants to return to Hollywood, and that he would like all of them to come in with him on the production of a film. Pebbel reacts to their refusals with reminders that it was through Shields and his belief in them that they achieved their success, and that they all owe him something. His reasoning fails to convince, but as they leave Pebbel's office Shields is on the line with Pebbel from Paris telling him the idea for his new film. In the outer office Georgia picks up an extension and listens in on the conversation as Amiel and Bartlow move in. *The Bad and the Beautiful* fades out with the implication that the crafty, magnetic Shields might, perhaps, possibly, get his old talent back.

One of the major assets of this film is the score by David Raksin, whose main theme is a long, flowing statement somewhat in the style of a siren song speaking for the lure of the picture business. Raksin agrees that this is one of the better films about Hollywood, but feels it is tinged with more than a little romantic nonsense. "It isn't that people in Hollywood wish to lie about themselves, but that they suspect the truth is not very glamorous. The truth is a strange apple, and it has little to do with whether it gives you a good picture, a good novel or a good poem. Talent is the point, not truth. The ability to tell the truth without talent means nothing. The things that really matter about Hollywood are those things few people would care about because they involve the drudgery of doing something decently or respectably. Hollywood prefers to think of its glamour and all kinds of jazzy things going on. Also, Hollywood is very cognizant of the world's notions of its myths."

The Bad and the Beautiful: Make-up man Del Armstrong, Lana Turner, hairdresser Helen King and Sammy White portraying an agent.

The Bad and the Beautiful: Kirk Douglas and Lana Turner.

The Bad and the Beautiful helps one to comprehend the Hollywood fever, and the nature of producers driven to assume great control; men who by their very nature must be opportunistic, complex and eccentric. The characterization of Jonathan Shields was thought by some to be inspired by David O. Selznick and to a minor degree by Val Lewton. Lewton is best remembered for a series of excellent low-budget horror pictures he produced at RKO in the forties, and one of the most amusing scenes in *The Bad and the Beautiful* is an early sequence in which Shields and Amiel look on doubtfully as a group of bored bit players clamber into tatty costumes to become cat men. Shields and Amiel decide instead to *suggest* horror by mood, reaction and what the imagination supplies. Lewton's first film was *Cat People* (1942), and this was his approach. But the parallel with Selznick (both David and his brother Myron) was much stronger. Lewis J. Selznick had been a Hollywood pioneer whose bankruptcy in 1923 went unaided—and, indeed, was thought to be brought on—by fellow leaders in the industry. His sad ending obviously affected his two sons. Myron became the toughest and most astute talent agent in Hollywood, and many feel that he tried to avenge his father by the ways in which he dealt with the studio heads. David reached early success as a producer—a producer who wanted to be

in command of every aspect of picture-making. David Selznick, a man of some humor, took no offense at *The Bad and the Beautiful*, telling one of this book's authors that it "relates to me only in insignificant details. I think some of my mannerisms were used, but I see no resemblance whatsoever in the story. I think what they did, out of the observations and memory of John Houseman (who had been my assistant at one time), was to use such things as my habit of taking off my shoes when I work, and my projection room behavior, and a few things that perhaps were remotely related to me. But there was nothing I could object to as regards my personal or professional life, since I saw nothing in the film that related to them."

In the view of Vincente Minnelli, *The Bad and the Beautiful* is a fair and accurate impression of Hollywood in the heyday of the big studios. "It was an industry that incurred great enmities and great friendships, and offered great rewards and great pitfalls. It was, and still is, a business that requires strength in order to survive and a driving desire to want to be in it. Jonathan Shields is a credible character. He's a composite—like a dozen photographs melded into one. When I first saw the script, it was called *Tribute to a Bad Man*, and MGM was surprised that I wanted to do it. But I didn't see it as the story of a heel. To me, Jonathan was a man of

The Bad and the Beautiful: Gilbert Roland and Lana Turner, and to the right, in the background, Kirk Douglas and Leo G. Carroll.

enormous charm and persuasiveness who used people to get what he wanted, which in this case was the best possible film, and although people may have suffered in the process, they also benefited from his use of their talent. There are producers in this business who are so devoted to their films they would push their own mothers aside if they got in the way. He was that kind. I always ask myself in tackling a script—is the story *possible*? *Could* it have happened? In the case of this film the answer is 'yes.' "

Ten years after *The Bad and the Beautiful*, many of the same talents made another picture about life in the film industry, *Two Weeks in Another Town*. Kirk Douglas, producer Houseman, director Minnelli, scenarist Schnee and composer Raksin regrouped to create this account of the activities of Hollywood people in Rome, the town of the title, but their efforts are less convincing than before and the tone is less sympathetic than *The Bad and the Beautiful*. Indeed, a major drawback of *Two Weeks in Another Town* is the lack of appeal of its major characters. Possibly it reflects the bitterness among Hollywood people in the early sixties, by which time it was apparent that the glory days were long gone. By 1962 a great many American film actors, directors, writers and technicians found it necessary to seek work in Europe, and Rome had come to be known as Hollywood-by-the-Tiber.

The Bad and the Beautiful: Dick Powell and and Kirk Douglas.

The Bad and the Beautiful: Barry Sullivan, Lana Turner and Dick Powell.

Two Weeks in Another Town (1962): Edward G. Robinson and Kirk Douglas.

Two Weeks in Another Town is not a sequel to *The Bad and the Beautiful*. Charles Schnee's screenplay is based on Irwin Shaw's novel about a once-popular movie star, Jack Andrus (Kirk Douglas), who has just emerged from three years in a sanitarium recovering from alcoholism, a nervous breakdown and a car crash, which left him with a thin scar across his face. An Academy Award winner, he is now just an actor trying to make a comeback. He goes to Rome, where the esteemed, but slipping, director Maurice Kruger (Edward G. Robinson) is making a film. Some of their best pictures had been made together in Hollywood, and now Kruger offers Andrus a small role. He finds Kruger in trouble with a leading lady, Barzelli (Rosanna Schiaffino), who barely speaks English, and a young leading man, Davie Drew (George Hamilton), who despises Kruger and refuses to take his work seriously. Kruger, a director famous for his "sound," persuades Andrus to take over the dubbing sessions on the disastrous film. The nervous Andrus is doubtful, but he meets a lovely Italian girl, Veronica (Dahlia Lavi), whose quiet charm Andrus finds helpful in this frenetic atmosphere. His ex-wife, Carlotta (Cyd Charisse), now turns up in Rome and irritates Andrus by trying to prove she still has a hold on him. She is a destructive, spoiled beauty who was largely responsible for his previous decline.

Two Weeks in Another Town: George Hamilton, Kirk Douglas, Joanna Rose and Moviola.

The dubbing sessions progress painfully, with Andrus struggling to get the best performances from the actors while trying not to return to drinking. At a party, Kruger's loud and vicious wife, Clara (Claire Trevor), accuses him of having an affair with his leading lady, and a few hours later the harried director is stricken with a heart attack. He begs Andrus to take over directing the picture. By reshooting previous scenes and cajoling good performances from his actors, Andrus manages to save what would surely have been a bad movie. But he finds no appreciation from the paranoid Kruger, who accuses Andrus of stealing his picture, a sentiment soundly seconded by Clara. However, having been able to pull the project together and having directed the picture has given Andrus a sense of security and the realization that he is now free of the likes of his ex-wife and of Kruger. He receives a call from his agent offering him another picture to direct, but Andrus decides to take things easy for a while, knowing that with the gentle Veronica by his side and the reclamation of his professional image his future is good.

Two Weeks in Another Town incorporates some footage from *The Bad and the Beautiful* as the actor and the director sit in a projection room and reflect on one of their past triumphs. It is a poignant touch, but it also serves to point up the painful fact that this film has little of the quality of the former one. Those involved in the production of *Two Weeks in Another Town* claim that it was robbed of much of its impact by brutal MGM editing at the command of a high-ranking executive. Says Kirk Douglas: "It seems this gentleman decided to supervise the editing himself, putting lines from one scene into another, trying to soften the picture and make it more marketable for the family trade. It just wasn't that kind of a story. Ironically, this same gentleman left the studio not long after. But by then it was too late to do anything about *Two Weeks in Another Town*."

Paramount's *The Carpetbaggers* is the story of a young business tycoon called Jonas Cord, Jr., who batters his way to wealth and power. Since the two industries in which he excels are aviation and motion pictures, it can hardly fail to invite comparison with the career of the eccentric, reclusive multimillionaire Howard Hughes. Hughes was twenty-five in 1930, when he completed *Hell's Angels*, one of the few major films about World War I aviation, and the picture that made a star of nineteen-year-old Jean Harlow. He went on to produce other films, notably *The Front Page* in 1931, *Scarface* in 1932, and *The Outlaw* eleven years

later. In 1948 he acquired the majority of shares of RKO studios. Hughes made no impact with his RKO productions, and by the mid-fifties he lost his interest in picture-making and turned his back on the industry.

Author Harold Robbins has become a millionaire by writing sensational chunks of fiction about power, affluence and sex in Western civilization, and the models for his *The Carpetbaggers* could hardly be more obvious, although denied. Prior to the release of the film, Hughes' chief attorney demanded a screening of the rough-cut, but concluded that there was no need to take action. In his opinion, the film was so wildly implausible that the best thing to do was to ignore it.

Joseph E. Levine's production, directed by Edward Dmytryk and scripted by John Michael Hayes, tells an unappealing tale of young Jonas (George Peppard), who hates his father (Leif Erickson), a cold, hard industrialist who has shown no love to his wife and son. Jonas inherits his father's chemical plant and resolves to conquer the world, which includes making love to his father's young, hedonistic wife, Rina (Carroll Baker). This wild widow becomes a movie star, Rina Marlowe, a high-living, champagne-guzzling sex symbol whose career is ended when she falls while swinging from a chandelier during a party. Robbins' character was clearly "inspired" by Jean Harlow, but it cannot be taken as an account of that much-maligned star's activities. Carroll Baker's performance did titillate the public sufficiently to move Levine to star her in his film about Harlow, but with lackluster results.

The ruthless, emotionally unstable Jonas Cord, tormented by memories of his thwarted childhood, moves from sundry industrial enterprises to Hollywood, where he gains control of a studio and makes successful pictures starring Rina Marlowe. Ever capricious and unpredictable, he also decides to make a star of a pretty, amiable call girl, Jennie Denton (Martha Hyer). The compliant Jennie is no problem to Jonas until the day her agent, Dan Pierce (Robert Cummings), is desperately in need of money and threatens to market a pornographic picture she had made years before unless he can be provided with a large sum of cash. Such people appear to be commonplace in the hectic life of Jonas, who has trouble maintaining relationships with women—including his gorgeous wife, Monica (Elizabeth Ashley).

One of the few admirable characters in *The Carpetbaggers* is Nevada Smith (Alan Ladd in his last picture, released a few months after his death in

(Opposite page)
The Carpetbaggers (1964): Carroll Baker and the chandelier escapade.

The Carpetbaggers: George Peppard and Martha Hyer.

The Carpetbaggers: Robert Cummings and Martha Hyer.

January of 1964). Smith is a soldier of fortune and something of a father figure to Jonas. He is a solid, no-nonsense fellow, a former Cord employee who drifts into Hollywood to find work as an extra and rises to become a cowboy star. Jonas makes a mess of his private and professional lives, and his wife and child leave him. Monica goes her own way and does well in business, but the humbled Jonas, in an unconvincing reformation of character, persuades her to return. This reformation is brought about by Smith, who visits the drinking Jonas to try to point out the errors of his way. The two men engage in a long and vicious fist-fight, thrashing each other to the point of exhaustion—and ending their long friendship. But the battle apparently brings Jonas to some sense of realization.

Levine's expensive, long (150 minutes), and florid epic pleased the customers but not the critics, who put it down as a lusty bit of vulgarity. As a depiction of Hollywood in the 1930s, *The Carpetbaggers* is garishly overblown, dwelling on the kind of sexy decadence found mostly in cheap novels. Any assumption that this film is an accurate description of how most producers, actors and agents conduct their business is an injustice. It certainly has little to do with Howard Hughes and Jean Harlow.

The trashiest of all movies about Hollywood is *The Oscar*, released by Paramount in 1966 and starring Stephen Boyd as an actor named Frank Fane. Since Fane is a vicious, heartless brute with no redeeming qualities whatsoever—and since there is no evidence given of his professional ability—the whole platform of the film is weak. It is unlikely that such a man could rise to stardom and become a contender for the Oscar, and producer Clarence Greene and director Russell Rouse, who collaborated with Harlan Ellison on the screenplay, further weakened their product by flooding it with clichés. Paramount advertised it as a picture about "The dreamers and the schemers, the hustlers and the hopefuls, the freeloaders and the phonies, the fakers and the famous . . ." With such a trite and implausible script it is incredible, and a sad comment on the spirit of Hollywood in 1966, that Greene and Rouse were able to interest a number of stars and respected character actors to do bits.

The picture opens at an Academy Awards presentation, with Fane one of the five nominees for Best Actor. He sits alone. His estranged wife, Kay (Elke Sommer), is seated on the other side of the hall with his friend Hymie (Tony Bennett). Bob Hope comes on stage as the Master of Ceremonies and gives forth with a patter that includes the line, "This is the night when war and politics are forgotten—and we find out who we really hate." Hymie looks across at Fane and his thoughts are given voice on the sound track, to the effect that Fane has come "a long way." The story is told in one long flashback, starting with Fane as a spieler in a bar for his strip-tease girl friend, Laurel (Jill St. John), and Hymie as their manager. They run afoul of the law in a small town and decide to head for New York, where Fane meets a fashion designer (Sommer) at a party. He woos her and gets a job with her company, and accompanies her one evening when she delivers costumes to a theatrical group. The confident, arrogant Fane jeers at the actors trying to perform a street fight with knives and jumps up to show them how it is really done. This impresses visiting Hollywood talent scout and drama coach Sophie Cantaro (Eleanor Parker), who senses he "has something." In Hollywood she persuades agent Kappy Kapstetter (Milton Berle) to handle him, saying "I haven't found anyone this exciting in years." Her professional judgment is a little biased, since she is also sleeping with him. Kenneth Regan (Joseph Cotten), the head of "Galaxy Pictures," feels that there is something about Fane that isn't quite right, but Sophie and Kappy prevail upon him to put him under contract. The cunning Fane now sends for Hymie and arranges a job at the studio for Kay, the fashion designer.

The rise of Frank Fane is swift. On the sound track narrator Hymie speaks of the narcotic of success. Fane uses everybody to his own advantage, and when he proposes to Kay she spurns him: "You represent everything I loathe," and she talks about the "rot" inside him. Despite these extreme views she later changes her mind and marries him, and on a trip to a Mexican border town they meet a couple, Barney and Trixie (Ernest Borgnine and Edie Adams), who are celebrating their divorce. He is a private eye and she a would-be actress, a sleazy pair soon to be of service to Fane. Studio head Regan's doubts about the actor are confirmed when box-office returns on his pictures and the comments of exhibitors prove him to have no popularity. This puzzles Fane, who feels he has just given a fine performance in a picture called "Breakthrough." Kappy now hits him with more unhappy news—Fane, through his high living, is broke and in debt. Cries Fane, "It's a nightmare, Kappy. You got to save me." Replies the kindly Kappy, "I'm an agent, there's just so much I can do." What he does is arrange a cheap television series for Fane, which would include his doing the commercials. But before the contract is signed, Hymie calls from the

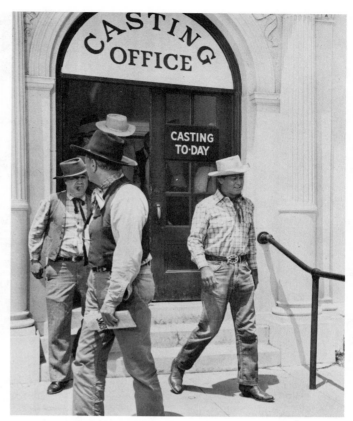

The Carpetbaggers: Alan Ladd.

The Oscar (1966): Stephen Boyd, Jack Soo and Tony Bennett.

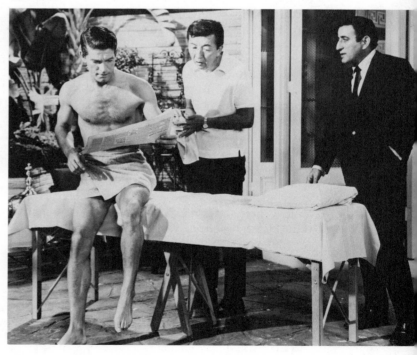

333

The Oscar: Elke Sommer and Stephen Boyd.

Academy of Motion Picture Arts and Sciences to tell him he has been nominated for an Oscar.

Fane's standing in the industry changes instantly. Hordes of people, many who had formerly rejected him, now shower him with congratulations. Determined to be the winner, Fane calls upon Barney to help in his scheme, telling him to leak to the press that he was once a spieler in strip joints, arrested and jailed for theft. This, incredibly, receives huge headlines and Hollywood is aghast that a nominee should be so maligned at this time. The onus is on the four other nominees, and Fane laughs when he explains this to the horrified Hymie: "Pull one plug and you drown the opposition. . . . I'll use a spiked boot on anyone who gets in my way." At a press conference Fane explains his background to the sympathetic reporters, and in referring to what everyone thinks is a deliberate smear he says, "I can't believe anyone would do it." Despite the sympathy, things get tougher for Fane. He appeals to his agent for money, but instead of cash Kappy hands him a release on their contract. The private detective attempts to blackmail him but Trixie, soft on Fane, foils the attempt. However, both Kay and Hymie decide the time has come to break with Fane, and as they leave his house he screams at them, "I'm no different from anyone else in this damn town."

At the Academy Awards presentations Bob Hope introduces Merle Oberon to present the Oscar for Best Actor. She alludes to Richard Burton and Burt Lancaster, and the camera cuts to Fane, who is so certain of winning he rises to his feet with the words, "The winner is . . ." For a second the audience is led to believe he may have won. Oberon announces the name, "Frank . . . Sinatra." The thunderstruck Fane joins in the applause, but his clapping becomes a desperate banging together of his hands in frustration. The camera pulls back on this pitiful, defeated man and the picture ends. And none to soon. As a dreary, degrading version of Hollywood life *The Oscar* wins its own award, and it is sad that Sinatra, Oberon, columnist Hedda Hopper and fashion designer Edith Head were persuaded to appear as themselves and lend it authenticity.

The Oscar met with little response from the public, and the critics were unanimous in denouncing it as a shoddy and implausible account of a screen actor's rise to fame. The film was released at the same time as *Inside Daisy Clover*, and coming a year or so after *The Carpetbaggers* and the two versions of *Harlow*, two of America's foremost critics were moved to express concern for these generally deprecating and poorly wrought depictions of the film industry. Writing in the March 25, 1966 issue of *Life*, Richard Schickel said:

When Hollywood turns the camera on itself it nearly always makes the astonishing discovery that the place is gaudy, vulgar, success-crazed, money-mad and generally suffering from bad values. The film capital has so earnestly scourged itself in the process of self-discovery that over the years it has made a kind of anti-myth about the quality of life around the kidney-shaped pools. Indeed, it seems that in the years of its decline, Hollywood has come to take a perverse pride in its rottenness; as if it were the last thing in which it still truly leads the world. It has made the cliché such a pervasive part of our culture that no audience could possibly take seriously an attempt to find some lurking good beneath the tinsel or believe a plot about ordinarily decent people going workmanlike about the job of making a movie.

At the same time Mr. Schickel was voicing his disapproval of *Inside Daisy Clover* and *The Oscar*, Bosley Crowther spoke up in a similar vein in *The New York Times*. Mr. Crowther gave his column the heading "Is Hollywood Killing Itself?," and several of his paragraphs strike a responsive chord with the authors of this book and surely for all those who are interested in the American film industry and the manner in which it presents its product and itself to the world:

The disgrace is not so much that these pictures have presented strange and squalid characters. That as a specific of content would be valid and reasonable. No one would claim for one moment that everybody in Hollywood is a paragon of virtue, an artist of the purest ray serene. Indeed, some of the most interesting Hollywood people—some of the most productive and sad—are (or have been) fantastic fakers, scoundrels, egomaniacs and scamps. A certain amount of aggressive self-serving goes with the territory, as they say.

The disgrace is that none of these [recent] pictures—not one of them, I would say—has shown the slightest bit of understanding or desire to understand and reflect the extraordinary business of making films. Not one has shown the faintest recognition of the kinds of toils and tensions involved in the process of creating movies, in uncovering and developing stars, in preserving manufactured illusions, in enduring disappointment and defeat. Not one has begun to give an idea of the kinds of triumphs and tragedies that can come from the glowing satisfaction and despairs of being involved with films.

The Oscar: Milton Berle and Stephen Boyd.

CHAPTER TWELVE

PREVUES OF COMING ATTRACTIONS

As this book goes to press (August 1975), a deluge of Hollywood-on-Hollywood movies are in preparation and production. In conjunction with the current accent on nostalgia and the growing interest in old movies and the movie stars of the past, the studios are forging ahead with big and some not-so-big productions about Hollywood during the so-called golden years. This cycle—threatening to replace the "disaster" epics of 1974–75—would seem to have been triggered by the previously mentioned *Day of the Locust*. Within the next six months Universal will release *Gable and Lombard*, *W. C. Fields and Me*. The studio is also currently preparing a feature film about Errol Flynn. At this point, no actor has been selected to play the swashbuckling Flynn.

Director Sidney Furie pointed out to us that the basic idea behind *Gable and Lombard* was to tell a love story—a kind of Romeo and Juliet set in the 1930s. But Furie, by his own admission not a man fascinated by the past, decided to low-key the period aspects of the production. He did not want to rely heavily on decor and costumes, but rather to put the emphasis on the characters and the story.

Furie says that *Gable and Lombard* is a story of two people whose love endured the narrow confines of the Victorian morality of the 1930s and the opposition of studio employers who were afraid of audience prejudice against "immorality" in public figures. One scene shows Louis B. Mayer (Allen Garfield) warning Gable (James Brolin) that he could end up scorned like Fatty Arbuckle or Mabel Normand if he continued to romance Carole Lombard (Jill Clayburgh) while still married to his second wife, Ria Langham, a wealthy Texas socialite (Joanne Linville.)

Lombard, to whom stardom came earlier than to Gable, had been married to William Powell and was divorced when she fell in love with Gable. The way for Gable's wedding to Lombard in 1939 was opened when Ria Langham agreed to a cash settlement of $260,000 to divorce him. Gable and Lombard's life together appeared to be relatively idyllic until an air crash tragically ended her life in 1942.

Jill Clayburgh's arresting performance as a prostitute in the 1975 television special *Hustling* attracted considerable attention, and made her the obvious choice for the very difficult-to-cast role of

337

Gable and Lombard: re-creating a scene from *Gone With the Wind.* James Brolin as Clark Gable playing Rhett Butler and Morgan Brittany as Vivien Leigh playing Scarlett O'Hara.

the glamorous, humorous, gutsy, sexy, sensitive Carole Lombard.

Some sequences from their films have been re-created in the feature—including moments from *Gone With the Wind.*

W. C. Fields contemporary appeal, says Rod Steiger, who was selected to play the famous comedian in *W. C. Fields and Me,* may stem in part from an attitude of "the individual in a vicious society. He attacked the sacred cows for all those people in the audience who wanted to. Fields was a street fighter. He was one of the few men who hit this town and became successful without kissing anyone's rear end. And that's an accomplishment."

The *Me* of the title is Carlotta Monti (Valerie Perrine), who, although unknown to the general public, lived with Fields as his mistress for fourteen years until his untimely death. A number of vignettes from Miss Monti's book, *W. C. Fields and Me,* are included in the film, but according to *Los Angeles Times* staff writer Lee Grant, the thrust will be an examination of Fields' psyche, attitudes, myths and postures. Included, too, are re-creations of Fields' classic routines from the stage and screen.

There are no fewer than four Rudolph Valentino projects planned for 1976, the 50th anniversary of the famed actor's death. The first Valentino biography to go before the cameras will be Mel Shavelson's version, which he is producing, directing and writing as a two-hour ABC television film. His story will deal wih Valentino's years as a superstar, the last five years of his life. Franco Nero portrays Valentino; Lesley Warren has been cast as his first wife, actress Jean Acker; Milton Berle is Jesse L. Lasky; Yvette Mimieux plays Valentino's second wife, Natacha Rambova; and Suzanne Pleshette portrays June Mathis, who wrote four of the actor's biggest pictures.

"In the various Valentino stories, all you you hear about are the glamour girls," Shavelson told *Hollywood Reporter* writer Ron Pennington recently. "But he had a strange relationship with June Mathis, who was much older and who had the power in Hollywood to get him his first starring job. Although he married two other women, June Mathis paid for his tomb and is buried beside him."

Another project, a scheduled two-hour NBC World Premiere Movie, will cover the last twelve years of Valentino's life. The most ambitious of the productions will be the new theatrical film version of *Valentino,* which Ken Russell will direct for United Artists release. This reportedly will concentrate on the star's early life, starting with his boyhood in Italy and covering his travels to Paris and his young adult-hood there and in New York. The fourth entry, *The Story of Valentino,* also for theatrical release, has been announced as an Anglo-Italian co-production.

Darryl Ponicsan, author of *The Last Detail* and *Cinderella Liberty,* recently completed the book and screenplay of *Tom Mix Died for Your Sins,* which deals with the cowboy star's life, and is being prepared for theatrical release,

Goodbye Norma Jean, concentrating on the teen-age Marilyn Monroe, commenced shooting in January 1975, with Misty Rowe in the title role.

Another Hollywood feature, completed some time ago and about to be released, is *The Wild Party.* The script is based on, and is partly written in the style of, a long narrative poem composed in 1928 by Joseph Moncure March. James Coco plays Jolly Grimm, a rotund, faded 1920s film comic who, with his mistress (Raquel Welch), throws a lavish party in order to show Grimm's new silent film and re-establish his dwindling career just as sound is coming in. The party takes place at his palatial Beverly Hills home (all the scenes were photographed at the fabled Mission Inn at Riverside, California) and begins apprehensively, continues through a dismal screening, then turns into a decadent, drunken debauch.

The rumored parallels with Fatty Arbuckle's story are so vague and remote as to be invalid. As *Variety* staff writer A. D. Murphy says in his review of *The Wild Party:*

Lest anyone think this a fictionalized Fatty Arbuckle story, it should be recalled that Arbuckle's scandal came when he was still hot (Coco plays a washed-up silent film comic who won't adapt to sound); there were no pistol homicides in the Arbuckle affair (Coco winds up killing Welch and [Perry] King, who have been off in a bedroom); and Virginia Rappe was known as a casual swinger (Welch's character has been with Coco for many years of close companionship).

Paramount's *Won-Ton-Ton, the Dog Who Saved Hollywood,* a satire on the career of Rin-Tin-Tin, with Madeline Kahn and Bruce Dern, is the story of a superstar movie dog who helps rescue a foundering studio from bankruptcy. *Bogart Slept Here,* dealing with an off-Broadway actor who gets lucky and becomes a Hollywood star, will be the first motion picture teaming for director Mike Nichols and writer Neil Simon, who collaborated on three Broadway hits. The title refers to a hotel in New York where Humphrey Bogart may have stayed during his career. The Warner Bros. film features Robert De

Niro and Marsha Mason. Mentioned elsewhere in this book are the forthcoming *Hearts of the West*, *The Screen Test: F. Scott Fitzgerald in Hollywood* and *The Last Tycoon*. Kirk Douglas (*The Bad and the Beautiful*) is playing another film producer in Paramount's recently released jet set melodrama, *Once Is Not Enough* (1975), an adaptation of Jacqueline Susann's novel that deals only peripherally with Hollywood and/or movie making. Even an offbeat item, *The First Nudie Musical*, an R-rated feature set in Hollywood and revolving around a movie-within-a-movie. is completed and awaiting release.

The Other Side of the Wind, Orson Welles' long-awaited film, which he wrote and directed, has been in production—on and off—for over three years. In it John Huston plays a senior Hollywood director whose life and career are both falling apart.

"It centers on a birthday party for the old director," Welles has been quoted as saying. "He's meant to be older than Huston, more like [Howard] Hawks. But he isn't Hawks, isn't John, isn't me, although the buffs will seek keys." According to critic Charles Champlin:

The party is given by an old friend of the director's, a Dietrich-like figure played by Lilli Palmer, and the idea is to introduce the great man to some of the New Wave washing over Hollywood and elsewhere, with the cool young director played by [Peter] Bogdanovich, chief among them. The Bogdanovich character has been a protege of the old man, and the movie watches the deterioration of their friendship. [Says Welles:] "I've assumed that the party is being covered by a documentary crew from the BBC and another from West Germany and by a whole lot of amateurs with cameras. You'll see only what they've recorded of this evening. It's a device that would only work once, I suppose, but God, it's fun, using three and four cameras at once. . . ."

The Other Side of the Wind will end amid the crumbling remains of a deserted back lot—an appropriate ending for a Hollywood fascinated by its bygone days of glory.

W. C. Fields and Me: Jack Cassidy as John Barrymore, Milt Kamen as Dave Chasen and Rod Steiger as Fields.

Gable and Lombard: James Brolin and Jill Clayburgh.

W. C. Fields and Me: Rod Steiger as Fields and Valerie Perrine as Carlotta Monti.

INDEX

342

343

344

PICTURE CREDITS

The authors are grateful
to the following individuals and organizations
for supplying still photographs

Academy of Motion Picture Arts and Sciences Library,
    Mildred Simpson and Staff
American Film Institute: The Charles K. Feldman Library,
    Anne G. Schlosser, Librarian
Bennett's Book Store
Eddie Brandt's Saturday Matinee
    Mike Hawks
Larry Edmunds Book Shop
Gina Ehrlich
Diane Goodrich
Ron Haver
Hollywood Poster Exchange,
    Bob Colman
Paula Klaw

Kenneth G. Lawrence
John R. Lebold
Museum of Modern Art,
    Mary Corliss
Chester Nelson
Gunnard Nelson
Ontario Film Institute,
    Gerald Pratley
Steffi Sidney
Ray Stuart
Bruce Torrence Historical Collection
c/oFirst Federal of Hollywood
UCLA Theatre Arts Library
    Audrée Malkin
Mae Woods